Everyday Vegan

300 Recipes *for* Healthful Eating

Jeani-Rose Atchison

illustrated by
Audrey Colman

North Atlantic Books
Berkeley, California

Everyday Vegan: 300 Recipes for Healthful Eating

Published by
North Atlantic Books
P.O. Box 12327
Berkeley, California 94712

Cover and book design © Ayelet Maida, A/M Studios
Cover art © Stockbyte
Illustrations © Audrey Colman, www.goodartstudio.com
Printed in the United States of America

Everyday Vegan: 300 Recipes for Healthful Eating is sponsored by the Society for the Study of Native Arts and Sciences, a nonprofit educational corporation whose goals are to develop an educational and crosscultural perspective linking various scientific, social, and artistic fields; to nurture a holistic view of arts, sciences, humanities, and healing; and to publish and distribute literature on the relationship of mind, body, and nature.

North Atlantic Books' publications are available through most bookstores. For further information, call 800-337-2665 or visit our website at www.northatlanticbooks.com.

Substantial discounts on bulk quantities are available to corporations, professional associations, and other organizations. For details and discount information, contact our special sales department.

ISBN-13: 978-1-55643-376-4

Library of Congress Cataloging-in-Publication Data

Atchison, Jeani-Rose.
Everyday vegan: 300 recipes for healthful eating / by Jeani-Rose Atchison.
p. cm.
Includes bibliographical references and index.
ISBN 1-55643-376-X (alk. paper)
1. Nutrition. 2. Vegetarian cookery. I. Title.

RA784.A84 2001
613.2'62—dc21 2001042793

5 6 7 8 9 10 11 12 13 14 DATA 14 13 12 11 10 09 08 07

When Health Is Absent . . .
Wisdom cannot reveal itself, art cannot become manifested; strength cannot be exerted, wealth is useless and reason is powerless.

—Herophilies, 300 B.C.

To my love, Eric,
and our precious little ones,
Rhiannon, Gwendolyn, and Nimue
who make my heart full.

Acknowledgments

There are so many people who have helped shape this book, many of whom before I even considered writing it.

My dear friend, Sharon Steele-McGee, who supported and believed in me through my shedding of old identities and the transformation to who I am today.

Arianne and Jean-Claude Koven, who were instrumental in my physical and spiritual paths back to health.

Randy Steer, who trusted my judgment in my change of careers.

Paul Burkett, for his infectious and irreverent sense of humor and friendship.

Sweet Terri Bona, whom I had so much fun with searching out answers to our life questions.

Elisabeth Carter, for creating a beautiful atmosphere for me to conduct classes.

Michael and Kim Strickland, for their enthusiastic support of the classes, the feedback on this project, our way of life, and their wide-open embrace of my self and my family, which I treasure.

To those of you at Life Grocery: Lisa, Ronnie, Arlene, Helen, and others who always made me feel like a special part of our wonderful Co-op.

To Myrna and Emery Atchison for never judging, always accepting, and being so supportive in what we do.

To Ronnie Hudson . . . hey girlfriend! Thanks for the critique and changes made on the text portion of this book.

And to Sue and Neal Tompkins. Especially Sue, whose work on this project was immense.

Thank you, all of you.

Table of Contents

Introduction

When I assist others' transitions to a plant-based diet, many people question what my belief system is in regard to the reasons I became a vegetarian.

Prior to changing my diet I had tried many therapies, conventional and complementary, to heal a myriad of ailments. Some therapies did not work and were discarded, others worked for a period of time, and a few continue to work to this day. Nothing, however, seemed to be "the answer." I was taking care of many aspects of myself, but there was something missing, some piece of the puzzle I had overlooked. In trying to find the missing link, I began to closely examine the food I was consuming and the relationship I had with it.

I grew up on a typical American diet with many missed meals in my preteen and teen years. When a meal was provided, it was eaten with no thought of nurturing, just the primitive notion of survival. My disassociation with food continued into my early thirties. Though I had always loved to cook, it was with a preponderance of rich sauces and gravies and, unbeknownst to me at the time, abominable food combinations.

After I changed my diet, I slowly began to see results. With compromised liver and kidney function, I found that eliminating meat was easier on my body. When I let go of my desire for dairy, I found dramatic results. My body felt more relaxed and I moved easier. My joints were not as stiff, and certain exercises and yoga postures were greatly improved. Eliminating refined foods and eating more raw foods allowed me to breathe easier, as well as feel a greater sense of peace. As I delved into nutritional research, I began to understand why this was happening. I was fascinated by the health benefits I was reaping and food became a whole new study, not only the preparation and selection of it, but also the emotional and chemical interactions of it as well.

I had been a real estate and securities broker during that time and found I was much happier completely letting go of those two careers.

With great enthusiasm, I jumped in with both feet to learn as much as possible why food was such a critical player in the physical as well as the emotional and spiritual parts of an individual.

Several years passed. A friend of mine offered me the use of his restaurant to teach cooking classes. Starting out was a little rough, sometimes there were only two students attending classes, but the word got out and eventually others joined. Soon after, interested individuals inquired about private cooking and health consultations. Most of them were working with a specific condition and/or illness. All had a common goal: to eat healthy, delicious fare without feeling "deprived." Most clients understood on an intellectual level that the quality, the quantity, and the types of foods were critical to their healing program, but the biggest challenge was to overcome their emotional attachment. Some of my clients could not cross over that barrier, but many others have, and they are enjoying their new life.

Along with my ongoing education on how food acts on the body, I became aware of the ecological and environmental benefits of eating low on the food chain. I felt proud that my family and I could make such a powerful difference in the preservation of our Earth.

The sacredness of life is another issue I consider. I strongly believe that all life is precious, whether it is plant, insect, animal, or human. Our society has been built without the consciousness of soul and so our intent has been warped as well. Most people who purchase their food at the supermarket are in denial that this was once a living being. The denial is so strong that when an average person finds out how I eat, they become defensive. I am not the type of person who would intentionally make anyone uncomfortable about his or her food or lifestyle choices. What happens, I believe, is that my beliefs or practices somehow touch their inner, most spiritual selves, the consciousness of their soul. Deep inside we know that this is the most natural and correct way to behave, but we are mired in so much confusion created by ourselves and by the food industry that we allow ourselves to become victimized. Blaming the media for the skewed messages sent to the consumer is oversimplified since it reflects the astronomical advertising budgets of the food industry. Both parties are irresponsible, giving a biased view of the benefits of the products being marketed, all for the sake of profit.

There are cycles of life that are as natural as the air we breathe. One of these cycles includes the lying down of the life of one being so that another may live. Many ancient and some present cultures recognize, respect, and honor this exchange of energy. Every day we all take in life in the food we ingest. Plants are as alive as animals. Through greed, our society has created an industry based on decaying flesh and denatured food products, effectively removing us from the conscious act of nourishment.

Whatever an individual chooses to eat should be respected, as long as that individual comes from a state of awareness. People need to take responsibility for their actions, whether it is how they treat their neighbor, how they use the resources of our Earth, or what they choose to eat. Once this consciousness occurs, certain practices such as factory-farmed animals, genetically engineered food, irradiation, pesticides, and manufactured foods will become intolerable. Intention in life is everything, but how can we have this without awareness?

I am not a religious person, though deeply spiritual. Simple whole foods allow my body to expend energy wisely and without difficulty. I believe this allows a heightened state of awareness within, creating a more receptive heart, mind, and soul. I try to walk with grace and reverence in my daily life and to guide my family in the same manner. My goals in life are very simple—to love, to be happy, to be of service to others, and to be at peace. I hope that this book will be of benefit to you.

This is the true joy in life, the being used for a purpose recognized by yourself as a mighty one; the being a force of nature instead of a feverish, selfish little clod of ailments and grievances complaining that the world will not devote itself to making you happy.

I am of the opinion that my life belongs to the whole community and that as long as I live it is my privilege to do for it whatever I can. I want to be thoroughly used up when I die, for the harder I work the more I live. I rejoice in life for its own sake. Life is no "brief candle" to me. It is a sort of splendid torch which I have got hold of for the moment, and I want to make it burn as brightly as possible before handing it on to future generations.

—George Bernard Shaw

Getting Started

Suggested Staple List

There are many, many products on the market, and new ones coming out daily, so it would be impossible to list them all. I have, though, listed what you might find in my kitchen. There are several items missing in my list that you may find in others, such as packaged convenience foods, seitan, certain sweeteners, cereals, etc. My family thrives on less-processed foods, and so I find no desire or added nutritional benefit in having them there.

I do list certain "cheeses," though the majority of them are not strictly vegan. There is an enzyme, rennet, that is taken from the stomach lining of calves (or other animals) that is used in the cheese-making process. Therefore, if your cheese does not specify vegetable enzyme, chances are it is not. There are a few vegan "cheese" products available. Try your local natural foods market. Dairy substitutes should not make up a great portion of your diet, rather they should be used as a condiment to enhance a specific recipe that may have traditionally been made with dairy. For those of you who are ready to give up dairy, there is a great little book called *The Uncheese Cookbook* by Joanne Stepaniak which is full of vegan renditions of favorite recipes. (See section on "Dairy" for more information.)

- Allspice
- Amasake
- Apple cider vinegar
- Arrowroot
- Artichoke hearts
- Baked chips
- Baking powder (nonaluminum)
- Baking soda

- Barley malt syrup
- Basil
- Bay leaves
- Beans (in enamel-lined cans)
- Black mustard seeds
- Bread, sprouted grain bread
- Brown rice vinegar
- Canned tomatoes (Muir Glen)
- Caraway seeds
- Cardamom
- Carob powder
- Chapatis
- Chervil
- Chili powder
- Chipotle powder
- Cinnamon
- Cloves
- Coconut milk
- Coconut, shredded unsweetened
- Coriander
- Corn tortillas
- Cumin
- Curry
- Dill
- Dried beans—garbanzo, northern, adzuki, black-eyed peas, navy, kidney, pinto, lima, mung, split peas, lentils, soybeans
- Dry mustard
- Fennel seeds
- Garlic powder
- Ginger

- Grain coffee
- Grains—barley (not pearled), oats, rye, brown and wild rice, grits, cracked wheat, quinoa, amaranth, millet, buckwheat, wheat berries
- Herbal teas
- Ketchup (natural brands)
- Kudzu
- Lecithin granules
- Marjoram
- Miso
- Mustard (whole-grain, natural)
- Nondairy cheeses
- Nonhydrogenated "natural" margarine (or make your own—see "Butter" recipe)
- Nut butters—almond, cashew, sesame
- Nutmeg
- Nutritional yeast
- Nuts and seeds—flax, sesame, sunflower, red clover, alfalfa, pumpkin, pine nuts, walnuts, pecans, almonds, cashews (no roasted nuts)
- Oils—flax, coconut, olive, sesame, toasted sesame
- Onion powder
- Oregano
- Paprika
- Parsley
- Peppermint
- Pickles
- Popcorn
- Poppy seeds
- Rice cakes

- Rice syrup
- Rosemary
- Sage
- Salsa
- Sauerkraut (all natural—no chemical preservatives)
- Sea salt
- Sea vegetables (arame, agar, kelp, dulse, nori)
- Slippery elm powder
- Soy milk powder
- Sprouted grain bread
- Stevia powder, liquid, and ground green leaf
- Superfoods—spirulina, chlorella, Kyogreen
- Tahini or sesame butter
- Tarragon
- Tempeh
- Thyme
- Tofu (in aseptic packaging)
- Turmeric
- Vanilla, maple, lemon flavorings by Frontier (all sulfur dioxide free)
- Vegan mayonnaise
- Vegan milk
- Vegetable broth cubes
- Vogue Vege Base
- Wheat-free pasta noodles or buckwheat soba (try not to eat noodles more than a couple of times a month)
- Whole-grain crackers

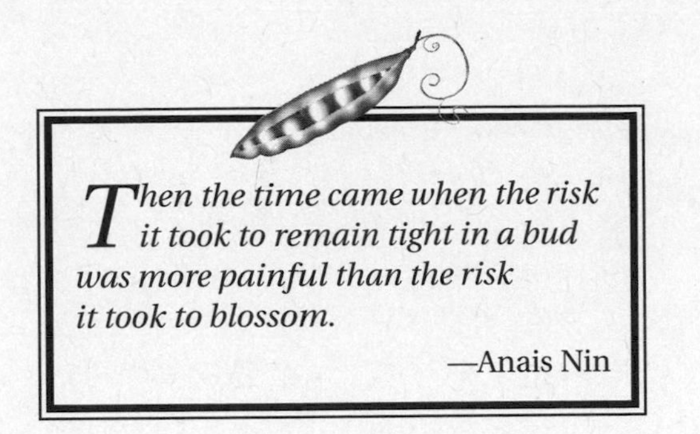

Substitutions

Baking powder—Many of the store-bought varieties contain harmful ingredients such as aluminum and lime, as well as too much sodium. Here are a few healthier alternatives:

- Blend 2 parts arrowroot, 1 part baking soda, 1 part cream of tartar.
- Use low-sodium or nonaluminum brands, such as Rumford.
- Make a paste with a small amount of yeast, water, and flour. Let it sit 30 minutes before using.

Cornstarch—Use arrowroot or kudzu.

Cocoa—Use carob powder. To help deepen the flavor, add a small amount of grain coffee substitute.

Coffee—There are many grain varieties available. Experiment to find your favorite.

Dairy

- **Milk** can be replaced with any soy or grain milk. Another option would be to use seed or nut milks. Simply grind a couple tablespoons of sesame or sunflower seeds, almonds (blanch and remove skins), cashews, etc., with 1/2 to 2 cups water. Add a pinch of sea salt and vanilla flavoring, if desired. When a recipe asks for milk powder, use soy powder instead.
- **Yogurt, sour milk, and buttermilk** can be replaced with soy milk (1 cup) curdled with 2 teaspoons lemon juice or with soy yogurt.

- **Butter** can be replaced with coconut oil (2/3 to 3/4 cup for each cup of butter), or other mild-tasting oils, but remember to use less. Natural, nonhydrogenated spreads such as Spectrum or Earth's Balance may be used as well. Try my recipe for "Butter" for a healthy, delicious substitute. Avocado is wonderful on a slice of bread or baked potato instead of butter. If baking sweet breads or cake, you can substitute applesauce, date paste, or prune paste.

- **Cream cheese** in recipes can be replaced with tofu. Or make a thick cashew cream or vegan mayonnaise. There are many faux cheeses on the market today. Experiment with the different types to find the one you like best.

- **Sour cream** is easy—try my Tofu Sour Cream, or use soy yogurt.

- **Heavy cream** can be replaced with my recipe for Cashew Cream.

Eggs—For one egg, use:

- 1 tablespoon flax seed, ground, mixed with 3 tablespoons water. This works very well. I favor it in most quick breads and cakes. It has a mild, nutty flavor. When mixed with water it becomes nice and "glooey," similar to eggs. The flax seed has been heavily researched and is rated very highly, nutritionally speaking. (See flax information in glossary).
- 1 tablespoon of any of these: tahini or sesame butter, garbanzo flour, lecithin granules, soy flour, or arrowroot mixed with 3 tablespoons of water.
- Make a blend of 2 parts arrowroot, 1 part tapioca flour, 1 part slippery elm, and mix 1 tablespoon with 3 tablespoons water.
- There is a product called "Egg Replacer." Follow directions on package.

Flours

Wheat flour was, once upon a time, a good food. But we have abused the use of wheat to the point that many of us are "wheat intolerant." This has caused me to be wheat defiant. Through hybridization, refinement, treatment with chemicals and preservatives, and a long shelf life, the wheat we purchase is oxidized and rancid and devoid of a great deal of its nutrients. If you are going to use wheat, then it would be best to grind your own, which is pretty easy to do. An inexpensive coffee grinder is ideal for small amounts of flour, spices, etc. (This is referred to as spice grinder in the Recipe section.)

Reduce or eliminate processed food products, and you will eliminate many allergens, and one of the biggest is wheat. It can be found in a lot of different foods, such as soy sauces, grain vinegar, hot dogs, luncheon meat, beer, catsup, nondairy creamer, many seasonings; "hidden" by names such as hydrolyzed vegetable protein, textured vegetable protein, hydrolyzed plant protein, modified food starch; and used as a binder, filler, or excipient in a phenomenal amount of packaged foods.

There are many of us who find it difficult to digest gluten, which is the protein found in glutinous grains. These grains include wheat, barley, sweet rice, rye, and oats. Oats, however, do not seem to cause the problems that the others do. Since wheat is the prevalent bad guy, I have pretty much rid my diet of it except in the form of sprouted bread on occasion, or sprouted berries (read the section on "Sprouting"). There is no need to feel deprived by removing one or a few grains from your diet.

When a recipe calls for flour, do not be afraid to substitute some or all of the wheat you would normally use with millet, rice, corn, oat, barley, rye, spelt, kamut, teff (a grain), etc. See "Breads" section for more information.

Salt—Use sea vegetables, powdered kelp or dulse, sea salt, miso, Bragg Liquid Aminos, tamari.

Sweeteners—For every 1 cup of white sugar or honey, measure:

- 3/4 cup maple syrup; decrease liquids in recipe slightly.
- 1 1/2 cups rice or barley malt syrup; decrease liquids in recipe slightly.
- 1 tablespoon ground stevia green leaf or 1 teaspoon stevia powder; add 2 tablespoons liquid to recipe.
- Date butter: Blend dates in a small amount of hot water until smooth.

Dietary Changes

1. Go slowly! Changing too much too quickly sets you up for failure.
2. Eliminate beverages such as coffee and soda.
3. Lower the concentrated protein portions on your plate and raise the vegetable portions.
4. Never drink water (or other beverages) with meals. This dilutes digestive enzymes, thus diminishing or halting the digestive process.
5. Man does not live on rice, beans, and green salads alone. Be creative. Use a wide range of cookbooks, experiment, and have fun.
6. Changing the way you eat is more difficult than changing religions or learning a new language. Not because a healthier diet is any harder to follow, but because we have to unlearn certain behaviors and beliefs at the same time, most of which have been with us since birth. Patience and a willingness to learn in time will enable you to nourish yourself and your family in a manner that is second nature.
7. Eliminate cookies, cakes, chips, pretzels, etc. If they are not in your house, you and your family will not be tempted. Always have a variety of healthier options available.
8. Eating healthy in our society today, sadly, is a learned behavior. There are no shortcuts. Do not be tempted to buy boxed or prepared "healthier" foods because it is easier. Otherwise, you will still have to train yourself to a whole foods diet.
9. Plan and organize! Plan weekly menus and stick with them. This makes shopping easier and supports your efforts in remaining on this new road you are traveling. Experts say it takes three weeks to change a learned behavior. Give yourself at least a month to see how much easier it is to live and eat in this healthier way.
10. Change the way you perceive food. So many times we make food selections based on emotions. An interesting exercise is to keep a food diary and write down how you feel prior to eating. Awareness is the first step to a healthier diet. Being conscious of our

choices makes us less a victim and more responsible for our actions. Nourishment is a gift of love, whether to one's self or to one's family. Each and every one of us deserves this gift.

Conscious Living

The scientific world has come a long way in identifying the roles that specific nutrients play in the way our body functions. We have only begun to scratch the surface of understanding how the body works. All components must work synergistically to achieve homeostasis, that is, balance and optimum health.

I sincerely believe that fad diets such as high-protein, low-fat, no-fat, etc., are detrimental to your health and bring you no closer to understanding how your body works. If you want to lose weight, gain clarity of mind, or help your body heal itself, you have to put some effort into it. Most people will not take the first step to health, which is learning what is or is not good for them. Rather, we tend to look to "experts" to give us a pill or herb or single therapy to cure us. This is because our psyches lean more toward the easiest route to take. Our ego would rather accept that outside influences are responsible for the way we feel, and that it has nothing to do with the hamburger, fries, and cola we had for lunch. We all must realize that healing comes from within. We must also understand that what we eat and drink, place on our skin and hair, breathe and clean our homes with have a direct effect on how our body will react.

Food manufacturers (now that's a term that should strike fear within us—being as far away from nature as you can get) and major food industries take certain information, revealed by research scientists, out of context and use it for their own monetary gain. One example is fortified packaged foods, which, through processing, lose many nutrients. Once the nutrients are lost, the powers that be decide which ones are important and process a few back in. Certain food industries campaign heavily in the media to make you aware of the importance of a specific nutrient found in their products without explaining the detrimental effects of other aspects of these "foods."

We are purposely kept in the dark, but we do not mind because it is too difficult to change the mindset of the years of programming that we have received from these industries.

There is considerable research on the effects of poor diet in the development of the unborn child and the young in our society today. Poor health is passed down from generation to generation. I, for one, do not want to leave that legacy behind. I am determined to understand what it is I can do to change this. It would not be a particularly difficult endeavor because learning how to eat and live is natural and instinctual. What does make it difficult, though, is that we have to unlearn many fallacies at the same time. Just think what a precious gift we can give our children if we never introduce these fallacies to begin with.

Often mothers come to me complaining that they cannot change their young ones' eating habits because the children refuse to eat anything other than what they are accustomed to eating. My answer is, if you want your children to eat healthier, then every member of the family must change. Throw away the junk from your cupboards, and do not bring it back in the house. If a child requests candy, soda, or potato chips, explain why you no longer buy these products. Look through this book for healthy snack options that have been kid tested! Even a two- or three-year-old child will understand the explanation that candy has bad sugar and fruit has good sugar. My eldest daughter (now five years old) understands that bad sugar will cause her body to work too hard to try not to get sick and not work hard enough to make her body strong. You do not have to get technical yet. However, you do need to have that knowledge, because children are naturally curious. As they grow older, they will want to know the reasons for your actions.

Your older child will eventually come around as well, especially when you are a good role model. There is also nothing wrong with telling them that you were wrong to bring those foods into the home to begin with—that you were not aware of their bad effects on the body. Include, not exclude, children in food decisions. Soon they will be on their own and will make decisions based on what they learned from you. You cannot stop them from making certain choices outside the home, and neither should you try. Rather, empower them with as much information as you can give and nurture their independence, which will give them the confidence to make decisions for themselves.

A child will not starve to death if she or he skips a meal in protest about the change of menu. Within a short period of time their adulterated taste buds will be cleansed, and they will enjoy with gusto the whole foods placed in front of them. Believe it or not, they will lose the desire for refined, high-sugar, high-salt, and high-fat foods.

Whole foods are more satisfying. They fill you up quicker. The texture is coarser. Full mastication is required. Therefore, a longer amount of time is needed at the dinner table, which invites more familial contact. This is another life practice sorely missing in our society.

Thirst is satiated easily on a whole foods diet, especially when you consume a large amount of fruits and vegetables in their raw state. Large quantities of soda, tea, or water are no longer needed to wash down the food. In fact, you begin to understand that liquid is not important at a meal and how it actually impedes digestion due to diluting the enzymes needed to break down the food.

Being conscious of our choices makes us less a victim and more responsible for our actions. Nourishment of the body is a great gift of love, whether to one's self or to one's family—each and every one of us deserves that gift.

The Natural Home

Using chemical cleansers in my home is not an option. I believe there are safer, less expensive, and easier ways to make cleansers that are just as effective. For anyone who is concerned about the toxic effects of chemicals on their family, pets, and environment, try these out!

White vinegar and lemon juice are fabulous cleansers to use for refrigerators, cupboards, and countertops. They have the added benefit of repelling ants. Simply dilute with water (1/2 lemon or splash of vinegar).

To wash floors, I add 1 tablespoon of castile soap and five drops each of the following essential oils to a bucket of water: clove, thyme, lavender, peppermint, and tea tree. It is highly aromatic, but diminishes quickly. It also works as a wonderful disinfectant. Research has found that molds, staphylococci, several bacillus strains, and other detrimental microorganisms are wiped out with applications of these oils.

Baking soda straight out of the box is wonderful for scrubbing pots and stovetops. It will not dissolve buildup as easily as some of the chemical brands, so a little elbow grease is needed—but it works! We purchased a thirty-some-odd-year-old house from a sweet old lady who fried all her food. There was tremendous buildup on the hood of the stove, as well as on the surrounding cabinets. The baking soda worked like a charm.

One-half cup of baking soda poured into the sink, followed by a half cup of vinegar, covered for a minute, will usually take care of minor pipe blockages. Use on a weekly basis to keep your pipes clean.

Vinegar diluted in water is my window and mirror cleaner of choice.

Insect repellents are also easy to make. Citronella, geranium (especially good), peppermint, eucalyptus, cloves, and rosemary may repel mosquitoes. Choose two or three of these. Add 1–2 drops of each to a tablespoon of lotion and rub onto skin. Experiment to find which ones work best for you. If you do get bit, add a drop of lavender directly on the bite or salt mixed with a touch of water, patted on like a poultice. For several bites from mosquitoes or "no-see-ums" (those irritating invisible attackers), try soaking in a bath with Epsom or sea salt for 15 minutes or more.

Pennyroyal is a common sight around my home. I toss the dried form (fresh is good too) into every corner, under the beds and couch, etc., to deter fleas. Smells nice. Lightly minty.

A flea comb is another product I would highly recommend for your animals. Combining that with frequent vacuuming controls fleas. For additional help, try a citrus-based flea dip and/or flea collar. Garlic fed daily to your animal helps as well as B vitamins.

Diatomaceous earth is what I use for the creepy crawlies. This fine, gray powder acts on a mechanical, not a chemical, level. It is completely safe around small pets and children as long as it is applied according to package directions. It can usually be found in natural food markets and some garden stores.

If cockroaches are a problem, try this simple recipe. Mix equal parts flour, sugar, boric acid, mixed with a little oil until it forms a paste. Roll into balls and tuck away into cupboard corners, under the sink, behind appliances, etc. Keep this away from children and pets.

Do not underestimate the power of the sun and fresh air! Opening windows daily for short periods of time (even in the winter) will rid your home of many contaminants and bring in a new supply of much needed nutrients. The sun will correct many of the mold problems you may have.

Plants are wonderful pollutant fighters, as well as oxygen recyclers. Some of the chemicals in a typical American home include benzene, trichlorothylene, and formaldehyde. Plants will absorb and transform them into nutrients that they can use. Nervous disorders, anemia, nausea, headaches, etc., are just some of the symptoms. My husband and then five-month-old daughter were greatly affected by the outgassing from new carpets and the fresh paint on the walls of an apartment we rented while we looked for a home. Both had severe allergic reactions, swelling, dark circles under the eyes, and inflammation of the mucous membranes of their mouth, eyes, and throat. We immediately went out and purchased spider plants, heartleaf philodendron, golden pothos, and a few other species, and hung them in every room. Daily vacuuming and open windows helped until we were able to move out.

Detergents, plastics, inks, synthetic fibers, wood finishes, dry cleaning, plywood, natural gas, and much more are also toxic. Plants can help. Limit or eliminate the use of these products. Conventional dishwashing detergents often contain phosphates, which rob our waters of oxygen, suffocating aquatic animals and plants.

We use laundry discs instead of detergent, do not dry clean, turn off the gas to our stove to prevent small leaks from escaping, and recommend the use of "chemically responsible" paints and varnishes such as those sold through Safecoat, which can be reached at 800-239-0321, or www.afmsafecoat.com.

There are many brands of cleansers available in your natural foods market from dish soap to toilet cleansers to hydrogen peroxide–based bleaching solutions. Though I prefer to make my own, usually for a fraction of the price, these are excellent alternatives.

For more ideas and recipes, pick up Casey Kellars's book, *Natural Cleaning for Your Home: 95 Pure and Simple Recipes.*

> **The word "organic" on the label stands for a commitment to an agricultural production system which strives for a balance with nature, using methods and materials which are of low impact to the environment.**
>
> —Katherine DiMatteo,
> executive director,
> Organic Trade Association

Organic Foods

What is the big deal about organic? This is a very common question. Many of us are in agreement that we would rather not have pesticides in our food. But most of us are not aware of the other contaminants used that affect our health, the soil, and the air. Herbicides, weed killers, synthetic fertilizers . . . the list goes on. Interestingly, even after something is grown, chemicals are used in its storage or transportation! We are inundated with poisonous substances wherever we turn. This is not said to strike fear; it is only said to bring about an awareness so that we all can make educated decisions regarding our food and health choices.

Organic farmers see beyond the use of chemicals. They are always looking to give back to the soil as much, if not more, of the nutrients used to produce our food.

Growing a wide selection of crops is one way in which organic farmers work. Typically, nonorganic farmers focus on growing only one type of crop. This depletes the soil of nutrients and makes the land unfit to grow any other type of crop.

I was speaking to a student of mine who lived in a small farming community. She remembers how the children, including herself, would run through fields that had just been sprayed or powdered with pesticides. She recalled how they would run behind the trucks that sprayed the chemicals, splashing their feet in the puddles left behind. She is in her early forties right now and says that more than three-quarters of the dozen people she grew up with either has cancer now or has died from cancer. It is rather depressing that someone's livelihood can also be his or her destruction.

Agriculture is the largest source of sewage in the United States today. This not only comes from the high volume feeding at production facilities (beef, dairy, pigs, chickens, and turkeys), processing plants and slaughterhouses, but also the nitrates from agricultural runoff. Pesticides for agriculture account for 75% of the 1.1 billion pounds of pesticides produced in the United States.

Once crops are sprayed, the chemicals do not just disappear. There is a considerable amount of runoff due to irrigation/watering systems. This in turn gets into our water supply. The techniques used by organic farmers not only protect our water supply, but also conserve it.

The flavor and the quality of organic produce is dramatically different from the conventionally grown. I always tell people to try a tomato test. Slice a tomato and see, smell, and taste why organic is superior.

A study from the Center for the Study of Biological Systems at Washington University in St. Louis, Missouri, found "a five-year average shows that the organic farms yielded, in dollars per acre, exactly the same returns. In terms of yield, the organic farms were down about 10%. The reason why the economics came out is that savings in chemicals made up for the difference."

One other point to consider. Over 70% of farmland is used to feed livestock. So if we lower our intake of meat, we could cut our yield in half and still have more than enough food at an affordable price for everyone.

After taking all of this into consideration, why wouldn't we support organic farmers?

Pesticides, Children, and Aggression

by Peter Montague

(Excerpted and reprinted with permission from *Rachel's Health & Environment Weekly, #648.)* For a complete, footnoted copy, or for subscription information, call 410-263-1584.

For the past twenty-five years, tens of millions of Americans in hundreds of cities and towns have been drinking tap water that is contaminated with low levels of insecticides, weed killers, and artificial fertilizer. They not only drink it, they also bathe and shower in it, thus inhaling small quantities of farm chemicals and absorbing them through the skin. Naturally, the problem is at its worst in agricultural areas of the country.

The most common contaminants are carbamate insecticides (aldicarb and others), the triazine herbicides (atrazine and others), and nitrate nitrogen. For years government scientists have tested each of these chemicals individually at low levels in laboratory animals—searching mainly for signs of cancer—and have declared each of them an "acceptable risk" at the levels typically found in groundwater.

Now a group of biologists and medical researchers at the University of Wisconsin in Madison, led by Warren P. Porter, has completed a five-year experiment putting mixtures of low levels of these chemicals into the drinking water of male mice and carefully measuring the results. They reported recently that combinations of these chemicals—at levels similar to those found in the groundwater of agricultural areas of the U.S.—have measurable detrimental effects on the nervous, immune, and endocrine (hormone systems).[1] Furthermore, they say their research has direct implications for humans.

Dr. Porter and his colleagues point out that the nervous system, the immune system, and the endocrine (hormone) system are all closely related and in constant communication with each other. If any

[1] Warren P. Porter, James W. Jaeger, and Ian H. Carlson, "Endocrine, immune, and behavioral effects of aldicarb (carbamate), atrazine (triazine), and nitrate (fertilizer) mixtures at groundwater concentrations," *Toxicology and Industrial Health* Vol. 15, Nos. 1 and 2 (1999), pp. 133–150.

one of the three systems is damaged or degraded the other two may be adversely affected. The Wisconsin researchers therefore designed their experiments to examine the effects of agricultural chemicals on each of the three systems simultaneously. To assess immune system function, they measured the ability of mice to make antibodies in response to foreign proteins. To assess endocrine system function, they measured thyroid hormone levels in the blood. And to assess nervous system function they measured aggressive behavior in the presence of intruder mice introduced into the cages. They also looked for effects on growth by measuring total body weight and the weight of each animal's spleen.

The experiments were replicated many times, to make sure the results were reproducible. They found effects on the endocrine system (thyroid hormone levels) and the immune system, and reduced body weight, from mixtures of low levels of aldicarb, and nitrate, atrazine and nitrate, and atrazine, aldicarb, and nitrate together. They observed increased aggression from exposure to atrazine and nitrate, and from atrazine, aldicarb, and nitrate together.

In the five-year experiment, thyroid hormone levels rose or fell depending upon the mixture of farm chemicals put into the drinking water. Dr. Porter and his colleagues present evidence from other studies showing that numerous farm chemicals can affect the thyroid hormone levels of wildlife and humans. PCBs and dioxins can have similar effects, they note. Proper levels of thyroid hormone are essential for brain development of humans prior to birth. Some, though not all, studies have shown that attention deficit and/or hyperactivity disorders in children are linked to changes in the levels of thyroid hormone in the blood. Children with multiple chemical sensitivity (MCS) have abnormal thyroid levels. Furthermore, irritability and aggressive behavior are linked to thyroid hormone levels.

Interviewed recently by Keith Hamm of the *Santa Barbara Independent,* Dr. Porter explained, "earlier work had shown that thyroid hormone typically changed when exposure to these pesticides occurred. Thyroid hormone not only affects and controls your metabolic rate, that is, how fast you burn food, it also controls your irritability level. For example, Type A personalities are more assertive, more aggressive, more hyper. These people tend to have higher levels of thyroid hormone. Type B personalities—people that are really laid back, really take things very easily—have lower levels of thyroid hormone. We expected that changes in thyroid [would] change irritability levels. This was a concern because there was information that kids are getting more hyper and [that their] learning abilities are going down," Dr. Porter said.

In the interview with Keith Hamm, Dr. Porter expressed concern for the overall effect of pesticides on the nation's children:

Hamm: "I would assume that most people in this country are eating conventionally grown food. If that's the case, wouldn't the problems be more apparent? Why are there not more hyperaggressive dim-witted people with poor immune systems?"

Porter: "If we really looked carefully at what's been happening in this country, you might find exactly that happening."

Because of recent violence in small cities and towns (such as Littleton, Colorado; Laramie, Wyoming; and Jasper, Texas), this is a time when Americans are searching for the causes of violence in their society. Some are blaming a decline in religious upbringing. Others are blaming households with the parents working and no one minding the kids. Some say the cause is violent movies, violent TV, and extremist Internet sites, combined with the ready availability of cheap guns. Still others point to a government that has often sanctioned the violence of "gunboat diplomacy" to open foreign markets for U.S. corporations.

No one seems to be asking whether pesticides, fertilizers, and toxic metals are affecting our young people's mental capacity, emotional balance, and social adjustment.

From the work of Warren Porter, Elizabeth Guillette [see below], and others, it is apparent that these are valid questions.

Pesticides and Children: A Case Study

by Peter Montague

A recent study of four- and five-year-old children in Mexico specifically noted a decrease in mental ability and an increase in aggressive behavior among children exposed to pesticides ("An Anthropological Approach to the Evaluation of Preschool Children Exposed to Pesticides in Mexico," *Environmental Health Perspectives,* June, 1998). Elizabeth A. Guillette and colleagues studied two groups of Yaqui Indian children living in the Yaqui Valley in northern Sonora, Mexico. One group of children lives in the lowlands dominated by pesticide-intensive agriculture (45 or more sprayings each year) and the other group lives in the nearby upland foothills where their parents make a living by ranching without the use of pesticides. The pesticide-exposed children had far less physical endurance in a test to see how long they could keep jumping up and down; they had inferior hand-eye coordination; and they could not draw a simple stick figure of a human being, which the upland children could readily do (see diagram).

Notably, in the Guillette study we find this description of the behavior of pesticide-exposed children: "Some valley children were observed hitting their siblings when they passed by, and they became easily upset or angry with a minor corrective comment by a parent. These aggressive behaviors were not noted in the [pesticide-free] foothills [children]." —P. Montague

Difference in drawing ability between children who have been exposed to toxic pesticides and those who have not.

Genetically Engineered Foods

Genetically engineered (GE) foods are just one more factor to consider in selecting what we put on the table. Some 70% or more of the foods in our supermarkets are altered, and the FDA projected that 100 to 150 new genetically engineered foods will be available by the year 2000. Well, that has happened, with most not being identified as such. Many companies voluntarily label their products GMO-free now as the pressure from concerned consumers has increased.

Genetic engineering is the cutting, splicing, and recombining of genes. Each gene in a DNA strand is responsible for a particular feature or function, such as whether a person will have blue or brown eyes. By taking a desired characteristic of one organism and injecting it into another, scientists can create what some consider a new and improved product. So far, some of the "successes" include combining a flounder "antifreeze" gene with a tomato to prolong the growth season, as well as creating potatoes that don't brown, corn that produces its own pesticide, and soybeans that are resistant to herbicides.

Some of these genes are derived from insects, bacteria, viruses, and other sources that have never been part of our diet in the past. No one knows if these are safe, as no long-term studies have ever been performed.

In the beginning, most genetically engineered crops were not segregated from non-genetically engineered crops, which means they were stored and processed together. Certain food manufacturers have attempted to identify and separate ingredients due to consumer demand, but it can be an overwhelming job to track down each distributor from an ingredient list.

The dangers of genetically engineered organisms are many, with mutations and side effects being two of the concerns. Not only can genetically engineered food lower the nutritional quality of a food, but it may also create new or higher amounts of toxins and allergens as well, resulting in untreatable conditions and even death by anaphylactic shock. If, for instance, someone is allergic to peanuts, how do they know if a GMO food has peanut DNA?

This science is alarming on an environmental level as well. A great portion of research is focused on the development of plants that can tolerate a greater amount of herbicides, which means more chemicals in our food and water supply. Along with that, insects, birds, and wind carry seeds and pollen great distances and can create new species with unknown dangers to wildlife. Through reproduction, migration, and mutation, these new organisms cannot be recalled. If a mistake is made, it is permanent!

For a more in-depth look at this technology and the debate surrounding it, contact:

The Natural Law Party and Mothers for Natural Law
P.O. Box 1900
Farfield, Iowa 52556
Website: www.natural-law.org
E-mail: info@natural-law.org
Telephone: 515-472-2040

I have included a partial list of foods to avoid if labels do not say organic or GMO-free:

Soybeans: Soy flour, soy oil, lecithin, soy protein isolates and concentrates. Products that may contain GE soy derivatives: Vitamin E, tofu dogs, cereal, veggie burgers and sausages, tamari, soy sauce, chips, ice cream, frozen yogurt, infant formula, sauces, protein powder, margarine, soy cheese, crackers, bread, cookies, chocolate, candy, fried food, shampoo, bubble bath, cosmetics, enriched flour, and pasta.

Corn products: Corn flour, corn starch, corn oil, corn sweeteners, syrups. Products that may contain GE corn derivatives: Vitamin C, tofu dogs, chips, candies, ice cream, infant formula, salad dressing, tomato sauce, bread, cookies, cereals, baking powder, alcohol, vanilla, margarine, soy sauce, tamari, soda, fried food, powdered sugar, enriched flour, and pasta.

Canola oil: Products that contain GE canola derivatives: chips, salad dressing, cookies, margarine, soap, detergent, soy cheese, fried food.

Cotton: Oil, fabric. Products that may contain GE cotton or derivatives: clothes, linens, chips, peanut butter, crackers, cookies.

Potatoes: Products that contain GE potatoes or derivatives: unspecified processed or restaurant potato products (fried, mashed, baked, mixes, etc.), chips, Passover products, vegetable pies, soups.

Tomatoes: No plum or roma tomatoes have been genetically engineered. But one cherry tomato has, as have regular tomatoes. Products that may contain GE tomatoes or derivatives: sauces, purees, pizza, lasagna, and all of those wonderful Italian and Mexican foods.

Dairy products: Milk, cheese, butter, buttermilk, sour cream, yogurt, whey. You have to ask several questions when you are looking at dairy products. Have the cows been treated with rBGH? What kind of feed have they been given? If they are not being fed organic grains, chances are quite likely that they will be eating GE animal feed. What does this do to their milk products? No one knows.

Animal products: Because animal feed often contains genetically engineered organisims, all animal products and animal by-products may be affected.

The above information was provided by Laura Ticciati, executive director of Mothers for Natural Law. She and her husband, Robin, have written a powerful little book entitled *Genetically Engineered Foods, Are they Safe? You Decide.* I strongly recommend this book to all.

One of the primary issues in the health food industry now is that we need verification, even from organic farmers, that the seeds they are getting are not GE. There has and will be pressure applied to organic farmers, as well as other organic producers, to make sure their labels certify GMO free. So far, the overwhelming response has been that we don't want GMOs in our food!

Irradiated Foods

Food irradiation is an FDA-approved process that exposes food to radioactive materials in order to kill insects and bacteria and to slow ripening. It has many other capabilities, which proponents for this technology ignore.

To put food irradiation into perspective, a chest x-ray delivers a fraction of one rad of radiation, yet FDA permits up to 100,000 rads in our food. It has been shown that irradiated food causes changes in human physiology. It is linked to cancer, kidney disease, and changes in white blood cells and chromosomes.

Along with killing insects and parasites, it also kills bacteria, but not the toxins created by the bacteria that wreak havoc in our bodies. It also destroys up to 80% of the vitamin content, specifically A, B, C, D, and K and almost entirely wipes out Vitamin E.

Most proponents for irradiation seem to be major food manufacturers, which is hardly a surprise since they would be the only ones benefiting, other than the nuclear waste management program from the Department of Energy, which recycles their waste into our food supply.

Buying organic is the only answer for those of us wanting to avoid buying genetically altered or irradiated products. Many people complain about the higher prices and the limited availability of organic products. This is changing quickly, though. With more and more people becoming aware and switching over to organic, it will increase demand and availability. Ask your supermarket. Most will be happy to bring in the products you request. Also, consider this: The most expensive organic products tend to be the refined and packaged convenience foods that I recommend you do without anyway!

If you are interested in more information on irradiation, contact Food and Water at 800-Eat-Safe.

Living Foods

On a daily basis, my family's diet consists of between 50% to 75% raw foods. This seems to be a good range, depending on the season (having less raw food in cold weather). Fresh, living foods give you the optimum nutrients possible. Heating food destroys a large portion of these nutrients as well as chemically altering a significant part. Enzymes are lost with cooking; therefore, your body will need to use its store of metabolic enzymes. This depletes our reserves, which sets us up for disease and rapid aging, which is, sadly, seen more often than not in our country. Nutrients are also diminished prior to actually eating a meal due to the type of preparation and the length of time it is allowed to sit. A prime example is fresh juices, which need to be consumed immediately for any benefit. If a juice bar is easily accessible to you, that is fine as long as you can see them prepare your selection for you. It is so easy to do your own, though. I cannot imagine going through the trouble of driving or walking to a juice bar. Bottled juice found in the market is not even worth discussing.

My girls enjoy fresh fruits, veggies, nuts, seeds, and sprouts every day. Although it is easier for children to accept and enjoy a whole foods diet from the beginning, it is not difficult to introduce these foods to older children.

For those of you unaccustomed to eating raw food, it can cause uncomfortable digestive symptoms, such as headaches, gas, and bad breath. This in no way means raw food is bad. Rather, your body is showing you just how toxic and weak it has become due to past abuse.

You must slowly work yourself into it. If you have never eaten a salad, eat one salad a day, or try steaming veggies until they are just tender (do not overcook!), which is better tolerated until your body adjusts.

Be sure to practice correct food combining. Melons should always be eaten by themselves. The reason is quite simple. A melon is made up of mostly water and can be digested very quickly (15 to 30 minutes). If you eat a meal with or before the melon, it is stuck in the digestive tract along with the other food. The sugars from the melon will start to ferment in this warm climate, which causes the remaining food to putrefy as well. All sugar has the same type of reaction, so sweetened drinks or desserts should not be ingested with meals either.

If you choose to use dairy, do not have milk with any other food product.

Concentrated proteins and grains do not work well together because it takes completely different enzymes to break them down and they need distinctly different atmospheres to do the job. Grains need a more alkaline atmosphere and protein needs an acid state, both of which will be diluted, diminished, or halted when combined. Keep your food choices simple.

As a nation we stuff our bodies with potions and pills to stop heartburn, gas, constipation, diarrhea, etc. This is quite laughable when, if we were combining our food correctly, eating healthier, and eating less, we would not need these products at all. Imagine, a whole industry based on gluttony would disappear!

Water

There is an overwhelming amount of information out on the unhealthy additions in our water. Most of us never bother to question the quality of the water that we use every day. I believe this is because we are not consciously aware of the reasons why our bodies need this vital nourishment. The majority of us survive on minimal amounts of water, replacing it with other beverages such as milk, soda, alcohol, coffee, and tea. Even those who strive to keep a clean, unadulterated diet dismiss the importance of the quantity and quality of their water intake.

An individual who eats large amounts of animal products has excess uric acid and other toxins in the system. Toxins are also created in those who ingest imbalanced nutrients through refined carbohydrates.

The kidney and liver functions are greatly enhanced by increased water intake. Pure distilled water with no toxins to add to the bloodstream is extremely beneficial in helping to disperse and clear out accumulated wastes. This eases the energy load on your organs, which frees them to perform their normal health-promoting activities.

Most of a city's tap water has already passed through a sewer or gone through an industrial and municipal service, giving us plenty of wastes, bacteria, or other toxins to enjoy with each glassful. Herbicides, pesticides, THMs, cysts, parasites, lead, mercury, and VOCs, are just some of the ingredients that may come through. Though the water is cleaned before it reaches your tap, there are questions on how effective that treatment is and what health risks are involved in the use of certain chemicals to clean the water. Not to mention how the environment may be affected.

Chlorine is one of the chemicals used in the "cleaning" of our water, though it can be harmful to eyes, mucous membranes, and skin. It also will destroy vitamin E and beneficial intestinal flora. The latest research shows that inhalation of chlorine, such as when we are showering, is even more detrimental to health than bathing in it. Chlorine will also combine with any organic substance that may be in the water and can form chloroform, which is a cancer-causing chemical.

Fluoride is another tap water additive.

Calcium fluoride was originally tested as a tooth decay preventive and touted as essential for children. In my opinion, if a child is in good health and eating wholesome foods, tooth decay would not be a major health issue.

Many cities were "sold" on the necessity of fluoridating their water. Ironically, it was not calcium fluoride that was being added but rather sodium fluoride. This is an extremely toxic by-product of the aluminum industry. Before being added to city water it was used primarily as a rat poison. There has never been any definitive evidence to back the use of fluoridated water and many countries have discontinued it or never deemed it necessary to have it. So why do we? Maybe because sodium fluoride as a waste product was very expensive to dispose of. More commonly used today (90%) is hydrofluorosilicic acid, a direct by-product of pollution scrubbers used in the phosphate fertilizer and aluminum industries. The government adds this highly toxic form of fluoride into water supplies even though it is trying to get rid of its own stockpile of fluoride compounds from years of stockpiling fluorides for use in the process of refining uranium for nuclear power and weapons. Sodium, rock, and hydrofluorosilicic fluoride are very toxic and are retained in great amounts in the body. There is a huge demand for this once-upon-a-time waste product and it is a lucrative side business of certain industries.

Fluoride disrupts thyroid disfunction. There are many medications with fluorine in them, such as Prozac.

Fluoride is also a mutagenic. In 1981, Dean Burk, head chemist at the National Cancer Institute, testified at congressional hearings, reporting that at least 40,000 cancer deaths in 1981 were attributable to fluoridation—40,000 cases that could have been prevented simply by not putting industry waste into the public water supply.

Recently a grievance was filed by the union representing all scientists at EPA headquarters in Washington, D.C., asking for fluoride-free bottled water for their offices, a request partly based on their recent findings that fluorides can seriously impair neurological functions and can reduce IQ level in children. The scientists at EPA are required by law to set a maximum contaminant level for fluoride in water, specifically to avoid a condition known as crippling skeletal fluorosis (CSF).

Tap water and toothpaste are not our only sources of fluoride. It is also found in beverages, processed foods, fresh fruit and vegetables, pharmaceuticals, teflon-coated cookware, vitamins and mineral supplements, teas, air, etc.

An unfathomable amount of pharmaceuticals and personal care products are entering our environment every year. Most of these are passed through humans and into our sewage treatment plants and then into our waterways.

This really brings the argument home that every action we take directly affects our health and the environment. Everything from perfume to sunscreen lotions to shampoos, fungal remedies, and prescription drugs. Most of us wonder if such minute amounts of these substances would really affect our lives?

Many of these products are used long term, which causes chronic exposure. There are unknown side effects with pharmaceuticals as well as, in many cases, unknown modes of action. There is also a combined concentration of similar drug mechanisms that could create a high exposure level. Physiological and endocrinological disruptors found in drugs will affect all life forms.

There has been years of research on pesticides and other chemicals. In fact, the National Institute of Health, the EPA, and the National Institute of Standards have "spectral libraries" to recognize them. Their libraries do not include identifying most pharmaceuticals, however. Alarming enough? Think about this: Personal care products and pharmaceuticals may also be found in our feces, otherwise known as sewer sludge, which is used on a great deal of our croplands.

Sewer sludge is not used on organic crops. And for those farmers who use manure, who's to say we don't get animals' pharmaceuticals?

This is not a new problem. For over twenty years, regulatory officials and drug corporations have dismissed it as having any potential adverse effects. The Genome Project is creating a huge array of new drugs, along with drugs that are being passed through the FDA, switching from prescription to nonprescription status. This increases their availability.

I am not crazy about my little girls getting subtherapeutic dosages of Viagra, Prozac, or Estrone. It is a real concern. Tests have been done that show low-level amounts in tap water.

Wells, streams, and springs may not be healthy either, if they are in close proximity to agriculture and livestock. Fertilizers, animal excrement, pesticides, and other substances can seep into the ground, affecting your water source.

What can we do to correct this problem? With proper care given to the body in the form of food, exercise, emotional and spiritual support, the need for pharmaceuticals will diminish. Most personal care products are not needed. If you do need one, try a natural brand, which will be kinder on you and the environment. There is a huge array of products available at natural food markets and frequently at your local supermarkets. You and your family can make a difference.

Distilled water is my drink of choice, coupled with a wholesome diet. I am confident I am receiving a greater amount of nourishment than most, and a dramatically decreased amount of chemicals, which none of us needs.

Your children are not your children.
They are the sons and the daughters of life's longing for itself.
They come through you but not from you,
and though they are with you, yet they belong not to you.
You may give them your love, but not your thoughts, for they have their own thoughts.
You may house their bodies but not their souls, for their souls dwell in the house of tomorrow, which you cannot visit, not even in your dreams.
You may strive to be like them, but seek not to make them like you.
You are the bows from which your children as living arrows are sent forth.
Let your bending in the archer's hand be for gladness.

—Kahlil Gibran, *The Prophet*

Thinking of the Children

Feeding Your Children

The American Academy of Pediatrics stated in 1995, "An American child has viewed about 360,000 advertisements before graduating from high school.... In 1750 B.C. *the Code of Hammurabi made it a crime, punishable by death, to sell anything to a child without first obtaining a power of attorney. In the 1990s selling products to American children has become a standard business practice."*

"So what can I feed my children?" or "But my child is such a picky eater!"

Sound familiar?

This is so often a source of frustration for parents as they transition towards a healthier lifestyle. It is certainly easier to feed a child who has always followed a healthy diet than it is to feed those who have already adulterated their palates and are led by peer pressure. It can be done, however, with persistence and a full explanation as to why.

Each child is so different. My eldest is a mono-diet type, which means she will only eat one thing at a time. My youngest, on the other hand, wants a variety of foods. What they both have in common, though, is the desire for simply prepared foods. They do not want fancy dressings, sauces, gravies, casseroles, etc. As I am writing this, it is late spring and the kids have been asking for asparagus and artichokes like crazy. I steam these and let them eat their fill. Shortly after, they want something more and are ready for a heavier food, say a protein or grain.

My eldest will also be obsessed with certain foods, asking for red bell pepper five days in a row. I think this is completely natural and her body knows what is needed. I always offer her two choices for a meal and stick with that unless she requests something equal to what I would have given her. I need to bend with my children's desires, but I am still firm about what they will eat throughout the day in regard to a balance of fruits, vegetables, grains, fats, and proteins. Rhiannon and Gwendolyn understand the importance of eating their vegetables before starting on something else. Most times any conflict about food choices has more to do with emotional control than with taste. That is where patience and the ability to treat your child with respect and as an intelligent individual comes into play. I have never forced them to eat a food with the words "Eat because I said so!" Or worse, "Eat it or you won't get dessert!" Instead I talk about the reasons why I give them these foods. Number one is because I love them too much not to give them good food. They are never too young to talk to about nutrition, how it works, or where food goes. When Rhiannon was two-and-a-half years old we made a game about where food starts in the mouth and how it ends up. Now, at the age of five, she has a good understanding of how the digestive system works.

If your child is transitioning to a healthier diet, it is easy to disguise foods into something they will enjoy eating. Shakes are a great way to get sprouts, nuts, and seeds into a child. Use a vegan milk (almond milk is my preference) and add the nuts, seeds, and/or sprouts, and some frozen raspberries. Whip it up in a strong blender. Cashews work well because they make the shake real creamy. A dash of vanilla and sweetener, such as stevia liquid, adds flavor and masks the sprouts, which have a distinctive taste. Rhiannon calls this her pink milk and requests it often. If your child is really adventurous, add some green to it, such as spirulina or barley grass. I highly recommend these green foods for children, as well as adults.

Raw cookies are a popular way to get children to eat foods they may not otherwise try. Children love finger foods, probably because it is easier for their little hands and sort of a taboo in most families. Making little balls, patties, or mini shish kebabs on toothpicks are favored.

More exotic foods such as sea vegetables may be a challenge at first due to their unusual appearance. Most children really like the distinctive taste. Dulse can be eaten out of the bag or dry toasted briefly for "chips." Arame and hijiki are fun. Kids like to gross out the parents by telling them they are eating worms! Nori is probably the most accepted, due to the popularity of sushi. I have rolled many combinations of food in a nori sheet with enthusiastic appreciation from young diners. The main thing is to lighten up on how we view food and the dinner table. It should be a joyful experience and a special time for the family to interact. Placing your own expectations on a child will only cause stress between you and your child.

Our perception of food has to change if we want good health for ourselves and our children. Getting connected to the whole cycle of life can be a very empowering feeling. Knowing that we are nourished by the sun, air, water, and earth, directly or indirectly, by eating a food that was, is a spiritual experience. We tend to view life in a more gentle way and journey through the years with more respect to living beings.

The long-term ramifications of this way of thinking are both infinite and awe-inspiring. I am so proud of the fact that my children are being raised in an atmosphere of awareness. Intelligence is not something given to children when they reach a certain age, but rather it is innate. Allowing the information and tools to be readily available to them enables them to sort out and make knowledgeable decisions for their own welfare. The impact that parents have on their children reaches far past the time they have grown and left home. I believe it is our responsibility to be as informed as possible, and to share this with them. Many of us have unresolved issues from our childhood, which have caused us not to take care of our own bodies. It would be very selfish of us if we did not work on these issues, as they most assuredly will affect our children.

Love of self must come before love of another.

Children's Food List

In this section, I have listed all the recipes in my book that children especially like, and included some ideas for meals throughout the day. These are suggestions that will provide a springboard for you and your child's creativity.

Never try to force a child to eat in the morning unless there is hunger. It is not true that a big breakfast is your most important meal of the day. Heavy food actually impedes the body's functioning, making it work harder to break down, assimilate, and remove toxins. This can give a lethargic feeling, headaches, cloudy brain functioning, etc. My children tend to like fruit upon waking, then a couple of hours later ask for something more substantial. There is no reason to feel rushed or pressured in the morning. If you find yourself running out of time, wake up a little earlier and go to bed a little earlier. Planning meals the night before helps tremendously.

The following list is varied, and children will find it difficult to become bored with their meals. For breakfast, try:

- Fresh or dry unsulphured fruit and raw nuts or seeds
- Shakes or smoothies (most all of the recipes in the Beverage section)
- Baked sweet potatoes
- Yogurt (I prefer Nancy's nondairy) with or without fruit
- Soups (Why not? Leftovers from the night before are great, especially on cool mornings.)
- Creamy rice cereal with oat milk
- Quicky Oats
- Hot millet cereal (1/2 cup rinsed and toasted millet cooked in 2 cups of water or vegan milk)
- Pancakes (Measure ingredients the night before and mix dry ingredients into wet ingredients in the morning.)
- Waffles (Soak grains at night, then blend in the morning.)
- Cashew French Toast

At home, small children will appreciate a variety of "grazings" for snacks and lunch. Try a large platter or lazy Susan filled with lightly steamed or raw veggies, dips, spreads, etc., and watch as it is devoured throughout mid-morning and afternoon.

Dinner should be more formal, with everyone sitting down together and sharing conversation, food, and laughter. This is a special family connection time.

- Banana Miso Tahini Spread
- Carrot Butter
- Quick and Easy Hummus
- Dulse Gomacio
- Fresh Tomato Sauce
- Vegan Sour Cream
- Broccoli Soup
- Fresh Tomato Soup
- Lemon Soup
- Pea and Carrot Soup
- Spinach Soup
- Tomato Carrot Soup
- Cashew or Almond Butter and Shredded Carrot Sandwiches
- Vegetable Sandwiches
- Carrot Salad Sandwiches
- Fresh green salads with child's choice of veggies
- Quinoa and Lentils (Rinse 1/2 cup quinoa, add to 1 3/4 cups boiling water with 1/4 cup lentils. Cook until liquid is absorbed. If lentils are still too chewy, add a little more water and cook a few more minutes.)
- Sprouted chickpeas and brown rice simmered in vegetable broth
- Potato, Corn, and Cherry Tomato Salad
- Coleslaw
- Sesame Carrot Salad with Arame
- Tabbouleh
- Chopped Main Salad Rolled in Nori
- Mock Egg and Chicken Salads (Serve with baked corn chips.)
- All recipes in the Breads section

- Nori Rolls and Rice Balls
- Potato quarters with Vegan Sour Cream and Dulse Gomacio
- Wilted Spinach
- Sautéed Kale with a splash of Bragg Liquid Aminos
- Spaghetti Squash and Green Beans
- Coconut and Cashew Veggies
- White Beans with Tomato and Sage
- Any plain beans and rice dish
- Bean Croquettes
- Asian Spring Rolls
- Pecan Patties
- Polenta Pizza
- Italian Beans 'n Greens
- Spinach and Rice Casserole with Toasted Almonds
- Squash and Bean Casserole
- Veggie Rolls
- Mediterranean Stuffed Collard Greens
- Squash and Leek Turnovers
- Spinach Fritters
- Cashew Burgers
- Earth Burgers
- Millet Nut and Seed Balls
- Rosemary Tofu Sauté
- Stuffed Pockets
- Tempeh Millet Loaf
- All dessert recipes

Other snacks may include avocado (my youngest daughter's favorite), frozen berries as finger food, toasted pumpkin seeds with or without a splash of Bragg's, cashews or almonds . . . and on and on. Don't forget lots and lots of water throughout the day!

Food Group Facts

Fats

One U.S. study showed that from 1991 to 1998, obesity increased in every state. The authors of the study said: "Rarely do chronic conditions such as obesity spread with the speed and dispersion characteristic of a communicable disease epidemic."

Many dieters cringe when they see my family enjoying avocados, nuts, and other full-fat whole foods. Most shake their heads in disbelief when I explain these are good fats, essential for optimum body functioning. I grin and add that eating fat actually helps maintain my weight.

It is important to know what a fat is and understand how it works in your body. Fats are as important as protein and carbohydrates. In fact, the basic composition of all foods includes these three components in differing degrees.

A lettuce, tomato, and cucumber salad has fat and so does a handful of almonds. This is natural and the way it should be, with the food also having the proper balance of nutrients needed for it to metabolize in the body.

Fats are similar in makeup to carbohydrates, composed of hydrogen, carbon, and oxygen. The difference between the two is that there is less oxygen and more carbon and hydrogen in fats. So, though they will be broken down similarly, it takes more bodily energy to metabolize fat.

Fats in humans and animals come from two sources—from the food we eat, and from excess carbohydrate intake (and the body's need to break down and store this excess as fat).

Fats are composed of glycerin and fatty acids. Glycerin is broken down into sugar, which may be used as fuel by the body. Fatty acids are described as chains of oxygen, carbon, and hydrogen atoms. These chains have links where additional atoms may be attached.

If hydrogen is attached to these links, the fat becomes solid, as in products like shortening and margarine. If oxygen is attached, the fat turns rancid.

Unsaturated fats are fatty acid chains with one or more carbon atoms missing their hydrogen atom accompaniment. Open links in these fatty acid chains are desirable. This is the way the body can combine certain nutrients with the fatty acids, allowing them both to be transported through the body where they can be used. Nuts and seeds are our chief sources of unsaturated fats, while animal fats contain very little.

Polyunsaturated fats (P.F.s) have a larger number of fatty acids with two or more open links in their chains. Polyunsaturated fats have harmful effects. It is generally known that P.F.s lower the cholesterol level in the blood. What is not generally known, though, is that P.F.s will move the cholesterol from the bloodstream into the tissues where it is more harmful. Researchers have also shown that P.F.s will inhibit white blood cells.

The hydrogenation process of fats destroys any nutrients that may be present. These added hydrogen atoms fill the empty links on the fatty acid chain and block additional nutrients as well.

Saturated fats are found mainly in animal products and coconuts (though fats from coconuts have a different chemical makeup). Saturated fats act like hydrogenated fats and do not allow nutrients to bond onto the fatty acid chains.

The good fat found in whole foods is used by your body as a source of essential fatty acids, as a source of heat and energy, as padding for organs and nerves, as well as a regulator of the fat-soluble vitamins A, D, E, and K.

The bulk of the fat in your diet should be derived from whole foods and not cooking oils. If you do sauté or stir-fry, try adding a little water. Baked goods containing oil should be looked at as occasional treats and not as a daily addition to the diet. Do not use low-fat or nonfat food products. They could be detrimental to your health, being deficient in nutrients needed for proper assimilation.

My Beloved is the mountains,
And lonely wooded valleys,
Strange Islands,
And resounding rivers,
The whistling of love-stirring breezes,
The tranquil night
At the time of rising dawn,
Silent music,
Sounding solitude,
The supper that refreshes and
deepens love.

—St. John of the Cross, mystic

If foods are cooked in high-heated oil, they can become carcinogenic. That means healthy cells may become cancerous.

In order for fats to be digested, they must be emulsified. High-heated oil cannot be emulsified. Your body will try to expel what it cannot use. If your body cannot expel all of it, it will store it in areas where it will cause the least harm.

You have to be aware of this even when you shop in health food stores. Potato chips, doughnuts, french fries, etc., are not healthier for you when purchased at these establishments! If you really want something like this, try baked chips, which may be a better selection.

Most food value found in oil will be lost when heated. The heated oil breaks down, and the fat-soluble vitamins will not be absorbed. So not only is the heated oil devoid of nutrition, it contributes to nutrient starvation of the body.

Eating whole foods lets go of the need to count calories and fat, and your body will feel satiated with a smaller intake. There are built-in safety factors in the natural food provided for us which prevent us from becoming obese.

The benefits of eating avocados, raw nuts, seeds, and legumes include: protection from cancer, heart disease, and arthritis; enhanced immune system; weight loss, mental clarity, hormonal balancing, smooth skin, strong nails, and lustrous hair.

The essential fatty acids found in whole foods are necessary for adults and children for brain and nerve functioning. I make sure my daughters have ample fat daily. I know I am doing well by how they glow with good health!

Coconut oil is an exception to the rule. It is one of the few plant foods that contain saturated fat. The critical difference between coconut and animal fat is that coconut is comprised of medium-chain and not long-chain saturated fatty acids. Medium-chain saturates digest easily and are used for fuel and energy, whereas the long-chain saturates are stored as fat in your body.

Coconut oil has many attributes, a few of which are:

- It contains almost 50% lauric acid in its makeup, which is a disease-fighting fatty acid, ideal for immune-suppressed individuals.
- It is a source of medium-chain triglycerides, which enable your body to digest fat efficiently.
- It is very stable and contains no harmful trans-fatty acids. This makes it a desirable oil for sautéing and stir-frying. No oil is good for deep-frying.
- Less is needed. Use approximately 1/4 measure less in any recipe.
- It has a mild taste, complementing all types of cooking and ingredients.
- It adds a richness of texture and taste to baked goods.

Many natural food stores carry coconut butter. If yours does not you can order it directly through Omega Nutrition, whose coconut butter is organic, processed, and packaged in a much healthier manner than most others. Their website is www.omegaflo.com and the phone number is 800-661-3529. They also carry a terrific line of other oils such as flax, hemp, and borage.

The food processing industry would like you to believe that coconut oil is unhealthy. It was in the news several years ago that coconut oil (especially that used in movie theaters) was detrimental to health. I would have to agree with that. If the oil used was nonorganic, processed with solvents and other chemicals and hydrogenated, then of course it would be unhealthy. One of the fears of the oil industry is that if you choose to use a pure source, carefully extracted oil over one of theirs, then theirs will no longer be wanted. Secondly, they will have to admit that most of the oil in today's markets is harmful. If this were to happen, it would alert us to the fact that perhaps other processed foods need to be questioned.

Some tips on oil:

- Buy small bottles of cold or expeller-pressed oil.
- Never buy hydrogenated.
- Do not fry.
- Do not let oil smoke in pan.
- Refrigerate oil after opening.
- Keep oil away from direct light.
- Smell your oil—if it smells rancid, do not use it.
- Keep your oil intake to a minimum.

My personal choices:

- Olive
- Sesame
- Coconut
- Flax—not for cooking
- Hemp—not for cooking

What we need to always keep in mind is that a fractionated food of any kind will never be healthier than a whole food. When using oils, do so wisely ... a little bit can go a long way.

Roughly 25% of U.S. children are overweight or obese. Children who are overweight turn into adults who tend to be overweight as well.

The day of my spiritual awakening was the day that I saw—and knew that I saw—All things in God, and God in all things.

—Mechtild of Magdeburg, mystic

Proteins

There are many different proteins functioning in our bodies. All proteins are composed of amino acids, which are, simply stated, the building blocks of proteins.

Our body cannot use protein in its original state. Instead, it will break it down into separate amino acids. Once this takes place, the body will then construct the specific protein it needs. When a protein is broken down, it is used immediately or absorbed by the liver and stored for future use. We have a reserve, or pool, of amino acids from which the body can draw at any time. There is no need, therefore, to try to consume foods or combinations of foods to achieve a "complete protein" in one meal. When we think of protein needs, we should realize that an understanding of amino acids is what is important in evaluating the true ultimate value of a food.

There are two ways our body receives protein. One is by diet—what we consume. The other is by catabolic cell processes, where other cells digest an expired cell. The waste is broken back down into amino acids and then used again to synthesize their own protein.

Of the twenty-three recognized amino acids, eight are considered essential because they must be found in a food source. With a varied whole food diet, you will have no problem attaining these.

Quality of protein is more important than quantity. Too much will wreak havoc in the body. It was originally recommended that people consume approximately 120 grams of protein a day. This conclusion was based on the misconception that since muscles are composed chiefly of protein, then protein must supply energy to the muscles. (Today, it is understood that plant-based food supplies the best fuel for muscular activity.) This recommendation was supported by further research in the late 1800s when experiments on dogs were done to determine safe amounts of protein intake. Unfortunately there was no adjustment made for the differences between humans and dogs. At around the same time, experiments in Germany showed that 40 grams of protein was sufficient. However, since the old standards were so well fixed in the minds of the medical establishment, it remained at that level until even more research forced them to lower it to 60 or 70 grams, twice the amount considered safe by the aforementioned experiments.

In the past sixty years, independent researchers have concluded that only 24 to 30 grams of protein are necessary to maintain good health. A study done by Dr. Jaffe at the University of California at Berkeley showed that the diets of large healthy groups of people around the world included 15 to 35 grams. Today, a typical American meat eater consumes over 90 grams of protein a day.

So, is too much protein detrimental? Definitely!

A high-protein diet will eventually destroy the entire glandular system. Protein metabolism leaves waste products such as uric, sulfuric, and phosphoric acids. This causes your body to become highly acidic, which forces your body's buffer systems to work very hard at trying to get rid of these substances. Buffer systems are those organs that maintain normal body pH, the major ones being your liver and kidneys.

Back in the early 1950s, scientific research showed that breast milk contained 60% less protein than the infant needed, according to RDA standards. A formula was created with 2½ to 3 times the amount of protein in breast milk, plus salt. Disastrous results from using this new formula began to appear. Symptoms included kidney damage, hyperacidity with osteoporosis, dangerously high phenylalanine and tyrosine content in the blood, poor protein metabolism, and increased acceleration of physical growth without mental growth.

Potassium and magnesium are deficient in the typical American meat eater's diet. Magnesium deficiency syndrome is apparent in arteriosclerosis, high blood pressure, migraine headaches, eclampsia, the leaching of calcium from teeth and bones, liver damage, and disturbance of the neuromuscular vessel system. The kidneys are deeply affected by all the above factors. Sports medicine services in the U.S.

have had to treat an extraordinary number of kidney injuries and breakdowns after athletic competitions due to high protein intake. The American Heart Association concluded that almost all of these diseases—arteriosclerosis, high blood pressure, and coronary disease—are significantly related to kidney function and, therefore, more than half of the population die of kidney disease.

Points to remember:

- The more protein you ingest, the more calcium (and other alkaline minerals) is excreted from your body. Remember: Dairy is a protein as well, so it would be best if you did the opposite of the popular milk campaign!
- If your calcium levels are low, your body will extract it from the bone to use in other functions.
- One in four women have lost 50% to 75% of original bone material by age sixty-five.
- If our blood becomes too acidic, the body extracts calcium, an alkaline mineral, from the bones to balance our pH. Meat, eggs, and fish are the most acid-forming foods.
- Eskimos have the highest dietary calcium intake of any other people (more than 2,000 milligrams per day from fish flesh and bones). They have the highest protein intake, 250 to 400 grams a day. They also have the highest rate of osteoporosis in the world.
- Protein exists in all whole foods in varying degrees. There should be no concern in where we can find it, but rather in the quality and the ease in which our body utilizes it. Especially good sources are whole grains, such as quinoa, millet, and amaranth, sea vegetables, kale, spinach, broccoli, nuts, seeds, beans, lentils, tofu, and tempeh.
- If you eat a wide spectrum of whole foods, you receive ample amounts of protein and calcium. In fact, it would be difficult not to.

There are so many drug residues in cow's milk that many consumers are in agreement that it should be purchased by prescription.

Dairy

When first transitioning my diet to a plant-based one, I still relied heavily on dairy for protein and calcium, predominantly with cheese. I was never a milk drinker. As a child I found it unappealing and I never felt good after drinking it. I did, however, enjoy buttermilk on occasion. Becoming more in tune with my body allowed me to connect how I felt from the effects of dairy, usually immediately upon ingestion. Symptoms included constipation, edema, abdominal pain (nausea and gas), difficulty breathing, excess mucus, and others. The most surprising symptom I was not even aware of until I eliminated dairy completely was the stiffness I felt in my joints and muscles, which I had considered normal. Movement is now more fluid and without discomfort. I feel wonderfully free of any constriction and my yoga postures have improved dramatically.

I weaned myself from dairy several years ago and have not brought it into my home or made it available to my children. I do not consider it a healthy option.

Both my daughters were breastfed beyond the age of two. And it was the sole source of nutrition in their first year.

Cow's milk and human milk are so completely different in makeup that it boggles my mind how much we rely on it as a food source. A human child grows slower, lives longer, and has the most rapidly growing brain of all animals. A calf has a smaller brain and rapid body growth.

Human milk contains lecithin and high amounts of taurine, an amino acid, both of which are needed for proper brain development. Cow's milk is deficient in these. Human milk also contains much more cystine and tryptophan (two more amino acids). Cow's milk is also deficient in iodine, iron, phosphorus, and manganese. Human milk contains six times more selenium and twice as much vitamin E.

The Composition of Foods, Agriculture Handbook No. 8 showed that 100 grams of human milk provides 1.1 grams of protein and 9.5 grams of carbohydrates, whereas cow's milk provides 3.5 grams of protein and 4.9 grams of carbohydrates. During the most rapidly growing period of our life, we only need modest amounts of protein, and the proper kind!

Rennin is a curding enzyme important in the digestive processes of infants, where it prevents the too-rapid passage of milk from the stomach. It starts to diminish when a child reaches approximately two years of age and begins to secrete the enzyme ptyalin, which is necessary for starch digestion. This is your body's way of signaling that it is ready to be weaned.

Pasteurized milk has its own set of problems, mainly that heating the milk will make it even more difficult to digest. The casein is coagulated and toughened, and the vitamin and mineral components are spoiled and made unavailable to your body. The lactic acid bacilli, which are beneficial intestinal flora, are destroyed. Milk is subjected to many other processes before it reaches your table. These processes are never put on the label.

Those knowledgeable about milk state that it has become more of an excretion of the cow than a secretion, due to the fact that the milk today also contains alarming amounts of drugs, including antibiotics, and concentrated levels of pollutants from the environment, such as pesticides. It has been shown that one dose of penicillin given to a cow will appear in the milk after four to seven milkings. Cows are given hormones for greater milk output. The average cow produces 1½ to 2 gallons of milk per day. With hormone use they can produce 8 to 9 gallons!

Bovine growth hormone is another big issue with many health risks. An article in the *Los Angeles Times* on March 20, 1994, stated the following:

- Growth hormone is not destroyed by pasteurization or digestion and is readily absorbed across the intestinal wall.
- Growth hormone induces rapid division and multiplication of normal human breast epithelial cells in tissue cultures.
- "The breast tissues of female fetuses and infants are sensitive to hormonal influences. Imprinting by IGF-1 (insulin-like growth

factor-1) may increase future breast cancer risks and sensitivity of the breast to subsequent unrelated risks such as mammography and the carcinogenic and estrogen-like effects of pesticide residues in food, particularly in pre-menopausal women" (*A Needless New Risk of Breast Cancer* by Samuel S. Epstein).

The protein content of human milk is mostly albumin, while that of cow's milk is mostly casein. Casein forms large, difficult-to-digest curds. Humans have problems with it but a cow (which has a four-stomach digestive system) can handle it just fine. A wonderful book to read is *Don't Drink Your Milk* by Frank Oski, M.D.

The Nutrition Committees of the American Academy of Pediatrics and the Canadian Pediatric Society jointly issued a report in 1979 strongly favoring breastfeeding, giving the following reasons:

1. The fats obtained from human milk are more easily absorbed by the human infant than those found in cow's milk.
2. The cholesterol in mother's milk serves a valuable purpose in the development of the infant.
3. The protein in mother's milk is a near-perfect source for infants—much better than cow's milk!
4. Infants are able to absorb about 50% more iron from mother's milk than from cow's milk. Infants on cow's milk for extended periods are at risk for iron deficiency, whereas full-term breast-fed infants receive sufficient iron from mother's milk until their birth weight has tripled.
5. Mother's milk also provides important protective factors not available from any formula. Two substances, lactoferrin and transferrin, prevent potentially harmful bacteria from growing in the intestinal tract. In addition, the infant is provided with important immunities by a fluid (colostrom) secreted by the breast during the first few days following birth. Finally, breast milk contains lysozymes, enzymes that attack and break down harmful bacteria, as well as a substance known as the bifidus factor, which promotes the growth of protective bacteria in the infant's body.

Mother's milk is the optimal food for mammals during the period of their most rapid growth, not for adults.

Some people react more severely than others when consuming dairy. Anyone who has asthma, allergies, frequent colds, bronchitis, etc., should get off milk immediately. Other problems connected with dairy consumption include heart disease, colic, cramps, skin rashes, acne, gastrointestinal bleeding, diarrhea, iron deficiency, anemia, arthritis, ear infections, diabetes, osteoporosis, cataracts, ovarian cancer, and autoimmune diseases such as MS.

Babies who are breastfed are 74% less likely to develop symptoms of asthma. American children miss 10 million school days every year because of asthma.

Some 50% of all grain grown in the U.S. is consumed by livestock. The standards for the spraying of pesticides on the grain eaten by livestock are lower than the standards for the grain eaten by humans. Thus, pesticides are found in high concentration in cow's milk.

A study of 1422 Norwegians who drank two or more glasses of milk per day showed 3.5 times the incidence of lymphatic cancer (*British Medical Journal,* 1990).

The use of cow's milk can contribute to juvenile diabetes and autoimmune diseases by interrupting the ability of the pancreas to produce insulin (*The New England Journal of Medicine,* 1992).

The late Dr. Benjamin Spock stated that cow's milk causes internal blood loss, allergies, indigestion, and contributes to some cases of childhood diabetes as well as anemia in babies.

Europe and New Zealand have banned the importation of rBGH milk. Several states in the U.S. now require labeling on packaging of rBGH products.

So how do we get calcium if we should not ingest milk? By eating a varied plant-based diet you will never fear getting too little. Dark greens, such as kale and collards, are my favorite. Sea vegetables, almonds, sunflower seeds, broccoli, figs, and parsley are all good sources. Plant-source calcium is also much more readily utilized by our bodies.

There is another factor essential for absorbing and utilizing calcium. All the minerals in the body are in a delicate, dynamic balance.

If a deficiency in calcium exists, other minerals will also be out of balance.

Remember this as well. Digestion of meats result in acids that must be neutralized by calcium (an alkaline mineral). Meat eating contributes to a phosphorus/calcium ratio in Americans that is four times greater than desirable. Phosphorus is essential for calcium utilization, but too much will deplete it. Sulphur, which is concentrated in meat, limits calcium absorption, and saturated fats combine with calcium to form a soap-like compound that is eliminated by the body. Simply put, the more meat and dairy consumed, the more calcium is excreted out of the body.

And just when you think that is enough to turn someone off dairy, here is some more interesting research that has come out recently.

In 1999, the World Health Organization held a dioxin conference in Geneva, Switzerland, and determined that 90% of dioxins ingested by humans come from milk, dairy products, and meat. Dioxins are the most toxic substances ever produced by man and are said to be extremely carcinogenic.

Rocz Panstw, a Polish journal, reported in 1999,

> Dioxins are highly toxic by-products of many industrial processes, e.g., chemical and municipal waste incineration or production of chlorophenols. These compounds penetrate the environment via air, water, and soil and are then incorporated in food chains. The major source of human exposure (90% of total exposition) is consumption of a wide variety of common foods (meat, fish, and dairy products) containing small amounts of dioxins. Food contamination with dioxins leads to enhanced accumulation of these compounds in human tissues to the extent of exceeding an acceptable level.

And who do you think ingests the highest amounts of dioxins? Breastfeeding infants whose moms eat meat and dairy.

A study published in the April, 2001, issue of the *Journal of Toxicology and Environmental Health* presents an ongoing study by Dr. Arnold Schecter and his colleagues to determine the extent and effect of dioxin exposure.

Schecter, working at the University of Texas School of Public Health, has determined that Americans are getting 22 times the maximum dioxin exposure suggested by the U.S. Environmental Protection Agency from their food. Nursing infants receive between 35 and 65 times the safe dosage.

A group of European scientists have been testing butter for levels of organic pollutants. Scientists at the University of Lancaster have discovered that dioxins remain in fat. Since butter is pure fat, scientists test samples of it, by region, to determine flows of dioxins.

In an effort to limit dioxin exposure, Ben & Jerry's ice cream company started using dioxin-free packaging. Unfortunately for them, Steve Milloy, author of junkscience.com, tested samples of Ben & Jerry's ice cream for dioxins. The *Detroit Free Press* said on November 8, 1999: "The level of dioxin in a single serving of the Ben & Jerry's World's Best Vanilla Ice Cream tested was almost 200 times greater than the virtually safe (daily) dose determined by the Environmental Protection Agency."

The *Journal of Animal Science* stated in a report in January, 1998, "The lipophilic nature of dioxins results in higher concentrations in the fat of animal and fish products, and their excretion via milk secretion in dairy cattle may result in relatively high concentrations of dioxin contamination in high-fat dairy products."

An Associated Press article on March 30, 2001, stated, "Meat and dairy products are considered the biggest sources. Dioxins concentrate in animal fat, and the best way to avoid them is to eat more fruits and vegetables."

"This is just one more reason for having less animal fats in our diets," Schecter told the *Houston Chronicle*. "Blood samples from pure vegans, who consume no animal products, show that they have less dioxins in their bodies than average Americans."

Traditional people in many countries have used dairy in their diet, usually by boiling it or fermenting it into yogurt and cheese. These were enjoyed in small amounts in addition to a plant-based diet. Americans, on the other hand, have overused dairy in all of its forms, including butter, milk, cheese, and ice cream. Overconsumption is something we have done in all areas of our lives, but I am specifically interested in addressing this issue in our diet. Overconsumption has affected our health in dramatic ways. Americans look at gluttony as acceptable, and we are paying a heavy price.

Milk Alternatives

There are so many milk alternatives to choose from. I have used soy in the past exclusively, but began to feel uneasy about eating and drinking it in excess. (Remember: Too much of a good thing can be bad.)

There is some research that indicates that the protein in cooked soy products becomes denatured, and thus is not properly absorbed in the body. Whether or not that is true, I have not come across enough data to draw a definite conclusion. I do know, though, that my family does not feel great when eating or drinking soy on a daily basis. However, the soy and dairy milk alternatives are equally delicious. Here is a list:

- **Soy milk**—The number-one milk substitute on the market. Available in full- and low-fat, as well as fortified. Available in plain, vanilla, carob, and cocoa flavors.
- **Rice milk**—This is thinner and sweeter than regular soy milk. Another very popular drink. Available in plain, vanilla, carob, and cocoa flavors.
- **Multigrain milk**—Has a rich, creamy texture. Available in plain or vanilla.
- **Oat milk**—Also has a creamy texture. Available in plain or vanilla.
- **Almond milk**—This has a light texture, with just a hint of almond flavor. This is my preference. Available in plain or vanilla.
- **Other nut/seed "milks"**—These can be made with coconut, sesame seeds, cashews, etc. Whatever your choice, you can whip them up and enjoy them in just minutes! Check out the Beverages section for an awesome recipe.

Carbohydrates

Only 25% of U.S. medical schools require future doctors to take nutrition courses.

Carbohydrates are poorly understood. They are a critical component of the foods we eat. Yet, in an extracted or fractionated form, they can create many imbalances in your body. Refined carbohydrates (such as sugar, flour, and cereals) are, I believe, more detrimental to your health than meat or dairy.

All refined carbohydrates are an incomplete food. Most of the nutrients are processed out. In the case of sugar, the body must take vital nutrients from healthy cells to metabolize it. Sodium, potassium, magnesium, and calcium are drawn from various parts of the body to make use of the sugar.

When sugar enters the stomach, glutamic acid and other B vitamins are denied to the body. The loss of these specific vitamins result in a confused mental state and there is a tendency to become sleepy during the day. Since refined sugars are removed from their natural sources, which contain the necessary nutrients for their metabolism, eating sugar causes the body to rob itself of already present vital elements.

For those of you who think you don't eat a lot of sugar products, think about this. Most of the sugar consumed today (about 75%) is hidden in processed foods. This means you, the consumer, are responsible for only about 25% of your sugar intake, meaning what you are physically adding to your food.

On average, we eat approximately 130 pounds of sugar each year. (A *New York Times* article dated May 6, 2001, stated that the average American consumes 70 pounds annually, not including what we get from soft drinks, sauces, and syrups.) Sugar is used extensively in packaged foods to prevent spoilage, to retain moisture, to maintain texture and appearance, and, of course, as a sweetener.

In the new food pyramid, carbohydrates are the heavy favorite. The problem is that there is no differentiating a good carbohydrate from a bad one. Refined grains, like white rice, grits, couscous, wheat flour, etc., are not recommended. Most flours, breads, cereals, noodles, and pastries fall into this category. They are acidic in nature, devoid of natural fiber, and low in water content, making them constipating.

It is a sad statistic that 75% of America's food comes from factories and not farms. We are so far removed from a natural foods diet, and it will just continue to worsen because of the increased domination and control of a few giant food companies. Their only concerns seem to be how they can create cheaper large-scale production and increased shelf life. There is very little thought given to the nutritional value of these nonfoods, and then only when they are pressed by the media to do so. Even then, their attempts are feeble, just enough to satisfy the immediate outcry. But if someone were to go beyond the feeble attempts, they might learn some very upsetting facts.

Such findings might be something like this: The mineral cadmium always exists along with the mineral zinc in foods. Zinc acts as a balancing mineral for the cadmium and prevents it from being absorbed in large quantities by the body. Cadmium, in excessive amounts, is hazardous to human health. It is one of the poisonous elements in cigarette smoke. When grains are refined, zinc is destroyed, but the cadmium is not.

Both iron and copper are destroyed when grains are refined. Copper is necessary for the utilization of iron by the body to build a healthy bloodstream. The food industry was pressured into adding inorganic iron back to the stripped flour, but of course the copper is not added.

Any refining quickly destroys B vitamins. Interestingly enough, the body requires B vitamins to metabolize or use the grains, which is why they are present in the food in the first place. If these vitamins are removed, then the body must once again rob from the current supply of B vitamins in the body so that these refined grains can be digested.

Two of the most popular ways of eating refined grains are in the form of bread and cereals. It is appalling what can be found in a typical store-bought loaf of bread. The real scary part is that it is not mandatory to list these added substances on the label. Chlorine gas may be blown into the flour to bleach it white. Hundreds of chemicals may be used, which have not been adequately tested (such as BHT). Other additives include raising agents, preservatives, emulsifiers, yeast stimulators, coloring agents, acids, and more. In order to make these products more palatable to the consumer, large amounts of salt and sugar are added.

What can we do? Stop buying cereals and make your own bread. Or go to a reputable health food store to buy good-quality bread, such as the sprouted variety. Children and adults do not need boxed cereals. Reading through this book will give you many fresh and innovative recipes for the first meal of the day—without spending much time on preparation, which always seems to be the biggest argument. It is not difficult to change. You just need to want to change.

If each American consumes ten pounds of chemicals a year in food, that may not sound like a lot. But remember, most of these chemicals have been inadequately tested or not tested at all. Our bodies are not able to cope with this. When all of these chemicals and refined foods are eaten together, a multitoxic effect occurs that has never been thoroughly studied. What we do know, however, is that most of our lives are spent gradually dying, and that every day we create new illnesses to die from. This unsettlingly parallels the degeneration of our diets. The ultimate shame is that it is so very easy to correct.

Sweeteners

The average American eats only 129 pounds of fresh fruit every year, yet consumes 130 pounds of refined sugar every year.

Almost everyone loves sugar in one form or another. It is natural. What is not natural, however, is the way our society has destroyed and abused this once healthy food component. Refining and processing are just part of the story. Excessive use is the other part of the story. On an average, Americans consume approximately 50 teaspoons of sugar a day!

We were meant to thrive on whole foods containing sugar. That is indicated by the sweetness of mother's milk and by the availability of and natural inclination to eat succulent fruits. Over the past two hundred years, though, we have gradually replaced the good sugars in our diet, such as grapes, melons, or apples, with corn syrup, refined cane sugar, or aspartame. Unfortunately, our metabolism cannot handle sugars devoid of all nutrients. Instead, it depletes our own reserves.

Though there are many substitutes for white sugar, some should never be used, and others only in small amounts. Nothing will replace whole fruits as the optimum "sweet" food. Here is a partial list:

Aspartame (Nutrasweet) contains methyl alcohol, a poison that converts first to formaldehyde and then to formic acid. Another component is phenylalanine, which breaks down into DKP, a brain tumor agent. Many symptoms are associated with its use, a few of which are memory loss, vision problems, chronic fatigue syndrome, birth defects, and heart and respiratory conditions. For more information, read *Excitotoxins—The Taste That Kills* by neurologist Dr. Russell Blaylock.

Stevia, a small shrub native to South America, is extremely sweet, from 10 to 300 times sweeter than sugar. It regulates blood sugar so it is safe to use by those with blood sugar imbalances. It has been shown to arrest the growth of plaque in your mouth and regulates blood pressure. A noncaloric herb, it is the only sweetener safely used for candida and yeast-type conditions. Many countries such as China, Japan, South America, and Germany use it extensively with no known adverse reactions. Here in the United States it can only be marketed as a supplement and is available in powdered, leaf, and liquid form. Other than whole fruit, I favor this herb.

Agave nectar is extracted from a cactus-like plant. It is comprised of 93% fruit sugar. When using it to replace sugar or honey, decrease the amount in the recipe by 25%.

Honey is highly refined by bees and has more calories than white sugar. Honey is made by bees eating pollen, then regurgitating several times. While in the bee's stomach, it is mixed with formic, manite, and other acids. Unlike bees, humans lack the enzymes to break down these acids. Acid-forming foods need alkaline minerals to neutralize them, thus they are decalcifying.

Raw honey is better than heated and filtered honey, but the minute amount of mineral material found in it provides minimal nutritional value. It acts like white sugar in the body and is assimilated directly into the bloodstream very quickly. Most health claims stem from the fact that it does have minerals and can be had with little processing. Used with longer-digesting foods (which is the norm, since most people do not eat it alone), honey and all other sweeteners, except stevia, readily ferments. Honey is a dehydrated "food," which when ingested immediately begins to reabsorb moisture from the stomach and stomach flora. This will destroy the bacterial population (the "good" along with the "bad"). The arguments for the use of honey are weak. I prefer to use other sweeteners that, in my opinion, are better utilized by the body.

Maple syrup undergoes high heat processing, which concentrates it beyond its natural strength. There are some nutritional benefits, though not enough for me to even classify it as a minor food source, though you will occasionally see it in my recipes. Be careful of your source. Most supermarkets rarely carry it in its pure form. Sugar, corn syrup, and other refined sugars can be used to stretch out the more expensive maple syrup. Also, it may be contaminated by paraformaldehyde, which is used during the tapping process. Water, stevia powder, and alcohol-free maple extract may be a good substitute for those who want to eliminate maple syrup from their diet, yet still want a maple flavor in their food.

Blackstrap molasses is one of the most highly heated and processed sweeteners. It is touted for its high mineral content, though it may contain many impurities, being the final dregs of sugar production. Some of the impurities it contains may be carbon dioxide, sulphur dioxide, phosphoric acid, bone char, and chlorine. If you choose to use this product, only purchase organic and unsulphured brands.

Rice syrup and barley malt syrup, whether in the form of syrup or powder, are not as highly processed. They are processed by fermenting and/or sprouting techniques. Only about a third as sweet as white sugar, they still have many nutrients intact, as well as complex sugars that take much longer to digest than simple sugars. These sweeteners are primarily composed of maltose and are less destructive to the body's mineral balance. I favor these after stevia.

Unrefined cane juice powder is made simply by evaporating the water from cane juice. It retains a great deal of its mineral and other nutrient content, though it is not recommended due to its high sucrose level. Many food producers are aware of the marketing advantage of not listing sugar as an ingredient. Instead, cane juice or dried cane juice, etc., may be used. Make sure the label reads unrefined cane juice if you choose to use this product.

The most important factor to remember when using sweeteners is to look at quantity as well as quality. Do not trick yourself into eating more than small amounts just because you chose a healthier option. Too much of a good thing is not a good thing. Eating sweets should be for special occasions, not a daily occurrence.

Sprouting

This is an important part of my daily regime. Sprouting is fun, economical, and also very nutritious. The vitamin and enzyme content increases dramatically with a sprouted food—as much as four to ten times the value. Many people who are allergic to grains, nuts, and seeds can tolerate them just fine when they are sprouted. The reason for this is that the sprouting process predigests the nutrients, which makes it easier for the body to assimilate and metabolize them, preventing an allergic reaction.

During sprouting, the starch is converted into simple sugars. Protein is turned into amino acids. Fat is broken down into free fatty acids.

There is much more you can do with sprouts than tossing them on a sandwich or salad. Looking through this book will give you some ideas. Also, remember that sprouts can be added to smoothies or shakes, can be ground and added or used alone for bread making, can be dehydrated and used for cereals or faux meat patties, can be added to soups right before serving, and can even be used in desserts!

Almost any seed will sprout as long as it is in its whole state. My favorites are lentils, mung beans, chickpeas, alfalfa, red clover, barley, and buckwheat. When sprouting certain legumes, such as chickpeas and soybeans, it is desirable to steam them for approximately 15 minutes or until tender. This is so much more convenient than cooking for one to three hours.

How to Sprout

Put 1 tablespoon of seeds into a wide-mouthed 1-pint jar. Cover the seeds with spring water. Place a piece of cheesecloth over the top and secure with a rubber band. Soak overnight and drain in the morning. Continue rinsing and draining the seeds morning and night until sprouts reach the desired length. Be sure to always drain well to prevent mold. Use the sprouts immediately or store in the refrigerator in an air-tight container.

Sprouting Chart

Seeds	Sprouting Time (in days)	Optimum Length of Sprouts (in inches)
Alfalfa	3 to 4	3/4 to 1
Buckwheat	3 to 5	1 to 1 1/2
Clover	3 to 4	3/4 to 1
Garbanzo bean	3	1/2 to 3/4
Lentil	2 to 3	Length of seed
Mung bean	2 to 3	1/4 to 1/2
Oat	2	Length of seed
Pea	2 to 3	1/4 to 1/2
Radish	3 to 4	1/2 to 1
Rye	2	Length of seed
Sesame	2	1/16 to 1/8
Sunflower	2	1/16 to 1/8
Soybean	3	1/4 to 1/2
Wheat	2	Length of seed

Sprouting is a no-brainer activity that gives you so much. It would be crazy not to do it. Certain sprouts, such as alfalfa and red clover, can be placed in a sunny spot after the first couple of days to ensure getting maximum Vitamin A and chlorophyll.

Almonds and sunflower seeds need only be soaked overnight to start the germination process and increase nutritional value. These can easily be added to your fruit in the morning or blended into shakes or smoothies.

Everybody benefits from sprouted foods. It is one of my first suggestions to an individual who wants to transition to a healthier diet.

How to Make Tempeh

Store-bought tempeh tastes nothing like freshly made. The hours to incubate it may seem daunting to some, but it actually takes a minimum amount of time to make. The effort is worth it, so I've included a recipe and instructions in this section.

First, you will need a couple of things:

- Grain mill (not necessary but sure makes it easier)
- Large stainless steel pot
- 4 plastic sandwich bags that have been punched with air holes every inch or so (I use a large sewing needle to do this)
- Styrofoam cooler that has a "lip" several inches down from the top
- Rack to place in the styrofoam container on the "lip." If you have to make something, the idea is to have a space between your heat source on the bottom and the rack.
- Heating pad with multilevel control, which rests on the bottom of the cooler
- Thermometer, which you will tape onto the inside of the lid
- 2½ cups organic dry soybeans
- Dry culture, available from The Tempeh Lab, 615-964-3574
- Apple cider vinegar

Set up the styrofoam container with the heating pad on the bottom, turned on to high, then put the rack and thermometer in place. Close the lid and heat to approximately 100°. Once the soybeans are placed in the container, the temperature will go down slightly. The ideal range is 89–94°, so you will have to check every few hours or so and adjust the heat controls. Halfway through incubation the soybeans will naturally heat up, and you may have to turn the heat off at this time. Each heating pad is different. Always check, at least until you get to know how hot your pad gets.

Place beans in a pot with lots of water and bring to a boil. Let it boil for 20 minutes, then turn it off and let it sit for 2 hours. Rinse and drain the beans. If you have no grain mill, you will have to manually split the beans with your hand. With a grain mill, place the setting at the point where the beans crack in two but not so much that it crushes them. Rinse the beans several times while doing this. The skins will float to the top of the pan; scoop them out and discard them. Don't worry if you don't catch every single one! Refill the pot with fresh water 3–4 inches above the beans and bring to a boil. Simmer beans for an additional hour or so. Drain and let cool to room temperature.

Use only glass or stainless steel utensils throughout.

Once the beans are cooled sufficiently add 2 tablespoons apple cider vinegar and 1 teaspoon of dry culture (or whatever is recommended on the package). Stir in well. At this point you can get really creative, adding finely chopped veggies or sea vegetables, maybe some grains or seasonings. Plain is great, though, and I always suggest this for first timers. I have come up with some great combinations but always make sure to have plenty of the plain around as well.

Go ahead and divvy up the beans into 4 to 6 prepared sandwich bags. Flatten out and seal the bags, then place them on a rack in the preheated cooler. Over the next several hours you will see no visual difference in the beans, but around the 20-hour mark the tempeh is well on its way with a whitish gray covering, which actually is throughout the whole package, making it very dense. For optimal taste you will want to let it incubate for a total of 30–32 hours. You will notice some grayish black spots developing; do not panic! This is normal and desired, for the final hours are what give homemade tempeh the taste edge over store-bought. The final product should smell slightly like mushrooms. Let it cool completely, then wrap and refrigerate or freeze if you have more than can be used in a week. They freeze fine for many weeks.

That's it, and I have lots of recipes for you to try. There are also several tempeh cookbooks out there. For more nutritional information go to the Glossary of this book.

The Vita-Mix Total Nutrition Center

For grinding grains, blending, and whole food juicing, nothing compares to the Vita-Mix. This powerful blender is a versatile workhorse in your kitchen. I use mine at least once a day and usually more. No other machine is as easy to clean. Just add some water and a drop or two of dish soap and blend it on high, then rinse out.

It is an extremely efficient machine. When juicing it actually purees the vegetables or fruits into a smooth and highly nutritious beverage, complete with all the fiber and other components in fresh food that work synergistically together to give you the optimum health drink.

There are several other well-known machines that extract juice, disposing of the fiber and other nutritional components. The Omega and the Champion are highly regarded in "juicing" circles. I have several concerns, though, regarding the loss of fiber, the extensive cleanup after use, and the problem of sugar imbalances when consuming a fractionated food. A fractionated food is always less nutritious than a whole food. In the case of juicing, it can be downright dangerous for many individuals. Consuming the pulp of naturally sweet fruit and vegetables works as a safety mechanism by slowing down the assimilation of sugar into your system.

I personally blend many concoctions that include nuts and seeds of innumerable variety. I find that the Vita-Mix does this so well that you are not left with a grainy or gritty recipe. Almonds, cashews, sunflower seeds, and more are all ground and blended to creamy satisfaction.

Grinding grains are a breeze with this wonderful product as well. I highly recommend grinding grains as you go along, as opposed to purchasing flour with no idea of how long it has been on the shelf or even in the bins of a health food market. Remember, the longer a food is left out after processing, the more nutrients it loses, and in the case of grains, they will become rancid rather quickly. By grinding as needed you get the freshest product with nutrients intact.

Throughout the recipe sections of this book there are recommendations to blend, juice, or grind ingredients. The Vita-Mix does it all in a more than satisfactory manner, and as mentioned before, with a minimum of cleanup. The only two exceptions, which I mention in certain recipes, are the use of an inexpensive spice grinder or a food processor. The spice grinder is used for small jobs, such as grinding herbs. My food processor is used when I want chunky texture in certain salads, etc.

For more details contact Vita-Mix Corp., 800-VITAMIX.

Vitamin B12

Poor digestion is the main reason why so many of us cannot absorb ample B12. It has nothing to do with the fact that we are meat eaters or vegetarians. It is a fallacy when "experts" say that it is impossible for vegans to get enough B12 in their diet.

B12 is not only ingested with the foods we eat but also created in our own digestive tract. A healthy digestive tract with a normal supply of enzymes ensures a consistent amount of B12 being made. Some professionals claim that there is a particular substance (called intrinsic factor) in gastric juices that help with B12 absorption. Others, however, state that intrinsic factor is really just another word for a normal supply of digestive enzymes. For those of you who take oral B12 supplements, it is recommended that you make sure these include "intrinsic factor" for proper absorption.

Intrinsic factor is thought to be a glycoprotein, which is secreted by the parietal cells of the gastric mucosa. B12 needs to be broken down and separated from the compounds it is normally attached to, which are protein or peptide. Only after being separated can the B12 be combined with the intrinsic factor, then transported and utilized. Normal absorption occurs in the ilium and, some experts say, in the upper small intestine as well.

There are lots of reasons why B12 is not absorbed. Disease conditions created by poor diet are the main cause.

If we have defective gastric secretions and defective intestinal absorption due to years of abuse, is there any way to reverse this?

Living hygienically, which means living as close to nature as possible, removes the causes of disease, which will allow the body to heal itself. In most cases fasting, rest, exercise, and fresh air with sunshine will restore the body's ability to absorb B12 and other nutrients. Better food combining after fasting is beneficial as well, since there will be fewer types of bacteria that use B12 to exist in a healthy digestive tract.

Many people become vegetarians because of ill health, others for ethical, environmental, or spiritual reasons. Though all these reasons are valid and honorable, there is still a great lack of knowledge among vegetarians on how to eat healthfully. I have worked with a great deal of "unhealthy" vegetarians over the years, correcting their diet and educating them on how food affects their health.

Common sense tells me to eat as close to nature as possible, yet I see, over and over, vegetarians and nonvegetarians who stock their cupboards with soda pop and coffee, refined flour and sugar, boxed goods, all accompanied with a chemical and dye list of ingredients on their labels. Wake up, folks! Elbow macaroni, yellow dyed mustard, white flour salted crackers, and chocolate syrup are not healthy. Most bagels and boxed cereals are not nutritious. Abusing the body with candy bars and potato chips, even most of those purchased from a natural foods market, will degenerate your digestive tract, diminishing the amount of enzymes that should be your normal supply. A subnormal amount, therefore, will certainly prevent nutrients, such as B12, from being absorbed.

Remember, B12 is part of the B complex of vitamins. In nature this complex is generally found in the same foods. B12 can be found in a large variety of fresh food, though usually in very small amounts. Small amounts are all that is needed. Because it is found in such small amounts, most experts don't bother stating that it is in the food. I have not come across any informational source that states that vegetables contain absolutely no B12. Rather, it is normally stated to be minuscule or trace amounts.

The idea that we all need to take specific vitamin or mineral supplements is absurd. One vitamin needs to work synergistically with others for us to get any benefit from it. Isolation of one nutrient from others is foolhardy and dangerous, keeping your body struggling to achieve the balance needed for an easy-flowing and energy-efficient workplace.

Supplementation for a short period of time, during a physical crisis, may be acceptable, though only if other avenues such as fasting have been found ineffective in resolving a problem. And then, it is my belief, recommendations should be made by an individual with a hygienic background or an understanding of it. A partial list of such individuals can be found by contacting the International Association of Hygienic Physicians (IAHP), through the National Health Association in Tampa, Florida.

Those who were born secreting no intrinsic factor, or those who were born with a defect in metabolizing B12, can still improve their digestion with proper diet after fasting, along with strict food combining afterwards. Quite a few books go into detail on food combining. Being a strict vegan, I don't have to worry as much about combinations, though I do eat high-water-content fruit alone and normally do not eat other fruits with grains. The warm nature of the stomach seems an ideal atmosphere to create fermentation (gas), rot, and nonfriendly bacterial growth. I also am aware that grains start breaking down through mastication and enzymes found in the saliva in our mouths. Protein, on the other hand, needs a more acidic environment, which can be found in the stomach. Thus, chewing well and eating high-protein and high-carbohydrate foods separately makes sense.

It is critical that individuals who have had parts of their stomachs or intestines removed also understand this.

Food Sources

Fermented foods such as miso or cultured veggies (natural sauerkraut) and pickles are rich in digestive enzymes and may aid in the absorption of B12. I personally love to eat cultured veggies daily.

Homemade tempeh can be a good source of B12. Check the easy technique to make this food in the recipe section of this book. Nutritional yeast (check to make sure it is grown on a B12-enriched medium) is a mainstay in vegetarian diets rich in B complex vitamins, including B_{12}. For more info, go to the Glossary.

Micro algae such as spirulina, chlorella, and wild blue-green are a good source of B_{12}. Originally it was thought that there were rich stores of B_{12} in these superfoods. With newer "radioassay" testing, however, it was found that the amounts thought to be contained in them were actually made up in large part by B_{12} analogues. Even with this, micro algae is still a good source. It is also an excellent addition to the diet in general, offering chlorophyll, iron, protein, and other nutrients in an easily digestible form.

Sprouts, sunflower seeds, nuts, bananas, grapes, burdock, comfrey, and peas are other food sources of B_{12}.

Each molecule of B_{12} contains a molecule of cobalt, so our diet must include a source of cobalt. Sea vegetables are a tasty way of getting this. There is still some confusion about whether it is only B_{12} analogues in sea vegetables or the real thing. But if it is like the micro algae, where it occurs in smaller amounts, I still insist on sea vegetables being an excellent food for the rich array of other nutrients they provide. See the Glossary for more information.

Food Philosophy

Aggression, Violence, and the Food Connection

Most mental disorders are supported by chemical and physical imbalances. Most of these can be corrected with a good diet as well as certain lifestyle changes. Our children are consuming vast quantities of nonfoods, many times with parental awareness. A young body that is continuously abused like this will degenerate quickly. Nutrients are needed for every bodily function and in a child more are needed due to their rapid growth and development. I've said much already on how certain foods work in our system and the detriments of refined foods. I feel the need to bring it home and reemphasize what it is that we are doing to these young ones, our future.

- Pesticide residues have been found in the amniotic fluid of pregnant women. See "Pesticides and Children" for an interesting look at pesticides and how children react to them.
- Infant formulas are lacking in essential fatty acids, which can alter neuron development.
- Tryptophan deficiency in formula-fed babies can lead to aggression and sleep disorders.
- Soy-based formulas can affect the neurological and endocrinological functioning of a child.
- Some children are ingesting large amounts of estrogen through soy-based formulas. Not only that, but as they grow older they get hormones from meat and dairy and even city water as well. Little or no research has been done to determine the effects of this on young bodies.
- Insecticide residues found in many baby foods will do the same.
- The EPA requires chemical manufacturers to prove that their products do not cause cancer or birth defects, but it does not require

them to provide data on neurological effects. Scientists researching the chemical industry have classified certain compounds such as pesticides, mercury, and PCBs, called neurotoxicants, that are found in things like tuna, lawn sprays, vaccines, and head-lice shampoo, to name a few, and that are linked to certain childhood disorders. One out of every six children in America suffers from problems such as autism, aggression, dyslexia, and ADD.

- MSG, a chemical that overstimulates brain cells, is added to processed foods in the amount of millions of metric tons.
- Nine billion servings of soft drinks are purchased daily.
- Filling up on empty calories from sodas and other junk foods leaves children with no appetite for healthy "real" food. Deficiencies in nutrition do have an effect on the emotional and chemical balance of an individual.
- Caffeine, found in many soft drinks, is mood altering and breeds physical dependence on it. Over 70% of soft drinks have caffeine.
- In 1997 the average American consumed 576 12-oz. servings of soft drinks. There is no exclusion for those of us who don't drink these beverages, which means that amount is much higher for certain individuals.
- One-fifth of all one- and two-year-olds drink nearly 1 cup of soft drinks daily.
- Exclusive contracts for vending machines are given to companies such as Coca-Cola and Pepsi from schools. This proves quite lucrative for both parties.
- Over $750 million is spent annually on vending machine sales, many of which are placed in schools.
- The few fresh vegetables and fruits children eat are more than likely to be genetically altered, with no testing or research on the effects they will have on their systems.
- Prepackaged lunches have amazingly high amounts of sodium and sugar.

- There is a definite link between mental illnesses and diet. Many mental health professionals treat nutritional deficiencies in their patients by dosing them with B12, folic acid, C, zinc, manganese, B3 and B6, etc. Many others find mental illnesses vanish when they treat their patients for candida yeast overgrowth, hypoglycemia, and allergies.

- "A rapidly expanding body of research shows that heavy metals such as lead and pesticides decrease mental ability and increase aggressiveness," Robert Hatherill, a researcher at the University of California, Santa Barbara, wrote in an editorial for the *Chicago Tribune.*

- Carol Simontacchi, a certified clinical nutritionist and author of *The Crazy Makers,* has much to say about diet and violence. Working with clients to change their diets and to introduce the concept of whole foods as nurturing for their minds and bodies, she has helped many to make wonderful changes in their lives.

- Some prisons, hospitals, and nursing homes have agreed to make drastic changes in their food programs. A preliminary study showed that aggressive behavior and other infractions were reduced by 45% after removing sugar from the prisoners' food and snacks at the Tidewater Detention Center in Chesapeake, Virginia.

- Kathleen DesMaisons, author of *Potatoes not Prozac,* states, "sugar sensitive people . . . usually have low levels of beta endorphins. Beta endorphin levels have a direct impact on a person's self-esteem, tolerance for pain, sense of connectiveness and to the ability to take personal responsibility for action."

Profit before health has become the silent motto of the food industry. It is evident that there is no regard given to life. Shame on our school systems, the secondary caretakers of our children, for supporting these industries in poisoning young minds and bodies. We are all responsible, though, for this happening. Living in ignorance or denial is no excuse. Awareness is the beginning. Taking action will bring an end to such insanity.

Co-Creation

We are all co-creating our reality. When our soul entered our body and became earthbound, there were certain responsibilities that went along with it. First and foremost is to revere life in all forms, beginning with ourselves. Many of us have deviated from this simple rule. It is evident by the atrocities that we inflict upon our physical and spiritual being. The road back to reverence is one of the most challenging and greatest acts of love there is. It takes discipline and courage.

Once back on that path, though, we learn compassion for ourselves and in turn we learn compassion for others. The gentle waves of awareness that originate from our new understanding lap at the consciousness of everyone we come in contact with. For those who are ready to hear, their hearts and souls will be awakened and they will bring along their gifts.

For this is the beauty of life. Each and every one of us has a unique gift to give. It is our purpose for living. We were born with certain goals to accomplish, whether it be raising a family or raising the consciousness of others. How do we know our goals? By how your heart responds to what you do. When I saw my midwife's face light up with joy and wonderment each time she touched my womb and connected with my then unborn child, I knew she was living her soul's task. When what you do is so deeply gratifying that you wake up each day with the anticipation of service to others, you are doing what you were meant to be doing.

There is a fine line between service to others and martyrdom, though. It has to be a genuine love that you give to others with no strings attached. This can only happen if you love yourself. Loving yourself means keeping each part of you—emotional, spiritual, and physical—healthy. If one part is out of balance it throws everything else out of balance too. You see many healers, for example, who focus and work on one aspect of being and forsake others. It is difficult to accept advice from a therapist with apparent unresolved issues or to follow the suggestions of an overweight healthcare practitioner in the proper way to eat or exercise. People can tell if you are a believable person by the way you take care of yourself. More importantly, you will believe in yourself if everything in your house is in order. No one is perfect, but striving for perfection (balance) is a noble pursuit. True love of self is not neglectful.

Feeding the body correctly, then, seems to be of monumental importance. To do so will make it easier for the mental, emotional, and spiritual aspects of ourselves to grow and express themselves.

Looking at impoverished families in this way enhances an already disturbing picture. How many great minds and spiritual leaders lie wasting away behind crumbling, stench-filled walls, their bodies degenerating with each mouthful of the denatured foods of commerce?

Poor nutrition breeds confusion, bitterness, despair, and finally apathy.

There are a few noble souls who recognize this and try to make a difference with certain educational programs geared for the poor.

Educating the middle class is important too, for poor diet is an insidious evil influenced heavily by the money food manufacturers place in advertising. The emphasis is always on convenience and immediate gratification. These are poor standards to expose our children to. The effects are being seen in more frequent episodes of violence, many of which take place in nice communities, nice schools, by nice children. We need to understand and teach our children how nutrition affects the way we think, feel, and react.

A tremendous amount of research shows how food affects us on a chemical level and how easy it is to keep our bodies running at their optimum level. There is some margin for error, but not for continual abuse. And abuse is what it is, making us self-destructive perpetrators.

If there is no effort to change, then the frequent episodes of violence will escalate into an epidemic of fear-based mayhem. Fear is the most basic negative emotion from which all other negative emotions stem. But, by diminishing our own fear, we diminish it in our world. All it takes is the realization of just how remarkable each of us is. Realization occurs when clarity is restored. Clarity is restored by removing as many toxins as possible, creating the climate for recovery of our consciousness, and the remembrance of our life's work.

Recipes

Appetizers, Dips, and Spreads

Germinated Sunflower Seed Spread

This has been a very popular spread for entertaining and at my many demos and workshops. It is quick and nutritious and the plate is cleaned quickly. Try it with baked blue corn chips or as a sandwich spread and even just on a bed of crisp greens.

- 2 cups raw, hulled sunflower seeds, soaked overnight and drained
- 1 carrot, diced
- 2 green onions, chopped
- 1 small handful of parsley, minced
- 1 leaf of kale, or other hardy green
- 1/4–1/3 cup vegan mayonnaise (try cashew/sunflower seed mayonnaise in next section)
- 2 tablespoons whole-grain mustard
- 1 heaping tablespoon Vogue Vege Base or other vegetable broth powder
- sea salt to taste
- 1/2 cup arame, soaked in warm or hot water 30 minutes, rinsed, drained, and coarsely chopped
- 2 stalks celery, diced small

Place sunflower seeds, carrot, green onion, parsley, and kale in a food processor and run until finely mixed.

Add mayonnaise, mustard, Vogue, and salt. Process just until blended.

Scoop into a serving bowl and stir in arame and celery.

Banana-Miso-Sesame Spread

- 1 banana
- 1 1/2 tablespoons sesame butter or raw tahini
- 1 teaspoon barley or rice miso

Combine all ingredients thoroughly.

Babaghanoush

For a smoky-tasting dip, roast the eggplant whole. Peel and puree.

- 1 1/2 pounds eggplant
- 1/4 cup sesame butter or raw tahini
- juice of one lemon
- 1/3 cup parsley, minced
- 2 large garlic cloves, minced
- Bragg Liquid Aminos to taste

Peel eggplant. Cut into 1 1/2-inch cubes. Steam eggplant until tender, approximately 5 minutes.

Blend in blender. Add remaining ingredients. Puree.

Serve warm or at room temperature. Garnish with olives, if desired.

Cheddar, Sunflower Seed, and Olive Spread

Try this spread on thick slices of fresh rye bread, or make a wrap sandwich with chapatis, sprouts, cucumber, and tomato.

- 4 ounces firm tofu
- 1/2 pound cheddar-style vegan cheese, chopped
- 1/2 cup pimento-stuffed or herbed green olives, patted dry
- 1 roasted red bell pepper, chopped
- 1/3 cup plain vegan yogurt
- 1/4 cup sunflower seeds, toasted lightly
- sea salt to taste

Blend all ingredients except sunflower seeds in food processor.

Stir in sunflower seeds until combined. Add salt if needed.

Guacamole

- 3 ripe avocados (preferably Haas)
- 2 cups tomato, seeded and chopped
- 1 red onion, chopped fine
- 1/4 cup coriander, finely chopped (or to taste)
- 1/3 cup fresh lemon juice
- ground chipotle pepper or cayenne to taste
- sea salt to taste

Halve and pit the avocados. Scoop flesh into bowl. Mash coarsely with a fork.

Stir in remaining ingredients.

Lentil Spread

This makes a fabulous sandwich spread, or use as a dip with daikon and carrot sticks.

- 2 cups lentils, cooked
- 1/4 cup sunflower seeds, toasted
- 1 tablespoon fresh oregano, minced
- 1 tablespoon whole-grain prepared mustard
- 1 tablespoon red wine vinegar
- sea salt to taste
- water

Process all ingredients in blender. Add water as needed to achieve a spreadable consistency.

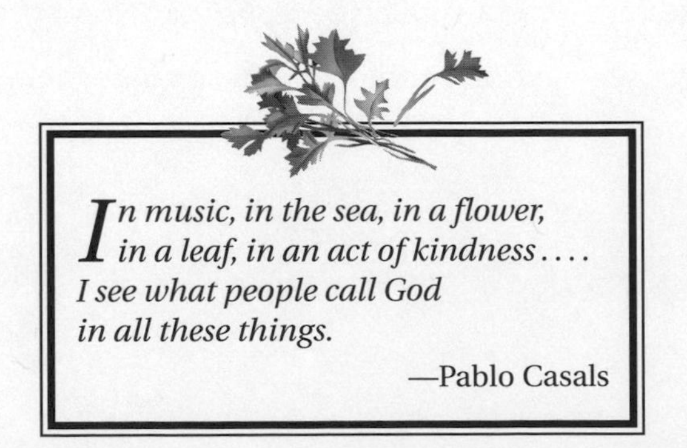

In music, in the sea, in a flower,
in a leaf, in an act of kindness....
I see what people call God
in all these things.

—Pablo Casals

Spinach Cheese Logs

1 pound vegan-style cheddar cheese
1 cup spinach, finely chopped
2 tablespoons Bragg Liquid Aminos
1 teaspoon lemon juice
1 teaspoon dill weed (optional)
scant 1/4 teaspoon onion powder

Grate cheese into large bowl. Add remaining ingredients. Mix well.

Press together. Form into roll. Cut into slices.

Roasted Garlic and Mushroom Spread

Garlic and mushrooms are a heavenly combination!

1 pound mushrooms, chopped
(try crimini, button, shiitake, or a combination)
1/2 cup onion, minced
2 tablespoons olive oil
3 tablespoons parsley, chopped
1 teaspoon whole-grain prepared mustard
1 tablespoon miso
1 head Roasted Garlic (see recipe in Condiments section)
sea salt to taste

Sauté mushrooms and onion in 1 tablespoon oil until soft and mushrooms release liquid. Add parsley, mustard, and miso.

Squeeze out garlic pulp. Add to mushroom mixture. Stir in another tablespoon of oil. Add sea salt, if using.

Spread on toast triangles.

Quick and Easy Hummus

- 3 tablespoons olive oil
- juice of 1 lemon
- 1 medium garlic clove
- 1/4 cup sesame butter or tahini
- 2 cups garbanzos (chickpeas), cooked or sprouted

Blend oil, lemon, garlic, and sesame butter in blender or food processor until smooth.

Add beans. Blend until creamy. Add 1 to 2 tablespoons of water, if needed.

Seed Spread

Use as dip or sandwich spread.

- 1/4 cup sesame seeds, coarsely ground
- 1/4 cup pumpkin seeds, coarsely ground
- 1/4 cup sunflower seeds, coarsely ground
- 2 tablespoons flax seed
- 1 large celery stalk, finely chopped
- 2 tablespoons oil
- 1 tablespoon apple cider vinegar
- 2 teaspoons Bragg Liquid Aminos

Combine seeds. Add celery.

Whisk together oil, apple cider vinegar, and Bragg's. Add to seed mixture.

Spinach-Mushroom Dip

- 1 clove garlic, crushed
- 1 cup onion, chopped
- 1/2 pound mushrooms, cleaned and chopped
- 2 tablespoons olive oil
- 1 1/4 cups spinach
- 1/2–3/4 cup stock
- 1/2 cup sesame butter or tahini
- 1 teaspoon sea salt
- 1/4 cup nutritional yeast flakes
- 3 tablespoons lemon juice

Sauté the garlic, onion, and mushrooms in oil over low heat until soft.

Stir in spinach. Combine all ingredients in a blender. Puree until creamy. Chill and serve.

Tzatziki *(Yogurt, Cucumber, and Garlic Dip)*

- 1 32-ounce container of vegan yogurt
- 2 cucumbers, peeled if not organic, seeded, coarsely grated
- 3 garlic cloves, minced
- 2 tablespoons olive oil
- 1 tablespoon apple cider vinegar
- 1–2 tablespoons fresh dill, minced
- sea salt to taste

Drain yogurt in a very fine sieve set over a bowl. Cover. Chill overnight. (You can also scoop out a hole in the center of the yogurt container and let sit overnight. Drain excess water.)

Squeeze cucumber to remove as much excess liquid as possible.

Stir together all ingredients in a bowl. Add salt.

Serve Tzatziki with bread, crackers, or veggies.

Brilliant Green Dip

1 10-ounce package frozen peas
1 tablespoon "butter" (from Condiments section) or vegan spread
1 tablespoon vegan mayonnaise
1 teaspoon ground cumin
1/2 teaspoon lemon juice
1/2 teaspoon sea salt

Place peas in a pot with 1 inch boiling water. Cover. Remove from heat. Let sit 2 to 3 minutes. Drain.

Place all ingredients in blender. Process until smooth.

Great with pita bread or toast triangles.

Carrot Butter

I like this best when the carrots are still warm!

2 1/2 cups steamed carrots
2 tablespoons cashew or almond butter
1 1/2 teaspoons Bragg Liquid Aminos
pinch of sea salt

Process all in blender until smooth. Add water, if needed.

Serve with chips or bread, or sprinkle with raw pumpkin seeds and serve as a side dish.

Condiments

Almonnaise

- 1/2 cup raw almonds
- 1/2 cup water
- 1/4 teaspoon garlic powder
- 3/4 teaspoon sea salt
- 1 cup flax, hemp, olive or any combination of these three oils
- 3 tablespoons lemon juice
- 1/2 tablespoon apple cider vinegar

Blanch almonds in a pot of hot water. When water cools, slip off skins.

Blend almonds, water, garlic powder, and sea salt until smooth.

Add flax oil slowly. Add lemon juice and apple cider vinegar.

Store in covered jar in refrigerator.

Cashew-Sunflower Mayonnaise

- 1/4 cup sunflower seeds
- 1/4 cup cashews
- 1/2 cup water
- 1/4 cup lemon juice
- 1/2 teaspoon sea salt
- 1/4 teaspoon garlic powder
- 1/4 teaspoon dry mustard
- 1/2 cup olive oil

Grind seeds and nuts if your blender is not strong. Place in blender. Add water and lemon juice. Add seasonings. Process until smooth.

Pour in olive oil while blender is running on a medium speed.

Process until thickened. Refrigerate.

Butter

Coconut oil is a natural saturated vegetable product that is made up of mostly medium-chain fatty acids. The body can metabolize this efficiently. Coconut oil does not elevate your LDL cholesterol levels.

- 1/2 cup water
- 1 small carrot
- 2 tablespoons powdered soy milk
- 1 teaspoon sea salt
- 1/2 cup flax, hemp, or olive oil
- 1 tablespoon lecithin granules
- 1/2 cup coconut oil

Process water and carrot in blender until smooth.

Add soy milk and sea salt. Blend well.

Add flax oil and lecithin granules slowly while blender is still running.

Add coconut oil. Blend until just thickened.

Pour into container. Chill to harden. Keep refrigerated.

Dulse Gomacio

My daughter dips carrots and other veggies in vegan sour cream, then gomacio. This can also be used as a table condiment in place of salt. High mineral content, especially calcium. Try it on a baked potato or salad.

- 2 parts sesame seeds, toasted
- 1 part dulse, toasted

Finely grind seeds. Finely grind dulse. Mix together.

Corn and Sun-Dried Tomato Relish

This is an awesome relish to serve alongside grilled veggie patties or alongside the Rio Grande Tempeh Meatloaf. Also great with baked corn chips.

- 1/2 cup sun-dried tomatoes, reconstituted
- 2 cups raw fresh corn (or frozen, defrosted)
- 1/4 cup red bell pepper, finely chopped
- 1/4 cup green bell pepper, finely chopped
- 1 teaspoon fresh jalapeno pepper, minced and seeded
- 1 1/2 tablespoons cilantro, minced
- 2 tablespoons fresh lemon juice
- 1–2 tablespoons apple cider vinegar
- 1 tablespoon olive, flax or hemp oil
- sea salt to taste

Soak sun-dried tomatoes in hot water until softened. Drain.

Toss together all the ingredients in a bowl. Add salt, as needed.

Cover. Chill for at least 1 hour.

Sesame Sauce

Great served with falafel or hummus wrap sandwiches, over steamed broccoli, or as a dip for a variety of fresh veggies.

- juice of 1 lemon
- 1 tablespoon miso, blonde or mellow white
- 2 tablespoons sesame butter or tahini water

Mix all ingredients well.

Cranberry Chutney

- 1/2 cup dried apricots, finely chopped
- 1/2 cup raisins
- 3 cups cranberries, picked over and rinsed
- 1 apple, cored, diced 1/4-inch (try Gala, Jona Gold, or Macintosh)
- 1 teaspoon freshly grated lemon rind
- 1/4 cup fresh lemon juice
- 1 tablespoon fresh ginger, grated
- 1/2 teaspoon dried hot red pepper flakes
- 1/8 teaspoon stevia liquid, or to taste

Soak apricots and raisins in 1 cup water overnight. Drain. Reserve water.

Place all ingredients in food processor. Pulse just to chunk—do not puree!

Add enough reserved soaking water to make chutney the desired consistency. Adjust seasonings, if necessary.

Let sit for a few hours before serving.

Cranberry, Orange, and Ginger Relish

This sure beats the canned cranberry gel my Mom used to serve!

- 2 teaspoons fresh gingerroot, peeled and chopped
- 1 large navel orange, including rind, chopped
- 1 12-ounce bag of cranberries, picked over
- stevia liquid to taste (start with 1/8 teaspoon)

Finely chop gingerroot and orange in a food processor.

Add cranberries. Pulse motor until berries are finely chopped.

Transfer mixture to a bowl. Sprinkle in stevia. Stir well. Cover. Chill for at least 30 minutes.

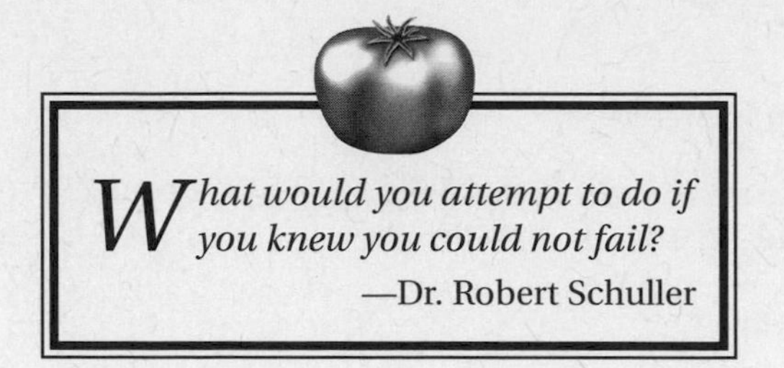

What would you attempt to do if you knew you could not fail?
—Dr. Robert Schuller

Eggplant, Tomato, and Bell Pepper Relish

This would also taste great over soba noodles or spaghetti squash.

- 3/4 pound eggplant, peeled and diced 1/4-inch
- 1 teaspoon salt, plus additional to taste
- 2 tablespoons olive oil
- 1 teaspoon garlic, minced
- 1/2 cup yellow bell pepper, finely chopped
- 6 plum tomatoes, seeded and chopped fine
- 1/4 cup red onion, finely chopped
- 2 tablespoons fresh basil, minced
- 1 tablespoon fresh parsley, minced
- 2 tablespoons balsamic vinegar
- 3 tablespoons fresh lemon juice

Toss the eggplant with the salt. Place in a colander. Cover with a plate that will fit inside the colander. Weight the plate. Drain eggplant for 20 minutes. Rinse eggplant. Pat dry.

Heat oil over moderately high heat in a large, heavy skillet until it is hot, but not smoking.

Sauté eggplant. Stir 2–3 minutes, or until eggplant is just cooked through.

Add garlic. Cook mixture. Stir 1 minute.

Cool to room temperature. Toss eggplant mixture in a bowl with remaining ingredients.

Add additional vinegar and lemon juice if desired.

Fresh Tomato Sauce

I believe it is totally unnecessary to cook your tomato sauce. This recipe bursts with flavor.

- 4 tomatoes, diced
- juice of 1 lemon
- 1 1/2–2 teaspoons fresh oregano, minced (or dried to taste, starting with 1/8–1/4 teaspoon)
- 1 teaspoon fresh thyme, minced (or dried to taste, starting with 1/8–1/4 teaspoon)
- balsamic vinegar, if desired

Place all ingredients in bowl. Add a splash of balsamic.

Toss with noodles, or try as a relish with spinach fritters.

Tomato Salsa

Serve with tortilla chips or on a legume, nut, or grain patty.

- 2 garlic cloves
- 1 lime, peeled
- 2 scallions, coarsely chopped
- 1 serrano chili, seeded (wear rubber gloves)
- 1 tablespoon fresh lime juice, or to taste
- 6 large plum tomatoes, seeded and chopped
- 3 tablespoons flax or olive oil
- 2 tablespoons cilantro, chopped

Finely chop all veggie ingredients by hand.

Stir in oil and cilantro.

Garam Masala

Can be added to your favorite Indian dishes. A traditional recipe from a friend of mine.

- 2 tablespoons cumin seed
- 2 tablespoons black cardamom seeds
- 5 teaspoons black peppercorns
- 4 1/2 teaspoons green cardamom, ground
- 1 tablespoon plus 1/4 teaspoon whole coriander
- 2 1/4 teaspoons fennel seeds
- 1 3/4 teaspoons cloves
- 2 1/2 teaspoons cinnamon
- 2 1/4 teaspoons ground mace
- 2 teaspoons black cumin seed
- 4 bay leaves
- 1 3/4 teaspoons ground ginger
- 1/2 whole nutmeg, coarsely chopped
- 2 tablespoons dried rose petals (optional)

Grind all ingredients as fine as possible in spice grinder.

Store in covered container.

Roasted Garlic

- 1 large garlic bulb

Preheat oven to 350 degrees.

Remove as much of the outer skin as possible without breaking the bulb apart.

Place in covered casserole dish. Bake for 30 minutes or until pressing a finger against a clove shows that it is soft.

Mushroom-Onion Gravy

My husband loves gravy and potatoes (don't all men?).

- 3 tablespoons olive oil
- 1 onion, diced
- 1 clove garlic, minced
- 2 cups mushrooms, coarsely chopped (shiitake are nice)
- 1 1/2 cups button mushrooms, sliced
- 2 tablespoons flour (oat, barley, rice, or spelt)
- 3 tablespoons nutritional yeast
- 2 tablespoons Vogue Vege Base
- 1 1/2–2 cups water
- 1 tablespoon Bragg Liquid Aminos

Sauté onions, garlic, and mushrooms in olive oil until just tender. Add flour, yeast, and Vogue. Cook for 2 minutes.

Add water slowly. Stir with a whisk until smooth.

Add Bragg's. Adjust seasonings.

Tofu Sour Cream

A simple recipe and very versatile. I love it on baked potatoes sprinkled with dulse flakes. My daughter scoops it right out of the bowl with carrot sticks. Also makes a good salad dressing base.

- 1 package of Mori-Nu silken firm tofu
- 1 tablespoon oil
- 1 tablespoon apple cider vinegar
- 1 teaspoon brown rice syrup
- 1 tablespoon lemon juice
- 1/2 teaspoon sea salt

Process all ingredients in blender. Cover. Refrigerate until ready to use.

Orange, Fig, and Pine Nut Relish

Serve with my Salisbury Steaks, a legume or nut loaf, or with traditional holiday sides, like stuffing.

- 1 cup dried figs, stemmed and cut into 1/3-inch pieces
- 1 tablespoon freshly grated orange zest
- 1/2 cup water
- 2 navel oranges, peel cut away with serrated knife and sections chopped (about 1 cup)
- several drops of stevia
- 2 teaspoons shallot, minced
- 1 teaspoon rosemary leaves, minced (or 1/4 teaspoon dried, crumbled)
- 1 teaspoon fresh lemon juice, or to taste
- 1/4 cup pine nuts, toasted lightly

Soak figs and zest in water overnight. Drain.

Stir in oranges, stevia, shallot, rosemary, and lemon juice.

Let mixture stand for at least 30 minutes and up to 2 days.

Stir in pine nuts.

You must understand the whole of life, not just one little part of it.

That is why you must read, that is why you must look at the skies, that is why you must sing, and dance, and write poems, and suffer and understand, for all that is life.

—J. Krishnamurti

Basic "Cream" Sauce for Steamed Vegetables

Basic Sauce:

1 tablespoon oil*
2 tablespoons flour (millet, rice, spelt, or oat)
1 cup vegetable stock, heated
1 tablespoon miso
dash of nutmeg

Heat oil in heavy saucepan. Stir in flour. Whisk 1–2 minutes over low heat. Remove from heat.

Add heated vegetable stock. Bring almost to a boil. Turn to low heat. Simmer until thickened.

Stir in miso and nutmeg.

*Oil can be omitted. Just dry-toast flour.

Variation 1:
Sauté shiitake mushrooms and 1 chopped onion. Add to sauce. Simmer a few more minutes.

Variation 2:
Add 1–2 teaspoons herbs to sauce while simmering. Include combinations such as thyme, nutmeg, garlic; thyme, sage, parsley; coriander, cumin, ginger.

Variation 3:

1 tablespoon peanut butter
1 onion, minced
1/4 cup orange juice

Combine all ingredients. Add to basic sauce. Omit oil in basic sauce recipe. Simmer 5–8 minutes.

Creamy "Mozzarella"

- 1/4 cup onions, diced
- 1 tablespoon olive oil
- 1 cup water
- 1/4 cup nutritional yeast
- 3 tablespoons rolled oats
- 1 tablespoon sesame butter or tahini
- 2 tablespoons arrowroot
- 2 tablespoons lemon juice
- 1/2 teaspoon sea salt

Sauté onion in olive oil until browned.

Place onions in blender. Add remaining ingredients. Process until smooth.

Pour into saucepan. Cook over medium heat. Stir constantly until very thick.

Soups

"Cream of . . ." Soups

Cooler weather begs for comfort foods and what better way to warm yourself from the inside out than with a steaming bowl of creamy soup? But what about the high fats and cholesterol in our favorite recipes that we have been trying to avoid? Try the following delicious and nutritious alternatives. I think you and your family will be pleasantly surprised!

Suggested "Cream" Alternatives

1. Oat or nut milk instead of milk or cream
2. Nutritional yeast (1/4–1/2 cup); 2 tablespoons sesame butter or tahini; 1/4 cup quick-cooking rolled oats; 2 tablespoons lemon juice; Bragg Liquid Aminos to taste. Blend all until smooth.
3. One potato, 1 tablespoon sesame butter or tahini, 1 tablespoon miso
4. Pureed starchy veggies or beans
5. One package silken tofu
6. 1/8–1/4 cup ground rice

Have fun! Experiment with different seasonings. Soups are not easily ruined—so be daring!

Try leftover "cream of" soups as a topping on rice, pasta, or other grains for a hearty main-course meal. Sprinkle with raw or toasted nuts and seeds for added nutrition and texture, if desired.

Autumnal Glory – Squash, Adzuki, Corn Chowder

1 1/2 cups adzuki beans
1 tablespoon oil
2 medium leeks, including greens, rinsed and thinly sliced
4 cups vegetable stock
1 1/2 pounds butternut squash, scrubbed, seeded, and cut into 2-inch chunks (peeling unnecessary if organic)

2 teaspoons dried tarragon
2 cups corn kernels, fresh or frozen
1/4 cup scallion greens, thinly sliced
Bragg Liquid Aminos to taste

Rinse beans. Soak 4–8 hours in water to cover. Drain and rinse beans. Set aside.

Heat oil. Sauté leeks for 2 minutes. Add stock, beans, squash, and tarragon.

Boil. Reduce heat. Simmer, covered, until beans are tender, about 60–90 minutes.

Stir in corn, scallions, and Bragg's to taste. Adjust seasonings, if necessary.

Broccoli Soup

5 cups water
1 onion, coarsely chopped
1 celery stalk, coarsely chopped
2 cloves garlic, chopped
4 cups broccoli, chopped
1 potato, coarsely chopped
2 tablespoons olive oil
2 tablespoons light miso
1 heaping tablespoon sesame butter or tahini
1 heaping tablespoon Vogue Vege Base

Sauté vegetables in olive oil until onion is golden. Add water and bring to a boil in a large soup pot. Reduce heat. Cover. Cook until veggies are tender, 8–10 minutes.

Puree in batches in a blender. Add miso, sesame butter, and Vogue. Adjust seasonings to taste.

Celery Soup

- 1 onion, chopped
- 1 carrot, chopped
- 1/2 fennel bulb, including green top, chopped
- 2 cups celery, chopped
- oil
- 4 cups vegetable stock
- 1/2 cup cashews
- 2 tablespoons arrowroot
- 1/4–1/2 teaspoon sea salt

Sauté veggies in oil for 5 minutes. Add stock. Boil. Simmer over low heat until carrots are just tender.

Process half of soup in blender with cashews, arrowroot, and salt. Pour into remaining soup. Stir.

Spinach Soup

- 1 tablespoon oil
- 1 small onion, diced
- 2 medium potatoes, diced
- 3 cups water
- 2 cups spinach, finely chopped
- 1 tablespoon Bragg Liquid Aminos
- 1 tablespoon miso (preferably mellow white)
- 1 tablespoon flax oil or "Butter" (see recipe in Condiments)

Sauté onion in oil until translucent.

Add potatoes and water. Cook until just tender. Mash potatoes in water (or puree in blender). Stir in spinach, Bragg's, miso, and flax oil.

Serve immediately.

My Favorite Curried Cauliflower and Carrot Soup

1 large onion, diced
1 medium cauliflower, flowerets diced
2 medium carrots, diced
oil
vegetable stock
1/4 cup nutritional yeast
1 heaping teaspoon curry powder
sea salt to taste

Sauté veggies in oil until softened slightly.

Add enough stock to just cover, then bring to a boil. Lower heat and simmer until just tender.

Process in blender, adding seasonings as you do so.

Fresh Tomato Soup

5 cups water
2 tablespoons fresh ginger, grated
4 cloves garlic, minced
1 jalapeno, minced
sea salt to taste
6 medium tomatoes, cored
1 tablespoon cumin seed, toasted
2 tablespoons cilantro, chopped
"Butter" (see recipe in Condiments)

Boil water, ginger, garlic, jalapeno, and salt. Lower heat. Simmer 5 minutes.

Pour into blender. Add tomatoes. Process until smooth. Add cumin seeds and cilantro.

Stir a small amount of "Butter" into each bowl before serving.

Cilantro Soup

Chipotle peppers are worth the hunt to find them. They impart a wonderful flavor.

1 tablespoon oil
1 onion, diced
8 cloves garlic, minced
1 teaspoon cumin seeds
4 medium potatoes, peeled and diced (russet works best)
4 cups water
chipotle peppers, ground (start with 1/8–1/4 teaspoon; adjust to your heat tolerance*)
1 cup cilantro leaves, minced
lemon juice
sea salt to taste

Sauté onion, garlic, and cumin seeds in oil in a large pot until softened.

Add potatoes, water, and chipotle peppers. Simmer until tender.

Process in blender with cilantro leaves. Return to pot. Add lemon juice and sea salt to taste.

*Chipotles are dried and smoked jalapenos. Very potent! If you cannot find them in dried form, you can usually find canned chipotles in adobo sauce.

Cold Zucchini and Red Bell Pepper Soup with Cumin

This is a delightful, late-summer soup.

3 cups zucchini, chopped
5 cups vegetable stock
4 red bell peppers, roasted*
1 cup plain yogurt (preferably soy-based yogurt)
1½ teaspoons cumin seeds
sea salt to taste

Combine the zucchini and stock in a large saucepan. Boil. Simmer for approximately 15 minutes. Cool.

Puree the mixture in a blender with the roasted peppers and yogurt.

Dry toast the cumin seeds in a clean pan, heated until quite hot. Shake the pan, being careful not to burn the seeds.

Pour seeds into a spice grinder. Grind coarse. Add to the soup.

Transfer soup to a bowl. Add sea salt, if necessary. Chill, covered, for at least 1 hour and up to 8 hours.

If desired, more cumin seeds can be toasted and sprinkled on top for garnish.

*To roast peppers, slice peppers in half and scoop out seeds. Flatten with your hands onto a broiler or cookie sheet and place under a preheated broiler about 2 inches from the heat, until the skins are blistered and charred. Transfer the peppers to a bowl and let them steam, covered, until they are cool enough to handle. The skin should peel away easily.

Lemon Soup

- 5 cups vegetable stock
- 1/2 cup rice
- 2 tablespoons lemon juice
- 1/2 cup carrot, shredded
- 1/2 cup green onion, shredded
- 1 cup spinach leaves, chopped
- 1 cup tofu, diced
- Bragg Liquid Aminos to taste
- lemon slices

Boil stock. Add rice. Cook, covered, until rice is tender.

Add remaining ingredients. Remove from heat.

Float a very thin slice of lemon in each bowl of soup for a pretty effect.

Corn and Rice Soup

- 1/4 cup brown rice
- 1/4 cup wild rice
- 5 cups vegetable stock
- 1 cup onions, diced
- 1 tablespoon olive oil
- 5 garlic cloves, minced
- 1 teaspoon cumin seeds
- 1 teaspoon salt
- 1/2 teaspoon thyme
- 1 teaspoon curry powder
- 1 cup tomatoes, peeled and chopped
- 1 cup corn, fresh or frozen
- 1/2 cup red bell pepper, chopped
- small handful cilantro, minced
- 1/4 cup green onion, minced

Simmer rice in stock until tender.

Sauté onions, cumin, and garlic in oil until soft. Add to rice and stock.

Add additional spices. Simmer 5–10 minutes. Stir in tomato, corn, and pepper.

Serve in bowls. Sprinkle with cilantro and green onion.

Creamy Mushroom Soup

- 1 large onion, diced
- 2 large celery stalks, diced
- 2 medium potatoes, diced
- 2 medium carrots, diced
- 2 cups mushrooms, chopped
- 2 tablespoons Vogue Vege Base
- 2 tablespoons raw sesame butter or tahini
- 2 tablespoons red miso
- water

Place all veggies in a large pot. Fill with water until water covers veggies. Bring to a boil. Simmer until potatoes are just tender. Add remaining ingredients.

Puree in blender, in batches if necessary.

Adjust seasoning to taste.

Curried Broccoli, Watercress, and Spinach Soup

- 2 cups vegetable stock
- 3 cups broccoli, chopped
- 1 cup parsley, chopped
- 1 cup spinach leaves, firmly packed, washed thoroughly
- 1 cup watercress, stems discarded
- 1/4 cup green onions, sliced
- 2 cups celery, including leaves, chopped
- 1/2 cup cucumber, sliced
- 1/3 cup green bell pepper, chopped
- 1 cup plain vegan yogurt
- 1/4–1/2 teaspoon curry powder
- sea salt to taste
- fresh dill

Simmer stock with broccoli in large saucepan until just tender. Add remaining veggies. Simmer 5 minutes.

Puree mixture in batches in a blender. Transfer to cleaned pan.

Stir in yogurt and curry powder. Heat soup over moderately low heat.

Add sea salt, if desired. Garnish with minced fresh dill.

Curried Coconut Noodle Soup

- 1/2 pound rice or soba noodles
- 2 tablespoons oil
- 2 garlic cloves, minced
- 2–3 tablespoons curry powder
- 2 cups vegetable stock
- 3 1/2 cups coconut milk, unsweetened
- 1 cup water
- 2 lemon grass stalks, outer leaves discarded, trimmed, and 5 inches of lower stalks, minced
- 10 slices fresh gingerroot, peeled, sliced 1/8-inch thick
- 1/2 pound frozen, defrosted tofu squeezed of water and cubed
- 2 tablespoons dulse flakes
- Bragg Liquid Aminos to taste
- 6 tablespoons fresh lime juice
- 1/3 cup fresh coriander or cilantro, chopped

Cook noodles according to package directions. Set aside.

Cook garlic in oil in a heavy saucepan over moderately low heat until fragrant. Stir constantly.

Add curry powder. Cook mixture for 30 seconds. Stir constantly.

Stir in stock, coconut milk, water, lemon grass, and gingerroot. Bring to boil. Simmer 15 minutes.

Add tofu, dulse, Bragg's, and lime juice.

Divide noodles among 6 bowls. Ladle soup over noodles.

Sprinkle soup with coriander.

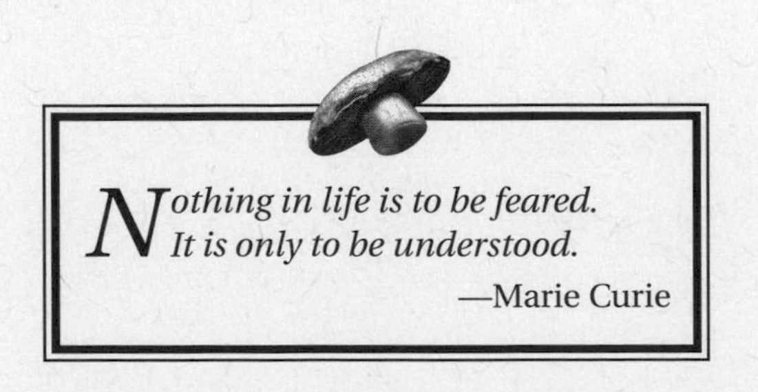

Curried Sprouted Lentil Stew

- 2 tablespoons olive oil
- 2 medium potatoes, diced
- 1 onion, diced
- 2 carrots, diced
- 2 celery ribs, diced
- 2 tablespoons Vogue Vege Base
- 1–2 teaspoons curry powder
- 1/2 teaspoon thyme
- 2 cups sprouted lentils
- 3–4 garlic cloves, minced
- 1/2 red bell pepper, diced (or 1/3 cup sun-dried tomatoes, minced)
- 1/2 bunch spinach, cleaned, stems removed and chopped

Sauté potatoes, onion, carrots, and celery in oil for 5 minutes.

Add Vogue, spices, and enough water to cover vegetables. Simmer until potatoes are just tender.

Add lentils, garlic, bell pepper, and spinach. Stir until spinach is wilted. Remove from heat.

Adjust seasonings, if necessary.

Pea and Carrot Soup

- 4 large carrots, sliced
- 1 large onion, chopped
- 1/4 teaspoon thyme
- 5 cups vegetable stock
- 2 1/2 cups peas
- 1/2 cup almonds or cashews, ground

Boil carrots. Simmer until just tender.

Add onion, thyme, and stock. Bring almost to a boil.

Add peas and almonds or cashews. Process in blender until smooth.

Pour back into pot. Add sea salt to taste.

Dal Soup

My friend, A.J., creates excellent Indian cuisine.

1/2 pound black dal
4 ounces chana dal
1/2 cinnamon stick
2 teaspoons turmeric powder
2 teaspoons paprika
2 curry leaves
2 teaspoons garam masala
sea salt to taste
2 teaspoons olive oil
1 teaspoon whole cumin seed
1 teaspoon whole mustard seed
1 medium onion, chopped
1 teaspoon garlic, minced
2 teaspoons ginger, minced
1 jalapeno pepper, finely minced
1 large tomato, diced
cilantro to taste, finely minced (start with 2 tablespoons)

Wash black and chana dal thoroughly. Add both dals to a 4–6 quart pot. Add water (6x by volume).

Add cinnamon stick, turmeric, paprika, curry leaves, garam masala, and salt. Boil. Simmer until dal is tender.

Separate dal from water. Puree. Pour back into water.

Heat a skillet. Pour in olive oil. Sauté whole cumin and mustard seed. Add onions. Sauté until golden brown.

Add garlic, ginger, and jalapeno. Sauté for 2 minutes.

Pour contents of skillet into simmering soup. Simmer for additional 30 minutes over low heat. Remove from heat. Add tomato and cilantro before serving.

Fragrant Oriental Soup

6 cups vegetable stock
1 teaspoon lemon peel, grated
1 tablespoon fresh ginger, grated
1 cup shiitake mushrooms, stems removed and caps sliced thin
2 slender carrots, sliced on diagonal, approximately 1/8-inch thick
1–2 jalapenos, seeded and minced
2 cups cabbage, shredded (napa or bok choy are nice if available)
1/2 package firm tofu, rinsed and cubed
Bragg Liquid Aminos to taste (start with 2 tablespoons)
1 2-inch x 2-inch piece of kombu
1/4 cup scallion greens, thinly sliced
1/4 cup fresh cilantro, minced

Simmer all ingredients except scallions and cilantro for 10–15 minutes.

Remove from heat.

Chop kombu into bite-size pieces. Return to pot.

Stir in scallions and cilantro. Adjust seasonings, if needed.

Serve immediately.

Freeze all vegetable ends and skins that would normally be discarded. When a large bag is created, you now have the ingredients for a rich vegetable stock. Just fill a stock pot with water and veggies. Bring to a boil, then simmer for 1 hour. Cool. Throw veggies in compost and store stock in refrigerator until ready to use.

Oriental Gazpacho

- 4–6 tomatoes (approximately 1½ pounds)
- 2 tablespoons cilantro, chopped
- 4 green onions, chopped
- 1 teaspoon fresh ginger, finely grated
- 1 heaping tablespoon Vogue Vege Base
- 1 tablespoon Bragg Liquid Aminos
- 1½ cups water mixed with 2 tablespoons miso
- 1 celery stalk, diced
- 1 cucumber, diced
- Thai curry paste to taste
- sea salt to taste
- 1 lime peel, finely grated or minced
- juice of 1 lime

Cut tomatoes in half. Chop flesh coarsely. (You should have about 4 cups.)

Place cilantro, green onions, ginger, Vogue, and Bragg's in a saucepan. Simmer over low heat for 20 minutes.

Pour mixture in blender. Add tomatoes, water/miso, celery, and cucumber. Puree in blender.

Add curry paste and salt to taste.

Stir in a small amount of grated peel, and the juice of 1–2 limes to taste.

Chill thoroughly before serving. Serve in chilled bowls.

Gazpacho

- 3 large ripe tomatoes (about 1½ pounds), quartered
- 1 large cucumber, peeled and halved
- 1 rib celery, cut in chunks
- 1 small green bell pepper, seeded and cut in chunks
- 1 small red bell pepper, seeded and cut in chunks
- 2–3 tablespoons Spanish or Vidalia onion, finely chopped
- 3 tablespoons fruity olive oil

approximately 1/2 cup tomato juice or water
3 tablespoons parsley, finely minced
2–3 tablespoons fresh cilantro, finely chopped (optional)
1 small garlic clove, peeled and finely minced
1 teaspoon apple cider or balsamic vinegar
sea salt to taste
croutons (optional)
tomato juice (optional)
avocado (optional)

Place all ingredients in a blender. Process, using the pulsing action, to create a coarse puree.

Thin soup by using tomato juice or water, if needed.

Adjust seasonings, if necessary. Chill. Serve in chilled bowls.

Garnish with croutons or slices of avocado, if desired.

Red Bell Pepper and Fennel Soup

2 tablespoons olive oil
1 large red bell pepper, seeded and chopped
1 large onion, diced
2 large stalks celery, diced
2 medium red potatoes, diced
1/2 bulb fennel (whole if small), diced, green top included
1/2–1 teaspoon rosemary, crushed
1/2 teaspoon sea salt
1 1/2 cups plain vegan milk
1 cup water

Sauté veggies in oil until onion is softened.

Add remaining ingredients. Simmer until just tender.

Puree until smooth.

Gingered Butternut Squash Soup

- 2 butternut squash (about 3½ pounds), peeled and halved
- 1 cup onion, chopped
- 3 tablespoons olive oil
- 1 tablespoon fresh gingerroot, peeled and grated
- 1 apple, peeled, cored, and chopped
- 1 teaspoon fresh nutmeg, grated
- 1–2 tablespoons white miso
- sea salt to taste

Discard the seeds and strings from the squash. Cut into ½-inch pieces. Combine the squash with enough water to just cover it in a kettle. Bring to a boil. Simmer squash, covered, stirring occasionally, for 30 minutes, or until the squash is tender. Drain, reserving the cooking liquid.

Sauté onion in oil in kettle over moderately low heat. Stir until soft. Add gingerroot, apple, nutmeg, and squash. Cook and stir mixture for 1 minute.

Add enough water to the reserved cooking liquid to yield 3 cups liquid. Add liquid to the squash mixture. Simmer 30 minutes. Stir occasionally.

Puree the soup in a blender in batches. Transfer to a bowl as it is pureed. Add the miso to the last batch.

Pour the soup into the kettle. Heat over low heat until it is heated through. Stir constantly. Adjust seasoning by adding more miso or sea salt to taste.

Lentil and Brown Rice Soup

- 1½ cups lentils, picked over and rinsed
- 5 cups vegetable stock
- 1 cup brown rice
- 3 carrots, diced
- 1 onion, chopped
- 1 celery stalk, chopped

- 3 garlic cloves, minced
- 1 tablespoon basil, minced (or 1/2 teaspoon dried)
- 1 tablespoon oregano, minced (or 1/2 teaspoon dried)
- 1 teaspoon thyme, minced (or 1/4 teaspoon dried)
- 1 bay leaf
- 1/2 cup parsley leaves, minced
- 3 medium tomatoes, diced
- 2 tablespoons apple cider vinegar
- sea salt to taste

Soak lentils in water overnight. Sprout until tails are approximately 1/2-inch long (about 2–2 1/2 days).

Combine stock, rice, carrots, onion, celery, garlic, basil, oregano, thyme, and bay leaf in a heavy kettle. Bring liquid to boil. Cover. Simmer for 45–55 minutes, or until rice is tender. Stir occasionally.

Stir in lentils, parsley, tomatoes, vinegar, and sea salt. Discard bay leaf.

Thin soup with additional water, if necessary.

Tomato Carrot Soup

- 2 leeks, white portions, washed well and chopped
- 1 1/2 cups carrots, peeled and sliced
- 3 tablespoons olive oil
- 5 cups vegetable stock
- 1–2 teaspoons fresh thyme, minced
- 2 pounds plum tomatoes, chopped
- 1/4 cup sun-dried tomato puree (after soaking tomatoes, process in mini food processor or blender until smooth)
- sea salt to taste

Sauté leeks and carrots in oil over moderately low heat until softened. Stir in stock and thyme. Simmer until carrots are tender.

Add remaining ingredients. Puree in blender. Season with sea salt, if desired.

Serve immediately.

Mulligatawny

olive oil
2–3 dried red chilies
3 garlic cloves, mashed
1/4 cup onion, diced
2 teaspoons fresh ginger, minced
2 teaspoons Madras curry
2 tablespoons chickpea flour
2 tablespoons coconut, ground
2 bay leaves
small handful cilantro leaves
3–4 cups mixed vegetables
3–4 cups vegetable stock

Sauté red chilies, garlic, onion, and ginger in olive oil until tender.

Add curry, chickpea flour, and ground coconut. Stir briefly.

Add bay leaves, cilantro, and vegetables. Stir 2 minutes.

Add stock slowly. Simmer until vegetables are just tender.

Remove vegetables. Discard chilies and bay leaves. Puree vegetables in blender until smooth. Add back to stock.

Serve as is, or pour through a sieve, discarding any solids. (You must discard chilies and bay leaves.)

Roasted Garlic and Mushroom Soup

1 medium yellow onion, diced
1 carrot, diced
1 large celery stalk, diced
1 potato, diced small
approximately 5–6 cups vegetable stock
olive oil
1 pound mushrooms, sliced
Bragg Liquid Aminos to taste
2 tablespoons fresh parsley, minced
1 tablespoon fresh marjoram, minced (or 1/4 teaspoon dried)

1 tablespoon fresh thyme, minced (or 1/4 teaspoon dried)
1 tablespoon fresh sage, minced (or 1/4 teaspoon dried)
1 bulb Roasted Garlic (see recipe in Condiments)
1/4 cup sun-dried tomatoes, reconstituted and minced
1–2 tablespoons miso
sea salt to taste

Bring onion, carrot, celery, and potato to a boil in stock. Simmer.

Sear mushrooms in oil on high heat until liquid is released. Add Bragg's. Add to soup mixture once the liquid is cooked out, and the mushrooms begin to brown.

Add spices. Simmer until veggies are just tender.

Squeeze each garlic clove. Discard the skin. Add roasted garlic, tomatoes, and miso to soup. Adjust seasonings, if necessary.

Serve immediately.

Zucchini Basil Soup

1 cup onion, chopped
6 garlic cloves, minced
2 tablespoons rice
2 tablespoons olive oil
1 quart vegetable stock
1/2 cup fresh basil leaves, chopped
1 teaspoon fresh thyme, minced
5 small zucchini, scrubbed and chopped
2 heaping tablespoons miso (preferably red)

Combine onion, garlic, rice, and oil in a large saucepan. Cook mixture over moderately low heat until onion is soft. Stir often.

Add stock, basil, and thyme. Boil. Lower heat. Simmer, covered, for approximately 25 minutes, or until rice is just tender. Add zucchini.

Remove from heat. Add miso. Puree soup in a blender in batches.

Serve immediately.

Soba Soup with Spinach, Tofu, and Arame

- 1/2 cup dry arame
- 1/2 pound dried soba (look for 100% buckwheat)
- 7 cups vegetable stock
- 2 carrots, thinly sliced
- 1/2 cup Bragg Liquid Aminos
- 1 tablespoon barley malt syrup
- 1 package Mori-Nu firm silken tofu, cut into 1/2-inch cubes
- 1/2 pound spinach, discard coarse stems, washed, drained, cut crosswise into 1 1/2-inch wide strips
- 3–4 tablespoons miso, or to taste
- 2 scallions, minced

Soak arame in hot water 15 minutes. Rinse. Drain. Set aside.

Cook soba according to package directions. Drain. Rinse under cold water. Set aside.

Boil stock, carrots, arame, Bragg's, and syrup for 5 minutes in saucepan. Stir in tofu. Simmer 1 minute.

Stir together 1/2 cup soup stock and miso in a small bowl. Pour into pan. Stir in spinach.

Divide noodles among 6 large bowls. Ladle soup over noodles. Sprinkle each serving with scallions.

Spicy Kale and Chickpea Stew

Sprouting chickpeas greatly reduces cooking time, increases nutritional value, and makes beans easier to digest.

- 1 1/2 cups dried chickpeas*
- 10 cups water
- 2 large onions, coarsely chopped
- 3 large garlic cloves, minced
- 2 green bell peppers, coarsely chopped
- 1/4 cup olive oil

1 1/2 pounds kale, coarse stems discarded and leaves washed well and chopped
2 28-ounce cans plum tomatoes, including the juice, chopped (preferably Muir Glen)
1 6-ounce can tomato paste
2 1/2 tablespoons chili powder
1 teaspoon dried thyme
1 teaspoon dried oregano
1 teaspoon dried hot red pepper flakes
1 teaspoon ground cumin
1 bay leaf
sea salt to taste

If you are not using sprouted chickpeas, soak chickpeas overnight in enough water to cover them by 4 inches. Drain. Rinse.

Simmer chickpeas in a large saucepan, covered partially in water, for 1 1/2 hours, or until tender. (Alternatively, sprout chickpeas first,* and reduce water to 6 cups.)

Cook onions, garlic, and bell pepper in a heavy kettle in oil over moderate heat until vegetables are golden. Stir occasionally.

Add the chickpeas with the cooking liquid, kale, tomatoes (including juice), tomato paste, and spices. Bring to boil. Simmer stew for one hour. Stir occasionally. Discard bay leaf. Season with sea salt. Serve over grains.

*To sprout chickpeas: Soak chickpeas overnight in a large jar. Rinse. Place cheesecloth or screen over top and tilt to 70–85 degree angle. Set in corner, away from direct light. Rinse once in the morning and once at night (3 times in summer) for approximately 36–48 hours or until sprouts are 1/4-inch to 1/2-inch long. Then sauté veggies as above. Add chickpeas. Add remaining ingredients. Simmer 5–8 more minutes. Add sea salt to taste.

Squash and Sweet Potato Chowder

- 1 cup carrots, diced and steamed
- 1 cup sweet potatoes, diced and steamed
- 2 cups butternut squash, diced and steamed
- 2 cups vegetable stock
- 1 bell pepper, diced
- 1 onion, diced
- 4 cloves garlic, minced
- 1/2 teaspoon thyme
- 1/2 teaspoon marjoram
- 1 tablespoon oil
- 1/2 cup nutritional yeast
- 1 cup vegan milk
- sea salt or Bragg Liquid Aminos to taste
- 1/4–1/2 teaspoon cinnamon

Process carrots, sweet potatoes, and squash in stock in blender. Set aside.

Sauté remaining veggies in oil with spices until softened. Add pureed veggies, nutritional yeast, milk, and seasoning to taste.

Ukrainian Cabbage Soup

- 2 tablespoons olive oil
- 2 cups leeks, sliced
- 1 onion, sliced
- 2 carrots, diced
- 1 medium cabbage, chopped
- 1 teaspoon thyme
- 7 cups water
- 2 tablespoons Vogue Vege Base
- 2 tablespoons white miso
- 3 tablespoons lemon juice
- 1 tablespoon barley malt syrup or a few drops of stevia liquid
- 2 medium tomatoes, chopped

Sauté leeks, onion, carrots, and cabbage in oil until softened.

Add thyme, water, and Vogue. Simmer for 10 minutes.

Stir in miso, lemon juice, and sweetener. Stir in tomatoes before serving.

Wild Rice and Shiitake Mushroom Soup

- 1 cup wild rice
- 1 onion, chopped
- 1/4 cup olive oil
- 1 cup shiitake mushrooms, chopped
- 1 cup white mushrooms, sliced
- 1/2 cup celery, thinly sliced
- 1/4 cup oat flour
- 6 cups vegetable stock
- 1 teaspoon curry powder
- 1/2 teaspoon dry mustard
- 1 1/2 teaspoons thyme, minced (or 1/2 teaspoon dried)
- 2 tablespoons miso
- 1/4 cup parsley, minced

Rinse rice in a sieve under cold water until water runs clear. Simmer rice in boiling, salted water, covered, for 35 minutes, or until tender. Drain in a sieve.

Cook onion in oil in a kettle over moderately low heat until softened. Stir occasionally.

Add mushrooms and celery. Cook until tender.

Stir in flour. Stir in rice, stock, and seasonings. Bring mixture to boil. Stir. Simmer for 5 minutes.

Scoop out approximately 1/2 cup stock. Stir miso into stock. Pour back into soup.

Stir in parsley.

Winter Greens Soup

- 1 tablespoon olive oil
- 1 large onion, thinly sliced
- 4 garlic cloves, minced
- 1 medium potato, thinly sliced
- 1 large carrot, thinly sliced
- approximately 4 cups vegetable stock
- 1 bunch kale, stems removed and chopped
- 1 bunch green chard, chopped
- 1 bunch spinach, chopped
- 1 tablespoon lemon juice
- 2 tablespoons white or blonde miso
- Bragg Liquid Aminos to taste

Sauté onion, garlic, potatoes, and carrots in oil until just tender.

Add vegetable stock, kale, and chard. Simmer at least 5 minutes. Remove from heat.

Add spinach, lemon juice, miso, and 1 tablespoon Bragg's. Process in a blender until smooth. Adjust seasonings, if necessary.

Serve immediately.

Chilled Curried Carrot Soup

- 1 onion, thinly sliced
- 4 carrots, thinly sliced
- 1 tablespoon oil
- 1 teaspoon curry powder
- 1 cup vegetable stock
- chopped fresh chives, for garnish

Cook onion and carrot in oil until onion is soft.

Add curry. Add stock. Simmer until carrots are just tender.

Puree in blender. Cool. Chill before serving. Garnish with chives.

Salads

Apple and Potato Salad with Mustard Cream Dressing

1 pound small red potatoes,
steamed until just tender, cooled
2 red Delicious apples
1 celery stalk, sliced thin
1 scallion, sliced thin

Dressing:

1/4 cup dry toasted dulse, crumbled
1 tablespoon fresh lemon juice
1 tablespoon whole-grain prepared mustard, or to taste
2 teaspoons fresh parsley, minced
1/4 cup plain vegan yogurt
1/4 cup vegan mayonnaise
sea salt to taste

Steam potatoes until just tender. Cool.

Add remaining vegetables in large bowl.

Prepare dressing. Whisk together all ingredients. Toss gently with vegetables.

Potato, Corn, and Cherry Tomato Salad

1–2 tablespoons apple cider vinegar
1/2 cup olive oil
1 cup packed fresh basil leaves
sea salt to taste
2 1/2 pounds small red potatoes, diced
corn kernels cut from 6 ears (or 2 10-ounce packages frozen corn, defrosted)
1/2 pound cherry tomatoes, halved

Blend together vinegar, oil, basil, and salt in a blender until dressing is emulsified.

Steam the potatoes. Cool. Combine all ingredients in a large bowl. Toss gently.

Collard Potato Salad with Mustard Dressing

Dulse is a great source of minerals.

- 2 pounds small red potatoes, scrubbed and diced
- 1 pound collards, stems discarded, leaves washed well, cut into 1-inch pieces
- 2 tablespoons whole-grain prepared mustard
- 2 tablespoons apple cider vinegar
- 1/3 cup olive oil
- 1/2 cup dulse, dry toasted and crumbled
- 2 green onions, thinly sliced
- salt to taste

Steam potatoes until just tender. Cool. Place in large bowl.

Place collards in heavy saucepan with 2 tablespoons water. Cover. Simmer for 5 minutes. Drain. Add to potatoes.

Whisk together mustard, vinegar, and salt in a small bowl. Add oil in a stream. Whisk until emulsified.

Pour over potato/kale mixture. Add dulse and green onions. Toss until well combined.

Warm Potato-Kale Salad

- 4 large red potatoes, cubed
- 1 large bunch kale
- 3 large cloves garlic, sliced or chopped
- 2 tablespoons olive oil
- 1/4 cup vegetable stock
- sea salt to taste
- 1–2 tablespoons apple cider vinegar

Steam potatoes until just tender.

Remove stems from kale. Tear leaves into bite-size pieces. Sauté with garlic and oil for 2 minutes. Add vegetable stock. Cover pan. Simmer 5 minutes.

Toss in potatoes, salt, and vinegar.

Potato Salad, My Way

- 1/2 package firm tofu, cubed in 1/2-inch cubes
- 3–4 cups red potatoes, cut into 1-inch cubes
- 2 large stalks celery, diced
- 1 cup mixed crunchy sprouts (lentils, peas, etc.)
- 1/4 cup parsley, minced

Dressing:

- 1/4–1/2 cup vegan mayonnaise (see recipe in Condiments)
- 1/2–1 tablespoon whole-grain prepared mustard
- 2 garlic cloves, minced
- 1–2 tablespoons lemon juice
- 1–2 teaspoons kelp powder or dulse flakes
- 2 tablespoons dill pickle, minced
- 1/8 teaspoon turmeric

Wrap tofu in a clean kitchen towel for 30 minutes.

Steam potatoes until just tender.

Mix all salad ingredients in large bowl.

Prepare dressing in a separate bowl. Stir into salad.

Serve warm or chilled.

Cole Slaw

- 4 cups cabbage, shredded
- 1 cup carrot, shredded
- 1/2 cup vegan mayonnaise
- 2 tablespoons whole-grain prepared mustard

Mix all ingredients well.

Far East Coleslaw

- 1 medium cabbage, quartered, core removed and discarded
- 1 large carrot, finely chopped
- 1 cup cilantro, minced and tightly packed

1/4 cup green onions, thinly sliced
1 cup cucumber, chopped
1/2 cup pumpkin seeds
1/4 cup sesame or flax oil
2 teaspoons peanut butter
4 tablespoons lime juice
3 tablespoons Bragg Liquid Aminos
1 jalapeno pepper, seeded and finely chopped
sea salt to taste

Shred cabbage by cutting very thin slices along the length of each quarter. Place in large serving bowl. Mix in carrots, cilantro, green onions, cucumber, and pumpkin seeds.

Whisk oil with peanut butter. Combine oil and remaining ingredients in a jar. Shake well to blend. Toss into salad. Adjust seasonings, if needed.

Sweet Potato Slaw

1 carrot, shredded
1 sweet potato, shredded
1/2 yellow or red bell pepper, chopped
1/2 cup kale, finely minced
2 green onions, minced
1/4 cabbage head, shredded

Dressing:

1/3 cup plain soy yogurt
1/3 cup vegan mayonnaise
1 teaspoon caraway seeds
stevia liquid, several drops to taste
2 teaspoons apple cider vinegar
1/4 teaspoon sea salt

Combine dressing with vegetables.

Serve immediately, or slightly chilled.

Chili Slaw

1 medium cabbage
1 1/2 cups red beans, cooked
1 red bell pepper, seeded and diced
1/4 cup scallion greens, thinly sliced
1 cup corn kernels
1/2 cup parsley, minced
2 stalks celery, chopped
1 teaspoon whole cumin seeds
1 teaspoon dried oregano
1 tablespoon chili powder
1/2–3/4 cup vegan mayonnaise
1 garlic clove, minced
3 tablespoons lime juice
sea salt to taste

Quarter cabbage. Cut away any hard core. Shred cabbage by cutting very thin slices along the length of each quarter. Place the shredded cabbage in a large bowl or storage container.

Toss in the beans, red pepper, scallion greens, corn, parsley, and celery.

Prepare dressing:
Heat a small heavy skillet for 30 seconds. Add cumin seeds. Stir constantly until they begin to brown and pop, about 10–20 seconds. Turn off heat immediately. Stir in the oregano and chili powder. Cool slightly. Grind mixture to a powder in a spice mill or with a mortar and pestle.

Combine the seasoning mix in a small bowl with the mayonnaise and garlic. Stir in 2 tablespoons of lime juice.

Toss enough of the dressing into the salad to thoroughly coat it. Add extra lime juice, if desired.

Celery and Apple Salad

- 2 tablespoons vegan mayonnaise
- 1 tablespoon whole-grain prepared mustard
- 1 teaspoon apple cider vinegar
- 1 teaspoon tarragon leaves, minced, or 1/4 teaspoon dried
- sea salt to taste
- 4 celery stalks, cut into 1 1/2-inch matchsticks, plus celery leaves for garnish
- 1 crisp tart apple, cut into 1 1/2-inch matchsticks

Whisk together mayonnaise, mustard, vinegar, tarragon, and salt in a bowl.

Toss with celery and apple. Garnish with celery leaves.

South American Jicama and Orange Salad

- 1/3 cup fresh lime juice
- 1 teaspoon sea salt, or to taste
- 1 teaspoon chili powder, or to taste
- 1/8 teaspoon cayenne
- 1 pound jicama, peeled, cut into 1/3-inch thick sticks
- 4 navel oranges, rind and pith cut free, sections cut away from membranes
- 2 scallions, minced

Whisk together lime juice, salt, chili powder, and cayenne in a large bowl. Add jicama. Toss to coat well with dressing.

Arrange oranges decoratively around edge of platter. Mound jicama with a slotted spoon in center.

Drizzle remaining dressing over oranges. Sprinkle scallions over salad.

Walnut and Apple Salad

1/4 cup flax or hemp oil
1 tablespoon whole-grain prepared mustard
1 teaspoon apple cider vinegar
sea salt to taste
2 cups salad mix
1 cup shredded red kale
1/3 cup walnuts, coarsely chopped
1/4 cup red onion, slivered
1/2 crisp apple, sliced very thin, then halved

Whisk the first four ingredients into a dressing.

Place remaining ingredients in a bowl and drizzle with dressing.

Corn, Kidney, and Cucumber Salad

This tastes best if allowed to rest up to 3 hours.

1 cup bulgur
1/2 cup raisins
1 1/3 cups water
1 tablespoon flax or hemp oil
1/3 cup vegetable stock
2 teaspoons orange rind, grated
1 1/2 tablespoons fresh parsley, minced
1 1/2 tablespoons fresh mint, minced
1 1/2 tablespoons fresh chives, minced
1 1/4 cups corn
2/3 cup cooked beans (kidney or other red bean)
1 cup cucumber, cut into matchsticks
sea salt to taste

Place bulgur and raisins in bowl with water. Set aside.

Place oil, stock, rind, and herbs in a separate bowl. Pour into bulgur mixture. Let sit until all liquid is absorbed.

Fold in corn, beans, and cucumber gently. Chill before serving.

Cucumber, Dill, and Wakame Salad

1 12-inch-long piece wakame
2 large cucumbers, sliced paper thin
1/4 cup apple cider vinegar
2 tablespoons green onions or sweet red onion, finely chopped
1 1/2–2 teaspoons dill weed, dried
sea salt to taste

Snip wakame into 1/2-inch pieces. Rinse briefly in cold water. Drain thoroughly.

Toss all ingredients together. Cover. Refrigerate until wakame is tender, about 4–6 hours. Stir occasionally to make sure the wakame is submerged in juice.

Serve slightly chilled or at room temperature.

Cucumbers with Tofu Sour Cream

1 cup Tofu Sour Cream (see recipe in Condiments)
3 cups cucumbers, chopped
1 teaspoon dill, minced

Mix all ingredients well.

Cucumber, Orange, and Aniseed Salad

1/4 teaspoon anise seeds
1 cucumber
1 navel orange
1 tablespoon apple cider vinegar
1 tablespoon olive oil
1/4 red onion, sliced thin crosswise
sea salt to taste

Crush the anise seeds lightly with the back of a spoon in a small bowl.

Peel cucumber, if desired. Quarter lengthwise. Cut crosswise into 1/4-inch-thick pieces.

Peel orange. Cut pith away with a serrated knife. Cut sections free from the membranes. Slice thin crosswise.

Combine all ingredients. Add salt to taste.

Spinach, Fennel, and Pink Grapefruit Salad

- 1 tablespoon apple cider vinegar
- 3 tablespoons fresh pink grapefruit juice
- 1/2–3/4 teaspoon whole-grain prepared mustard
- 1/4 cup olive or flax oil, or both combined
- sea salt to taste
- 1 pound spinach, stems removed, washed well, spun dry
- 2 pink grapefruits, zest and pith cut away, cut into segments
- 1 small fennel bulb, sliced thin crosswise

Blend vinegar, grapefruit juice, mustard, oil, and salt until emulsified.

Arrange salad on plates decoratively. Drizzle with dressing.

Cauliflower Salad

- 1 cup cauliflower, diced
- 1/2 red bell pepper, sliced into slivers
- 1/2 cup daikon radish, sliced into matchsticks
- 1 cup mung bean sprouts, blanched
- olive oil to taste
- balsamic vinegar to taste

Combine all ingredients. Mix well. Chill and serve.

Sesame Carrot Salad

Try adding 1/4 cup of reconstituted arame sea vegetable for an extra boost of flavor and nutrition!

- 1 garlic clove, smashed
- 3 tablespoons oil
- 1/4 cup sesame seeds
- 8 medium carrots, coarsely grated
- 2 tablespoons fresh lemon juice
- sea salt to taste

Cook the garlic in oil in a small heavy skillet over moderate heat. Stir until garlic is golden.

Add sesame seeds. Cook, stirring, until golden.

Toss together carrots, sesame mixture, lemon juice, and salt in a bowl.

Broccoli with Cheddar Vinaigrette

- 1 tablespoon olive oil
- 1 teaspoon apple cider vinegar
- 1 tablespoon water
- pinch cayenne or red pepper flakes
- 1/2 cup grated cheddar-style vegan cheese, coarsely grated
- 1/2 pound broccoli, cut into long flowerets
- sea salt to taste

Blend together all ingredients except broccoli in a blender. Add salt, if using.

Steam broccoli until crisp tender, or raw is great.

Serve topped with vinaigrette.

Broccoli Salad Italiano

1 bunch broccoli, cut into bite-size pieces
1/3 cup sun-dried tomatoes, reconstituted in 1 cup hot water
1/4 red onion, sliced into thin slivers
small handful sun-dried black olives, chopped

Dressing:

2 tablespoons balsamic or red wine vinegar
1/4 cup olive oil
1/2 teaspoon basil, dried (or 2 teaspoons fresh)
pinch red pepper flakes
pinch salt

Steam broccoli until crisp tender.

Drain tomatoes. Reserve liquid. Dice tomatoes.

Mix broccoli, tomatoes, onion, and olives.

Mix dressing ingredients in a jar. Shake well to blend. Pour over broccoli salad.

Rice and Broccoli Salad with Sunflower Seed Dressing

2 cups long-grain rice, sprouted or cooked (red rice would be nice)
1 bunch broccoli
1 cup slivered almonds, lightly toasted
1/2 cup scallion greens, thinly sliced
1/3 cup raw sunflower seeds, lightly toasted
4 teaspoons apple cider vinegar
1/2 cup flax oil
5 teaspoons toasted sesame oil
sea salt to taste
1 cup vegetable stock

Place cooked or sprouted rice in bowl.

Peel stems of broccoli. Slice thin. Cut flowerets into 1-inch pieces. Steam broccoli until crisp tender. Cool.

Add broccoli, almonds, and scallion greens to rice. Combine mixture well.

Puree sunflower seeds with the vinegar, oils, and sea salt in a blender. Add 1 cup vegetable stock in a stream. Blend until emulsified. Toss with salad.

Arame-Zucchini Sesame Toss

- 1/3 cup arame, soaked in warm/hot water for 20 minutes
- 2 cups zucchini, grated
- 1/2 red bell pepper, chopped
- 1/4 cup green onions, minced
- 3/4 cup sesame seeds, ground
- 1/2–1 tablespoon whole-grain prepared mustard
- 1 tablespoon Bragg Liquid Aminos
- 1/4 cup water
- 1 tablespoon Vogue Vege Base

Place veggies in a bowl. Mix remaining ingredients. Add to veggies. Toss well.

Moroccan Swiss Chard Salad

- 1 1/2 pounds Swiss chard
- 2 tablespoons oil
- 1 tablespoon garlic, minced
- 1 tablespoon paprika
- 2 teaspoons ground cumin
- 2 tablespoons fresh lemon juice
- sea salt to taste

Trim chard. Discard thick stems. Wash well. Chop coarse.

Heat oil in large skillet over moderate heat until hot, but not smoking. Cook garlic briefly, just until golden.

Add chard, paprika, cumin, lemon juice, and sea salt. Stir to coat well. Cook mixture for 5 minutes. Let cool.

Serve at room temperature or chilled.

Escarole, Spinach, Hijiki, and Red Onion Salad

1/4 cup hijiki, soaked in water overnight
4 cups packed escarole, rinsed, dried, and torn into pieces
3 cups packed fresh spinach, rinsed, dried, and torn into pieces
1/2 cup red onion, finely chopped
1/2 cup peas
2 tablespoons sunflower seeds

Dressing:

1 garlic clove, minced and mashed to a paste with 1/8 teaspoon sea salt
1 teaspoon apple cider vinegar
1 tablespoon fresh lemon juice
1/2 teaspoon whole-grain prepared mustard
1/4 cup olive or flax oil

Drain hijiki. Rinse well. Chop coarse.

Mix all salad ingredients together.

Process dressing ingredients in blender until smooth.

Combine well with salad.

Tabbouleh

1 cup bulgur wheat poured into 2 cups boiling water (or 2 cups cooked quinoa, which I favor)
1 cup parsley, finely minced
2–3 tablespoons mint, finely minced
1 carrot, finely diced
1 tomato, seeded and finely diced
1 cucumber, seeded and finely diced
2 tablespoons olive oil
4–6 tablespoons lemon juice
1/2 tablespoon whole-grain prepared mustard
1–2 garlic cloves, finely chopped

Let bulgur wheat sit in boiling water 15–20 minutes. Drain liquid, if any. Add vegetables.

Blend olive oil, lemon juice, mustard, and garlic. Stir into salad.

Let rest. Cool before serving, if desired. Adjust with lemon juice, if needed.

Tomato and Fennel Salad

- 5 tablespoons fresh lemon juice
- sea salt to taste
- 1/2 cup olive oil
- 2 large fennel bulbs, sliced paper thin
- 2 pounds tomatoes, sliced

Whisk together lemon juice with some sea salt in a large bowl. Add oil in a stream until emulsified.

Add fennel. Toss well. Marinate for a few minutes.

Arrange tomatoes decoratively on a platter. Spoon fennel mixture over them.

Insalata Caprese

- 2 large, firm, ripe tomatoes (about 1 pound), sliced thin crosswise
- 1/2 pound mozzarella-style cheese, sliced thin
- 1/3 cup basil leaves, thinly sliced
- 2 tablespoons drained capers
- sea salt to taste
- 1/4 cup olive oil (Spectrum Organic is my favorite)

Arrange tomatoes decoratively on platter. Add mozzarella.

Sprinkle with basil and capers. Season with salt. Drizzle with oil.

Chopped Main Salad

2 avocados
1/2 cup corn
1/2 cup peas
1/2 cup sprouts (preferably pea or lentil)
1/2 cup red bell pepper, finely diced
1/2 cup carrot, finely diced
1/2 cup celery, finely diced
1 cup cabbage, finely diced
1 cup ground almonds or sunflower seeds
1/4 cup onion, finely chopped
1/4 cup parsley, finely chopped
3 tablespoons apple cider vinegar
3 tablespoons Bragg Liquid Aminos

Mix all ingredients well.

Marinated Mushroom Salad

1 pound button and/or crimini mushrooms, cubed
1–2 cups bean sprouts
1 red bell pepper, sliced in slivers
1/4 cup toasted almonds, sliced
1/3 cup fresh parsley, minced

Dressing:

3 tablespoons apple cider vinegar
2 tablespoons Oriental sesame oil
2 tablespoons oil
pinch red pepper flakes
1/2 teaspoon salt
2 tablespoons cilantro, minced
2 tablespoons green onions, minced
1 tablespoon ginger, minced
2 garlic cloves, minced

Combine salad ingredients.

Mix dressing ingredients. Pour over salad. Marinate 30–60 minutes before serving.

Italian Chopped Salad with Pesto Dressing

1 cup broccoli, chopped
1 cup cabbage, chopped
1/2 red or yellow bell pepper, diced
1/2 cucumber, diced
1/2 cup corn
1 carrot, diced

Place all ingredients in large bowl.

*Pesto Dressing:**

1 cup parsley, chopped
1 cup basil leaves, chopped
2 tablespoons olive oil
1/2 head Roasted Garlic (see recipe in Condiments)
2 tablespoons pine nuts
1 tablespoon lemon juice
1 teaspoon lemon rind, finely grated
1 teaspoon balsamic vinegar
1 teaspoon mellow white or blonde miso

Add dressing to chopped salad, starting with half of the dressing and adding more as desired.

*Any leftover dressing can be used over beans, sliced tomatoes, or steamed potatoes.

Sprouted Wheat and Veggie Bowl

- 2 cups 48-hour sprouted wheat
- 1/2 cup celery, diced
- 1/2 red bell pepper, diced
- 1/2 cucumber, diced
- 1-2 ears of corn, removed from cob
- 1/2 cup kale or collard greens, stems discarded, minced

Place all ingredients in a large bowl. Toss with Lemon-Sesame Dressing or my favorite, Dried Tomato, Caper, and Olive Dressing (see recipes in Salad Dressings).

Spicy Chickpea Salad

- 1 cup dried chickpeas, soaked overnight (or 3 cups of sprouted chickpeas cooked until tender, about 15 minutes)
- 1 yellow or red bell pepper, finely diced
- 1 small bunch green onions, thinly sliced
- 1/2 cup cilantro, finely minced

Dressing:

- 2 tablespoons lemon juice
- 1 tablespoon apple cider vinegar
- 1 garlic clove, minced
- 1 teaspoon fresh ginger, grated
- 3/4 teaspoon cumin, ground
- 1/4 teaspoon cayenne or chipotle pepper
- 1/4 cup olive oil

Cook chickpeas until tender. While warm, combine chickpeas with bell pepper, onions, and cilantro.

Whisk together all ingredients to make dressing.

Add dressing to chickpea mixture. Stir well. Let rest for at least an hour before serving.

Bean Salad

1 pound green beans, cleaned
1 ripe tomato, diced
1/2 yellow bell pepper, cut in strips
2 tablespoons red onion, chopped
2 tablespoons olive oil
2 cloves garlic, minced
1/4 teaspoon dried thyme
sea salt to taste
1 tablespoon apple cider vinegar

Steam green beans until crisp tender. Keep warm.

Place tomato, pepper, and onion in bowl.

Heat oil in small pan. Add garlic. Sauté briefly, 1–2 minutes.

Pour over veggies. Add remaining ingredients. Toss well.

Millet Salad with Apricots, Pine Nuts, and Ginger

1/2 cup red onion, finely diced
1 tablespoon apple cider vinegar
1/3 cup millet cooked in 1 cup water
1/4 cup olive oil
6 dried apricots, diced small
2 teaspoons fresh ginger, grated
1/4 teaspoon salt
2 tablespoons pine nuts, toasted
1 celery stalk, diced

Boil water in a small pot. Place red onion in water for 15 seconds. Drain well.

Toss onion with a few splashes of vinegar to draw out its pink color.

Toss all ingredients together. Add salt or vinegar to brighten the flavor, if needed.

Quinoa Salad with Sun-Dried Tomatoes

- 1 cup quinoa
- 2 cups water
- 1/2 cucumber, seeded, skinned if desired, and minced
- 1/2 cup fresh basil, minced
- 1/2 cup rehydrated sun-dried tomatoes, minced
- 2 green onions, minced
- 2 tablespoons pine nuts, toasted
- 1/4 cup olive oil
- 1–2 tablespoons whole-grain prepared mustard
- 2–4 tablespoons lemon juice
- sea salt to taste
- 1 large garlic clove, minced

Rinse quinoa. Cook quinoa in water as you would rice, simmering for approximately 20 minutes until all moisture is absorbed. Cool.

Add cucumber, basil, tomatoes, and onions to quinoa in a large bowl. (The smaller you can dice the vegetables, the better.) Add pine nuts. Mix well.

Blend oil, mustard, lemon juice, salt, and garlic well. Toss into salad. Adjust seasonings, if desired.

Mexican Pasta Salad

- 1 pound pasta noodles such as rigatoni, elbows, or curls (preferably wheat free)
- corn kernels cut from 3 ears (or 1 10-ounce package frozen, defrosted)
- 1 small red onion, sliced into 1/4-inch rings, then halved
- 2 bell peppers seeded and diced (if available, use red and green)
- 2 tablespoons parsley, minced
- 2 tablespoons cilantro, minced
- 2–3 tablespoons sun-dried olives, sliced
- 2 teaspoons chili powder
- 1 teaspoon toasted cumin seeds, ground

1½ cups kidney or pinto beans, drained and rinsed
1½ cups Tomato Salsa (see recipe in Condiments), or bottled
½ cup Tofu Sour Cream (see recipe in Condiments)
sea salt to taste

Cook the pasta according to package directions. Drain. Rinse under cold water to stop the cooking. Drain again. Place in a large bowl.

Add the remaining ingredients. Toss well. Adjust seasonings if needed.

Pasta and Vegetable Salad with Basil Dressing

I favor Papadini Lentil Pasta, Lundberg Rice, or Quinoa Noodles.

1 pound pasta shells, fusilli, or other corkscrew pasta
2 cups basil leaves, firmly packed
½ cup olive oil
6–8 sun-dried olives, pitted
2 garlic cloves, minced
1 tablespoon apple cider vinegar
¼ cup vegetable stock
sea salt to taste
1 cup carrots, diced ¼-inch
1 cup fresh or frozen corn
1 cup peas
⅓ cup artichoke hearts, chopped
½ cup lentil sprouts
¼ cup pine nuts, lightly toasted
1 tomato, chopped
vegan-style parmesan (optional)

Cook pasta according to package directions. Rinse. Drain under cool water.

Blend basil, oil, olives, garlic, vinegar, stock, and salt in blender until dressing is smooth.

Toss all ingredients in large bowl, incorporating the dressing well. Sprinkle vegan-style parmesan over all, if desired.

Wild Rice Salad

- 4 cups water
- 1½ cups wild rice, rinsed and drained (replace with sprouted wild rice if desired)
- 1 medium red or yellow bell pepper, roasted and diced
- ⅓–½ cup sun-dried tomatoes, reconstituted in hot water, drained and chopped
- ¼ cup sun-dried olives, pitted and coarsely chopped
- 2 tablespoons fresh parsley, finely chopped
- ¼ cup pine nuts, lightly toasted
- ¼ cup olive oil
- 2 tablespoons fresh lemon juice
- sea salt to taste

Boil 4 cups water in a large saucepan. Add the wild rice. Cover. Simmer for 40 minutes, or until tender. (Alternatively, sprout wild rice first.)

Drain the wild rice in a sieve. Transfer to a large bowl. Toss rice with remaining ingredients. Add salt, if desired.

Serve at room temperature or chilled.

Wild Rice Salad #2

Sprouted rice is a nice substitution for cooked rice.

- ¼ cup wild rice
- ½ cup brown rice
- 2 cups water
- 1 cup peas
- 2 stalks celery, thinly sliced
- 4 green onions, sliced
- ½ red bell pepper, slivered
- ¼ cup orange juice
- 2 tablespoons olive oil
- 1 tablespoon Bragg Liquid Aminos
- 2 teaspoons brown rice syrup
- 3 tablespoons sesame seeds, toasted

Cook rice until liquid is absorbed. Cool. Add peas, celery, onions, and bell pepper to rice mixture.

Combine orange juice, olive oil, Bragg's, rice syrup, and sesame seeds. Pour over rice mixture. Toss.

Mock Chicken Salad

1 package tempeh
1/4 cup vegan mayonnaise
1 celery stalk, finely chopped
2 tablespoons dill pickle, minced
2 tablespoons onion, minced
2 tablespoons parsley, minced
1–2 teaspoons whole-grain prepared mustard
1–2 teaspoons Bragg Liquid Aminos
1/4 teaspoon powdered garlic

Steam tempeh 10 minutes. Cool. Cut into small cubes. Combine with remaining ingredients.

Mock Egg Salad

1 block firm tofu
1/2 cup celery, finely minced
1/4 cup green onion, finely minced
1–2 tablespoons whole-grain prepared mustard
1/4 cup vegan mayonnaise
1/2 sheet nori, shredded (or toasted and crumbled dulse)
pinch of turmeric
salt and pepper to taste

Crumble tofu. Leave chunky. Mix all ingredients well.

Mock Chicken

1 tablespoon Vogue Vege Base
2 tablespoons Bragg Liquid Aminos
2 tablespoons tomato sauce
1/2 teaspoon chili powder
1/2 teaspoon apple cider vinegar
1/4 teaspoon garlic powder
1/4 teaspoon onion powder
1/4 teaspoon sage
1/4 teaspoon paprika
1/4 teaspoon oregano
1 block firm tofu, crumbled

Preheat oven to 350 degrees.

Mix all seasonings together. Squeeze into tofu. Arrange on an oiled baking sheet. Bake for 30 minutes, stirring 2 or 3 times. Set aside.

Mock Chicken Taco Salad

1 prepared recipe of Mock Chicken
1 cup tomato, diced
3/4 cup Tofu Sour Cream (see recipe in Condiments)
1/2 cup red onion, diced
1/4 cup fresh cilantro, chopped
3/4 teaspoon ground cumin
1/4 teaspoon sea salt (delete if using salted corn chips)
4–6 cups salad greens
1 roasted anaheim chili, chopped
1/2 bag baked tortilla chips

Combine all ingredients, except tortilla chips, in a large bowl.

Crush tortilla chips with your hands. Stir gently into salad. Serve immediately.

Mock Chicken with Spicy Fruit Salad

- 1 mango, peeled and cut into 1/2-inch cubes
- 1 papaya, peeled, seeded, and cut into 1/2-inch cubes
- 1 pint strawberries, hulled and quartered
- 2 tablespoons brown rice syrup (or a few drops of stevia)
- 1 red serrano or jalapeno chili, seeded and minced (wear rubber gloves)
- 2 tablespoons mint leaves, minced
- 6 cups, approximately, mixed salad greens
- 1/4 red onion, thinly sliced into half moons
- 1 carrot, shredded
- 1 large rib celery, diced
- 1 tablespoon fresh lemon juice
- 1 tablespoon olive oil
- 1 prepared recipe of Mock Chicken (see recipe in Salads)

Stir together mango, papaya, strawberries, syrup or stevia, and chili in a bowl. Let mixture stand for 10 minutes. Stir in mint.

Toss together salad greens, onion, carrot, and celery. Whisk together lemon juice and oil. Combine well with greens.

Place salad greens on 4 individual plates. Divide Mock Chicken. Place in center of plates. Add a large dollop of fruit salsa on top.

"Egg" Salad with Jalapeno and Cumin

Serve with baked corn chips for a light, zesty lunch.

- 1/3 cup vegan mayonnaise (see recipe in Condiments)
- 1 tablespoon fresh lemon juice, or to taste
- 1 tablespoon Vogue Vege Base
- 3/4 teaspoon ground cumin, or to taste
- 1 block firm tofu, rinsed
- 1/2 cup celery, finely chopped
- 1/4 cup green onions, white and green parts, thinly sliced
- 1 1/2 teaspoons jalapeno pepper, seeded and minced
- 1–2 tablespoons dill pickle, minced
- sea salt to taste

Whisk together mayonnaise, lemon juice, Vogue, and cumin.

Crumble tofu. Add celery, onion, jalapeno, pickle, and salt. Stir mixture until combined well.

Curried "Tuna" Salad with Coriander

Try this salad on a bed of mixed greens with peas, cashews, and nori strips. Rim the plate with cucumber and tomato slices.

- 1 package tempeh
- 1/2 cup red onion, finely chopped
- 1/4 cup vegan mayonnaise (see recipe in Condiments)
- 1/4 cup plain yogurt (preferably vegan)
- 2 teaspoons fresh lemon juice, or to taste
- 1 1/2 teaspoons curry powder, or to taste
- 1/3 cup celery, finely chopped
- 3 tablespoons coriander, chopped, or to taste
- sea salt to taste

Steam tempeh for 10 minutes. Cool. Grate.

Soak onion in bowl of ice and cold water for 10 minutes. Drain well.

Whisk together mayonnaise, yogurt, lemon juice, and curry powder.

Add onion, tempeh, celery, coriander, and salt. Stir mixture until combined well.

Daddy's Favorite Salad

- 1 pound tofu, frozen, defrosted
- 1/2 cup arame
- 2 cups green beans, sliced into bite-size pieces
- 2 stalks celery, thinly diced
- 2 cups red cabbage, shaved
- 1 bunch romaine
- 1 cup lentil sprouts
- 1 yellow bell pepper, diced
- 2 tablespoons olive oil

- 1–2 tablespoons Bragg Liquid Aminos
- 1/2 teaspoon dry mustard
- 1 heaping tablespoon Vogue Vege Base
- 2 cloves garlic, minced
- 1/2 onion, sliced into half moons

Defrost tofu. Squeeze to release liquid.

Soak arame in hot water for 15 minutes. Drain.

Steam green beans until crisp tender.

Place all veggies and tofu in large bowl.

Whisk oil, Bragg's, mustard, and Vogue.

Sauté garlic and onion in a small amount of oil until onion is lightly browned. Toss all ingredients well.

Ginger Mint "Ceviche"

- 1 package smoked tofu, cut in 1/4-inch cubes
- 1 lime, juiced
- 1 teaspoon lime peel, finely minced
- 1 tablespoon ginger, finely minced
- 1 garlic clove, finely minced
- 2–4 small chilies, seeded and minced
- 2 tablespoons cilantro, chopped
- 2 tablespoons mint, chopped
- 1 green onion, chopped
- 1/2 red bell pepper, chopped
- 3 tablespoons hemp or flax oil
- 1 teaspoon fresh nutmeg, grated
- 1/8–1/4 teaspoon curry paste
- 1/2 teaspoon sea salt
- salad greens

Mix all ingredients well, except greens.

Refrigerate for at least one hour before serving. Serve over bed of greens.

Oriental Salad with Smoked Tofu

If you cannot find enoki mushrooms, fresh shiitake would be my next choice, though plain button mushrooms may be substituted.

Salad:

- 3 cups wild rice, cooked or sprouted
- 1 package smoked tofu, cubed
- 1 cup fresh mung or soybean sprouts
- 1 red bell pepper, slivered
- 1 package enoki mushrooms
- 1/2 cup sliced almonds, toasted
- 1/4 cup green onions, sliced

Dressing:

- 3 tablespoons red wine vinegar
- 1 tablespoon Bragg Liquid Aminos
- 1–2 tablespoons Oriental toasted sesame oil
- 1 tablespoon brown rice syrup
- pinch of red pepper flakes
- 1/2 teaspoon sea salt
- 1 tablespoon fresh ginger, finely minced
- 2 teaspoons garlic, finely minced

Mix together salad ingredients.Toss salad with dressing.

Salad Dressings

Basic Vinaigrette Dressing

2 tablespoons balsamic or red wine vinegar
1/4 cup olive oil
1/2 teaspoon basil, dried (or 2 teaspoons fresh)
pinch of red pepper flakes
pinch of salt

Mix all ingredients in jar. Shake well to blend.

Herbed Vinaigrette Dressing

2 tablespoons lemon juice
1/2 teaspoon whole-grain prepared mustard
1/3 cup olive or flax oil
1 1/2 teaspoons parsley, minced
1 1/2 teaspoons snipped fresh chives
1 1/2 teaspoons tarragon, minced
1 1/2 teaspoon chervil, minced
sea salt to taste

Whisk first two ingredients. Add oil slowly, until emulsified. Stir in remaining ingredients.

Miso Vinaigrette Dressing

2 tablespoons red miso
2 teaspoons Dijon or whole-grain prepared mustard
1 tablespoon water
1 1/2 tablespoons fresh lemon juice
1/4 cup hemp or flax oil
1 teaspoon fresh gingerroot, peeled and minced
1 scallion, minced

Mash together miso and mustard in a bowl. Whisk in water and lemon juice. Add oil in a stream, whisking. Whisk until emulsified. Whisk in gingerroot and scallion.

Basil Dressing

- 2 cups basil leaves, firmly packed
- 1/2 cup olive oil
- 6–8 sun-dried olives, pitted
- 2 garlic cloves
- 1 tablespoon apple cider vinegar
- 1/4 cup vegetable stock
- sea salt to taste

Blend all ingredients in blender until dressing is smooth.

Basil, Mint, and Orange Vinaigrette

- 1/2 cup packed fresh basil leaves, minced
- 1/2 cup packed fresh mint leaves, minced
- 1/4 teaspoon orange zest, freshly grated
- 1 tablespoon fresh orange juice
- 1–2 teaspoons apple cider vinegar
- 1 garlic clove, minced
- 1/2 cup oil

Blend all ingredients in a blender until emulsified.

Pesto Dressing

- 1 cup parsley, chopped
- 1 cup basil leaves, chopped
- 2 tablespoons olive oil
- 1/2 head Roasted Garlic (see recipe in Condiments)
- 2 tablespoons pine nuts
- 1 tablespoon lemon juice
- 1 teaspoon lemon rind, finely grated
- 1 teaspoon balsamic vinegar
- 1 teaspoon mellow white or blonde miso

Process all ingredients in blender until well combined.

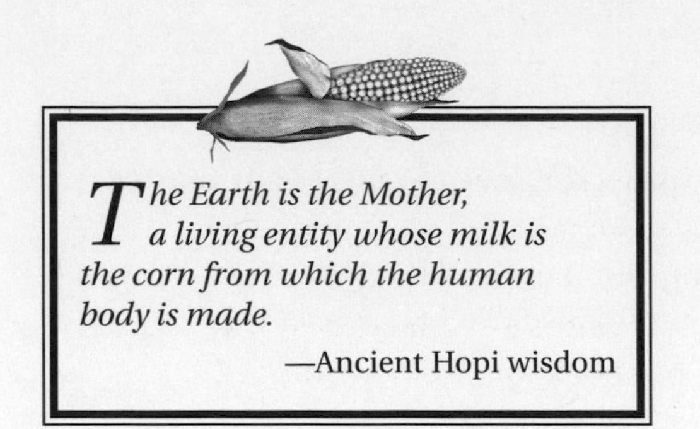

Cucumber Dill Sour Cream Dressing

- 1/2 cucumber, seeded and coarsely grated (about 1/2 cup)
- 1/4 teaspoon sea salt
- 2 teaspoons whole-grain prepared mustard
- 1 tablespoon apple cider vinegar or lemon juice
- 1/2 cup vegan sour cream
- 1/4 cup plain vegan yogurt
- 1 tablespoon snipped fresh dill

Toss cucumber with salt. Place in a small sieve, set over a bowl. Let sit 10 minutes.

Process remaining ingredients in blender until smooth. Stir in cucumber until combined.

Dried Tomato, Caper, and Olive Dressing

- 1/2 cup vegan mayonnaise (see recipe in Condiments)
- 1 tablespoon fresh lemon juice
- 2 sun-dried tomatoes, reconstituted in hot water and minced
- 1 tablespoon bottled capers, drained and minced
- 1 teaspoon sun-dried olives, pitted and minced
- 2 tablespoons water, or enough to thin dressing to desired consistency
- sea salt to taste

Whisk together all ingredients in a bowl. Add salt to taste.

Sunflower Seed Dressing

- 1/3 cup raw sunflower seeds, lightly toasted
- 4 teaspoons apple cider vinegar
- 1/2 cup hemp or flax oil
- 5 teaspoons toasted sesame oil
- sea salt to taste

Puree sunflower seeds with the vinegar, oils, and sea salt in a blender. Add 1 cup water in a stream. Blend until emulsified.

Eric's Favorite Dressing

Great over greens with sprouts, avocado, and toasted pumpkin seeds. For a heartier salad, add some diced marinated baked tofu (there are several packaged varieties).

- 1 heaping tablespoon Vogue Vege Base
- 2 tablespoons Bragg Liquid Aminos
- juice of 1 lemon
- 1/4 cup olive oil
- dry mustard to taste (optional)

Blend all ingredients well.

Garlic Mint Dressing

- 1 garlic clove, crushed
- 2 tablespoons fresh lime juice
- 1 teaspoon whole-grain prepared mustard
- 1 1/2 teaspoons fresh mint, minced (or 1/2 teaspoon dried)
- 1/2 teaspoon brown rice syrup
- 1/4 teaspoon sea salt
- 1/3 cup flax or hemp oil

Process all ingredients in a blender or mini processor until emulsified.

Green Goddess Dressing

- 1/2 cup vegan mayonnaise (see recipe in Condiments)
- 1/2 cup soy yogurt
- 1 tablespoon lemon juice
- 1/4 cup parsley, minced
- 1 green onion, minced
- 1 garlic clove, minced

Mix all ingredients well.

Roasted Shallot Vinaigrette Dressing

- 4 large shallots
- 2 cloves garlic
- 1/3 cup sesame oil
- 1/3 cup olive oil
- 4–6 tablespoons lemon juice
- 3/4 teaspoon sea salt
- 1/8 teaspoon dry mustard

Preheat oven to 375 degrees.

Place unpeeled shallots and garlic cloves in a casserole dish. Cover. Roast until very soft, about 15 minutes. Cool. Peel.

Combine with remaining ingredients in a blender or food processor until thoroughly blended. Adjust seasonings, if desired.

Lemon-Sesame Dressing

- 1/4 cup sesame butter or tahini
- 1/4 cup lemon juice
- 3/4 cup oil (part olive and hemp or flax)
- 1/4 cup water
- 1–2 teaspoons Bragg Liquid Aminos
- 1/4 teaspoon sea salt

Whisk all ingredients until emulsified.

Spiced Sesame Dressing

- 1/2 teaspoon whole cumin seeds
- 1/2 teaspoon whole coriander seeds
- 1/4 cup sesame butter or tahini
- 1/4 cup hot water
- 1–2 teaspoons apple cider vinegar
- 1/2 cup silken tofu
- 1 tablespoon lemon juice
- 1 tablespoon hemp or flax oil
- sea salt to taste

Toast cumin and coriander seeds over moderate heat in a dry, small, heavy skillet. Shake skillet until spices are fragrant, about 2 minutes. Cool completely.

Finely grind seeds in a mortar and pestle or in a spice grinder.

Whisk together all ingredients in a bowl. Add sea salt to taste. Thin with additional water, if desired.

Spicy Dressing

2 tablespoons lemon juice
1 tablespoon apple cider vinegar
1 garlic clove, minced
1 teaspoon fresh ginger, grated
3/4 teaspoon cumin, ground
1/4 teaspoon cayenne or chipotle pepper
1/4 cup olive oil

Whisk together all ingredients.

Raspberry, Orange, and Lemon Dressing

1/2 cup fresh orange juice
1/4 cup fresh lemon juice
1/2 cup raspberries
1/2 cup olive oil
pinch of cayenne or red pepper flakes
sea salt to taste

Process all ingredients in blender until smooth.

Mustard Dressing

2 tablespoons whole-grain prepared mustard
2 tablespoons apple cider vinegar
sea salt to taste
1/3 cup olive oil

Whisk together mustard, vinegar, and salt in a small bowl.

Add oil in a stream. Whisk until emulsified.

Mustard "Cream" Dressing

1/4 cup dry toasted dulse, crumbled
1 tablespoon fresh lemon juice
1 tablespoon whole-grain prepared mustard, or to taste
2 teaspoons fresh parsley, minced
1/4 cup plain vegan yogurt
1/4 cup vegan mayonnaise
sea salt to taste

Whisk together all ingredients.

Mustard Garlic Dressing

1 garlic clove, minced
1/8 teaspoon sea salt
1 teaspoon apple cider vinegar
1 tablespoon fresh lemon juice
1/2 teaspoon whole-grain prepared mustard
1/4 cup olive or flax oil

Mash garlic and salt to a paste. Whisk all ingredients until smooth.

Oriental Dressing

2 tablespoons rice vinegar
1 tablespoon oil
1 tablespoon Oriental sesame oil
1 tablespoon Bragg Liquid Aminos
1/2 teaspoon dry mustard
2 teaspoons ginger, finely minced
1/2 teaspoon garlic, finely minced
1 tablespoon green onion, finely minced
1 teaspoon sweetener

Combine all ingredients in a jar. Shake vigorously.

Variation:

- 3 tablespoons apple cider vinegar
- 2 tablespoons Oriental sesame oil
- 2 tablespoons oil
- pinch of red pepper flakes
- 1/2 teaspoon salt
- 2 tablespoons cilantro, minced
- 2 tablespoons green onions, minced
- 1 tablespoon ginger, minced
- 2 garlic cloves, minced

Breads

Everywhere people ask, "What can I actually do?" The answer is as simple as it is disconcerting—we can, each of us, work to put our own inner house in order.

The guidance we need for this work cannot be found in science or technology, the value of which utterly depends on the ends they serve; but it can still be found in the traditional wisdom of human kind.

—E. F. Schumacher, *Small Is Beautiful*

Before getting started in this section, please take a few minutes to read these notes:

Oil choices: My personal favorite is coconut oil, though other mild-flavored, unrefined oils can be substituted. Read the "Fats" section for more information on special oils. If you have problems finding coconut oil in stores, you may order it directly from Omega Nutrition at 800-661-3529. Keep in mind that when using coconut oil, slightly decrease the amount used by approximately one-quarter measure.

Stevia: Can enhance the effect of other sweeteners. Adding stevia to recipes as a dietary supplement can help reduce the amount of sweetener you would need.

Flours:

- **Kamut** and spelt are relatives of wheat, though most people tolerate them better.
- **Amaranth** is used in small amounts with other flours to add flavor.
- **Barley** is a flour I usually couple with another flour.
- **Buckwheat** is very dense. Use in small amounts with other flours. Great in pancakes.
- **Cornmeal** adds flavor and texture to quick breads.
- **Garbanzo** is a good wheat replacement, though I would use it with another flour, such as rice.
- **Oat** flour has a sweet, nutty taste, though it is dense and should be mixed with another flour.
- **Quinoa** has a strong flavor and is best used in small amounts.
- **Rice** flour lends wonderful flavor and texture.
- **Rye** flour is dense and hardy. It works well with cornmeal or can be used alone.
- **Soy** flour is dense, so use it in small amounts or mix it with other grains.
- **Teff** is rich in taste and is good alone, or in combination with other grains. Use in quick breads.

Pumpkin-Apricot Bread

This makes a moist, dense loaf—delicious warm or cooled.

2 cups flour (spelt, alone or in combination with others listed at beginning of this section)
1 teaspoon baking soda
1 teaspoon baking powder
1/2 teaspoon sea salt
1/4 teaspoon cinnamon, ground
1/4 teaspoon ginger, ground
1/4 teaspoon cardamom, ground
1/4 teaspoon coriander, ground
3/4 cup barley malt syrup
1/2 teaspoon stevia leaf
1/2 cup dried apricots, coarsely chopped
2 cups pumpkin puree
1 tablespoon Egg Replacer, dissolved in 4 tablespoons water
1/3 cup orange juice
1 tablespoon orange zest, grated

Preheat oven to 350 degrees. Lightly grease and flour a loaf pan.

Combine dry ingredients and apricots in a large bowl. Mix thoroughly.

Whisk together wet ingredients in another bowl. Stir into dry ingredients until liquid is absorbed.

Transfer batter to loaf pan.

Bake for 55–60 minutes, or until a toothpick inserted in center comes out clean. If it browns too quickly in oven, cover it halfway through baking.

Apple, Apricot, and Raisin Muffins

- 3 tablespoons flax seeds, ground
- 1/2 cup water
- 1 3/4 cups spelt, barley, or wheat pastry flour
- 1 1/4 cups oat flour
- 1 tablespoon grain coffee
- 1 tablespoon nonaluminum baking powder
- 1 teaspoon baking soda
- 1 teaspoon cinnamon, ground
- 1/8 teaspoon sea salt
- 1 apple, grated
- 1/2 cup dried apricots, diced
- 1/3 cup raisins
- 1/3 cup barley malt syrup
- 1/4 cup coconut oil
- 1 cup apple juice

Preheat oven to 375 degrees.

Stir flax seeds into water. Set aside.

Combine dry ingredients. Stir in apple, apricots, and raisins.

Combine wet ingredients in separate bowl, including flax seed mixture. Whisk until frothy.

Stir wet ingredients into dry, just until all flour is absorbed.

Spoon into oiled or papered muffin tins. Bake on middle shelf of oven until tops are lightly browned, and a toothpick inserted in center comes out clean, approximately 15–20 minutes.

Cool muffins on rack for 10 minutes before serving.

Banana Muffins

Light and not overly sweet.

- 1 1/2 tablespoons flax seed
- 1/4 cup water
- approximately 2 1/2 ripe bananas, mashed
- 2 tablespoons brown rice or barley malt syrup
- 1/4 cup coconut oil
- 1 teaspoon vanilla
- 1 1/3 cups barley or spelt (or combine with millet or rice flour)
- 2 teaspoons baking powder
- 1/4 teaspoon nutmeg, freshly grated
- 1/3 cup pecans or walnuts, coarsely chopped

Preheat oven to 350 degrees.

Grind flax seeds. Add to water. Let sit for a few minutes.

Add remaining wet ingredients.

Combine dry ingredients into wet until liquid is just absorbed.

Pour into oiled or papered muffin tins. Bake for approximately 35 minutes, or until a toothpick inserted in center comes out clean.

Cool muffins on rack for 10 minutes before serving.

Banana-Date Muffins

- 3 tablespoons flax seeds
- 1/2 cup water
- 1 3/4 cups oat flour
- 1 1/2 cups barley or rice flour
- 1 tablespoon baking powder
- 1 teaspoon baking soda
- 1/2 teaspoon cinnamon, ground
- 1/2 teaspoon nutmeg, ground
- 1/8 teaspoon sea salt
- 1 1/2 bananas

1/2 cup dates
1/4 cup coconut oil
1 cup apple juice

Preheat oven to 375 degrees. Lightly oil muffin tins or use paper cups.

Grind flax seeds. Place in blender with 1/2 cup water. Let sit.

Combine dry ingredients in a large bowl.

Process all liquid ingredients in blender until smooth (including bananas and dates).

Stir wet ingredients into dry ingredients until liquid is absorbed.

Pour into oiled or papered muffin tins. Bake for 15–20 minutes, or until a toothpick inserted in center comes out clean.

Carrot-Date Muffins

Soak overnight:

1/3 cup water
1/4 cup dates, chopped
1/4 cup rolled oats

Next morning, add:

3 tablespoons flax seed, ground, mixed with 1/2 cup water
1 cup grated carrots
1/4 cup coconut oil
1 teaspoon stevia leaf
1/2 cup walnuts, chopped

Combine in separate bowl:

1 1/2 cups flour (barley, spelt, or rye)
1 tablespoon baking powder
1 teaspoon salt
1/4 teaspoon nutmeg, ground
1 1/2 teaspoon cinnamon, ground
2 tablespoons soy milk powder

Preheat oven to 350 degrees.

Stir dry ingredients with wet ingredients. Mix until barely absorbed.

Pour into oiled or papered muffin tins. Bake for approximately 20 minutes, or until a toothpick inserted in center comes out clean.

Cool muffins on rack for 10 minutes before serving.

Date and Oatmeal Yogurt Muffins

- 1/3 cup walnuts
- 2 tablespoons flax seeds, ground
- 1/4 cup water
- 3/4 cup spelt flour
- 3/4 cup rolled oats
- 1 1/2 teaspoons nonaluminum baking powder
- 1/2 teaspoon sea salt
- 1/8 teaspoon cinnamon
- 1/3 cup pitted dates, chopped
- 1/4 cup barley malt syrup
- 1/2 cup plain soy yogurt
- 1/2 cup vegan milk
- 2 tablespoons oil

Preheat oven to 400 degrees.

Toast walnuts lightly. Chop fine.

Stir flax seeds into water. Set aside.

Stir together dry ingredients in bowl, including dates and walnuts.

Mix wet ingredients in another bowl.

Stir wet into dry until just combined.

Divide batter among 6 oiled or papered 1/2 cup muffin tins. Bake for 30 minutes, or until a toothpick inserted in center comes out clean.

Cool muffins on rack for 10 minutes before serving.

Lemon-Cranberry Muffins

Toasted almonds complement the lemon and cranberries in this recipe wonderfully!

- 3 tablespoons flax seeds, ground
- 1/2 cup water
- 1 3/4 cups barley flour
- 1 1/4 cups oat flour
- 1 tablespoon baking powder
- 1 teaspoon baking soda
- 1 teaspoon cinnamon, ground
- 1/2 teaspoon nutmeg, ground
- 1/4 teaspoon sea salt
- 1 1/2 teaspoons stevia leaf
- 1/3 cup toasted almonds, coarsely chopped
- 1 cup cranberries
- 1/2 cup lemon juice
- 1/2 cup apple juice
- 2 teaspoons lemon zest, finely minced
- 1/4 cup coconut oil

Preheat oven to 375 degrees.

Mix flax seeds and water. Set aside.

Mix all ingredients, except oil and lemon juice, in another bowl.

Blend together oil and lemon juice.

Mix all liquids (including flax seed mixture) into dry ingredients until just combined.

Pour into oiled or papered muffin tins. Bake for 20 minutes, or until a toothpick inserted in center comes out clean.

Cool muffins on rack for 10 minutes before serving.

Squash-Corn Muffins

One of my favorites.

- 1/3 cup coconut oil
- 1/2 cup brown rice or barley malt syrup
- 1 1/2 cups squash or pumpkin puree*
- 1 cup water
- 2 1/4 cups rye, barley, or oat flour
- 1 cup cornmeal
- 1 tablespoon baking powder
- 1 teaspoon cinnamon, ground
- 1/2 teaspoon ginger, ground
- 1/4 teaspoon cloves, ground
- 1/4 teaspoon nutmeg, ground

Preheat oven to 375 degrees.

Combine wet and dry ingredients separately. Blend together just until liquid is absorbed.

Pour into oiled or papered muffin tins. Bake for approximately 30 minutes, or until liquid is absorbed.

*I have used butternut, kabocha, or pumpkin with wonderful results. You need half a squash. Scoop out seeds. Cook cut side down on a baking sheet at 350 degrees until soft to touch, 30–45 minutes. Cool. Scoop out flesh. Either hand mash or run through processor for a few seconds.

Zucchini Muffins

- 1 1/2 cups zucchini, coarsely grated, tightly packed
- 3 tablespoons flax seeds
- 1/2 cup water
- 1 1/2 cups barley flour
- 1 cup ground oats
- 1 tablespoon baking powder
- 2 teaspoons cinnamon, ground
- 1 teaspoon ginger, ground

- 1/4 teaspoon cloves, ground
- 1 1/2 teaspoon stevia leaf
- scant 1/2 teaspoon sea salt
- 1/2 cup nuts, coarsely chopped
- 1/2 cup raisins
- 2/3 cup apple juice
- 1/4 cup coconut oil
- 1 teaspoon vanilla

Preheat oven to 375 degrees.

Place zucchini on a couple sheets of paper towels to absorb some of the liquid.

Grind the flax seeds in a spice grinder. Add to water. Let sit.

Combine all dry ingredients.

Add all liquid ingredients to flax mixture. Add dry ingredients.

Pour into oiled or papered muffin tins. Bake approximately 20 minutes, or until toothpick inserted in center comes out clean.

Wheat-Free Muffins

A very versatile batter—be creative!

- 1/4 cup flax seeds
- 3/4 cup water
- 1/2 cup coconut oil
- 3/4 cup rice or barley malt syrup
- 1 cup vegan milk
- 2 cups barley flour
- 1 3/4 cups oat flour
- 1 1/4 cups cornmeal
- 1 teaspoon baking soda
- 1 tablespoon baking powder

Preheat oven to 350 degrees.

Grind flax seeds. Add to water. Let sit a few minutes.

Add remaining wet ingredients.

Combine dry ingredients. Stir into wet.

Spoon into oiled or papered muffin tins. Bake for 35 minutes, or until a toothpick inserted in center comes out clean.

Variations:
For a sweet muffin, add 1 teaspoon vanilla to the liquids. And add 2 cups chopped fruit or nuts or a combination of both.

For a savory muffin, add 2 cups of finely chopped vegetables.

Sesame Biscuits

- $2\frac{1}{4}$ cups barley flour
- $\frac{1}{2}$ cup soy flour
- 3 tablespoons sesame seeds, toasted (black sesame seeds are a great choice)
- $\frac{3}{4}$ teaspoon sea salt
- 1 tablespoon baking powder
- $\frac{1}{2}$ cup water plus an additional 2 tablespoons
- $\frac{1}{4}$ cup coconut oil
- 2 tablespoons barley malt syrup

Preheat oven to 425 degrees. Lightly oil a baking sheet.

Combine dry ingredients. Stir in liquids to create a soft dough.

Knead dough briefly. Dust a flat surface with flour. Roll out to $\frac{1}{2}$-inch thickness.

Place on baking sheet. Cut into 2-inch squares.

Bake until lightly browned, approximately 14–16 minutes.

Corn Cakes

I love corn muffins, and these are the best whole foods rendition that I've come across.

Mix:

1½ cups brown rice, cooked
2 cups cornmeal
1½ cups boiling water

When cooled, add:

½ cup coconut oil
¾ cup brown rice syrup or barley malt syrup
2 cups vegan milk
½ cup plus 1 tablespoon flax seeds, ground, and added to 1¾ cups water

In another bowl, mix:

1½ cups barley flour
4 cups cornmeal
2 tablespoons baking powder
2 teaspoons sea salt

Preheat oven to 400 degrees.

Combine the dry ingredients with the liquid mixture.

Spoon into muffin tins or square pans (make sure these are well oiled).

For muffins:
Bake for 25 minutes.

For cakes:
Bake at 375 degrees for 35–40 minutes, or until toothpick inserted in center comes out clean.

This makes 24 large muffins or two 8-inch-square cakes. You can easily freeze these in individual serving sizes. Keeps well. Makes great toast or can be grilled in a pan with a little oil. You can also split the recipe in half.

Oatcakes

Simple stove-top biscuits—ready in 10 minutes.

- 2 cups oat flour*
- 1/4 cup coconut oil
- 1/4 teaspoon sea salt
- 1 tablespoon baking powder
- 1 1/4 cups water

Mix all ingredients.

Lightly oil skillet. Heat on medium heat.

Drop spoonfuls of batter into skillet. Cover with lid.

Cook until golden on both sides.

Serve immediately.

*Oat flour is simply oats ground in spice grinder.

Side Dishes

Baked Tomatoes

Preheat oven to 350 degrees. Cut off tops of tomatoes.

Place in baking pan. Bake at 350 degrees for 30 minutes. Sprinkle with tarragon, parsley, and coriander during the last 5 minutes.

Broccoli-Stuffed Tomatoes

2 large tomatoes, halved
1 tablespoon olive oil
1 medium onion, minced
1 small bunch of broccoli, minced (approximately 3–4 cups)
2 tablespoons fresh basil, minced
2 teaspoons Bragg Liquid Aminos
vegan cheese cubes (optional)

Dressing:

2 tablespoons olive oil
1 tablespoon apple cider vinegar
2 tablespoons fresh basil, minced
sea salt to taste
tomato centers

Preheat oven to 375 degrees.

Scoop out the centers of tomatoes. Reserve centers and shells.

Sauté onion in oil until soft. Add broccoli. Cook, covered, for 5–8 minutes.

Add basil and Bragg's. Blend in processor or blender until smooth. Add cheese, if desired. Divide mixture between tomato shells.

Place on a lightly oiled pan. Cover. Bake for 10 minutes, or until cheese just begins to bubble.

Process dressing in blender. Serve alongside.

Carrots in Orange Sauce

Black sesame seeds make a dramatic presentation.

Sauce:

- 2 cloves garlic, minced
- 2 teaspoons ginger, minced
- 1/2 teaspoon orange peel, grated
- 1 cup fresh orange juice
- 1 cup vegetable stock
- 1/3 cup red wine vinegar
- 1/4 cup brown rice syrup
- 1 1/2 teaspoons Bragg Liquid Aminos
- 1/4 teaspoon sea salt
- 1/4 star anise (optional)

- 1 pound medium carrots, diced
- 1 tablespoon sesame seeds, toasted

Boil sauce ingredients. Cook, uncovered, until sauce just begins to thicken, about 15 minutes. Remove anise if using.

Cook further, until it turns a caramel color. Sauce is ready when a spoon leaves a path in it.

Toss in carrots. Sprinkle with sesame seeds.

Ginger Carrots

- 4 carrots, sliced
- 1 teaspoon oil
- 1 teaspoon ginger, grated
- sea salt to taste
- 1 tablespoon arrowroot diluted in 1/2 cup water
- 1 tablespoon Vogue Vege Base

Sauté carrots in oil for 3 minutes. Add ginger and salt. Cook 20–25 minutes on low heat until tender.

Add arrowroot and Vogue. Stir. Simmer for 2 minutes.

Citrus Spaghetti Squash Noodles

Spaghetti squash, quartered

Sauce:

- 1 tablespoon garlic, minced
- 2 tablespoons olive oil
- 3 tablespoons Bragg Liquid Aminos
- 2 tablespoons brown rice vinegar
- 2 tablespoons toasted sesame oil
- 1 tablespoon brown rice syrup
- pinch of red pepper flakes (optional)
- 2 teaspoons orange peel, finely grated
- 1/2 cup green onions, minced
- 1/4 cup toasted sesame seeds*

Preheat oven to 350 degrees.

Scoop out seeds in spaghetti squash. Place cut side down on a baking sheet. Bake for 30–45 minutes. (Should be soft—but not mushy!—when you press a finger on the skin.)

Cool for a few minutes. Scrape out flesh with a fork into a bowl. Set aside.

Sauté garlic briefly in a small pan. Add remaining ingredients. Bring to boil.

Remove from heat. Add to squash. Toss well.

*To toast sesame seeds, place pan over high heat. Add sesame seeds. Shake pan until seeds start to turn light brown. Careful! They will burn easily. Tip out into a small bowl immediately. Set aside until ready to use.

Lemon Bulgur Mounds with Chives

- heaping 1/2 cup scallions, thinly sliced
- 1/4 cup olive oil
- 2 1/4 cups bulgur
- zest of 1 1/2 lemons, removed with vegetable peeler, making sure no white pith is included, minced fine

3 1/3 cups vegetable stock, hot
1 cup fresh chives, thinly sliced
3/4 teaspoons lecithin
sea salt to taste

Cook scallions in oil in a kettle over moderately low heat. Stir until softened.

Add bulgur and zest. Stir for 1 minute.

Add stock. Cover. Let stand for approximately 10–15 minutes, or until liquid is absorbed.

Fluff bulgur with fork. Stir in sliced chives, lecithin, and sea salt.

Cover. Let sit for one half hour before serving.

Nori Rolls

1 package smoked tofu, thinly sliced
4 cups cooked brown rice
umeboshi plum paste (optional)
miso or rice vinegar (optional)
sesame seeds, dry toasted
Bragg Liquid Aminos
fresh or steamed thinly sliced vegetables (such as cucumber, avocado, collard leaves, carrots, broccoli, garlic, green onions, etc.)
nori sheets, toasted or not

Mix all ingredients except nori. Set aside.

Place a sheet of nori on a small bamboo mat or heavy cloth napkin.

Spread 1/2 cup of rice over the sheet, leaving a 2-inch edge uncovered at the end of the sheet.

Arrange filling in a line across the middle on the rice.

Roll the nori tightly around filling using the mat to guide, lift, and roll over nori as well.

Place roll with seam down to seal. Slice 1-inch thick.

Rice Balls:
Shape cooked brown rice into balls the size of ping-pong balls. Dip hands in cold, salted water to prevent sticking. Roll balls in toasted sesame seeds, mashed and cooked beans, or chopped nuts. Wrap in toasted nori sheets.

Oriental Quinoa Pilaf

Quinoa has been a staple food to the natives of the South American Andes since 3000 B.C. The ancient Incas held it sacred, calling it "the mother grain."

- 2 cups vegetable stock
- 2 tablespoons Bragg Liquid Aminos
- 2 teaspoons orange peel, grated
- pinch red pepper flakes
- 1–2 tablespoons oil
- 2–3 garlic cloves, minced
- 1/2 onion, diced
- 1 cup quinoa
- 1/4 cup sesame seeds, toasted
- 1/2 cup green onions, chopped
- 1/2 cup red bell pepper, chopped
- 1/4 cup raisins, chopped (optional)
- 3 tablespoons cilantro, minced

Combine stock, Bragg's, orange peel, and pepper flakes. Set sauce aside.

Sauté garlic and onion in oil. Add quinoa.

Pour in sauce. Cover. Simmer until all liquid is absorbed.

Add sesame seeds, green onions, red bell pepper, raisins, and cilantro to quinoa.

Serve immediately.

Pine Nut, Pinto Bean, and Scallion Pilaf

1 cup brown rice
2 cups vegetable stock
1 cup cooked pinto beans
1/2 cup scallions, including green tops, chopped
1/4 cup pine nuts, lightly toasted
1/4 teaspoon lecithin
sea salt to taste

Cook rice in vegetable stock. Toss together all ingredients.

Special Mashed Potatoes

5 medium potatoes, diced
1 stalk celery, minced
1/2 onion, minced
1/4 cup parsley, minced
1 bulb Roasted Garlic (see recipe in Condiments)
vegan milk
2 tablespoons olive oil
sea salt to taste

Simmer potatoes, celery, onion, and parsley in just enough water to cover. Drain when fork tender. Reserve stock for future use.

Squeeze the roasted garlic cloves into potato mixture.

Mash the potatoes well, either with a hand masher or mixer, starting with 1/4 cup vegan milk. Add olive oil and sea salt as you mash. Add more milk to achieve desired consistency.

Serve immediately.

Suzhou Potatoes

3 large potatoes
1 tablespoon Oriental sesame oil
1 tablespoon curry powder
1 tablespoon Vogue Vege Base
1/2 teaspoon sea salt
oil
4 cloves garlic, finely minced
1/2 red bell pepper, cut in slivers
1/2 cup green onions, minced

Wash, dry, but do not peel potatoes. Cut into 1/4-inch cubes (enough to make 4 cups). Rinse well. Cover potatoes with cold water until ready to cook. Set aside.

Mix the sesame oil, curry powder, Vogue, and salt in a small bowl. Set aside.

Drain and pat dry potatoes.

Heat oil in large pan over medium high heat.

Add the potatoes. Brown on all sides.

Add the garlic. Cook briefly.

Add sesame oil mixture. Mix with a small amount of water to loosen (no more than 1–2 tablespoons). Cook until liquid is absorbed.

Add red bell pepper and green onions.

Serve immediately.

Ratatouille

1/3 cup olive oil
1 pound eggplant, cut into 1/2-inch pieces
4 medium onions, coarsely chopped
2 green bell peppers, cut into 1/2-inch pieces
2 garlic cloves, minced and mashed to a paste
1/2 teaspoon dried oregano

- 1/2 teaspoon dried thyme
- 1/2 cup packed fresh basil leaves, torn into pieces
- 2 pounds tomatoes, coarsely chopped
- sea salt to taste

Heat the oil in a heavy kettle over moderately high heat until it is hot, but not smoking.

Sauté the eggplant. Stir until golden. Reduce heat to moderately low.

Add remaining ingredients, except basil leaves, tomatoes, and salt. Cook mixture over low heat for approximately 15 minutes, or until the eggplant is just tender.

Add tomatoes and basil. Add sea salt to taste.

Cook until just heated through.

Serve hot or at room temperature.

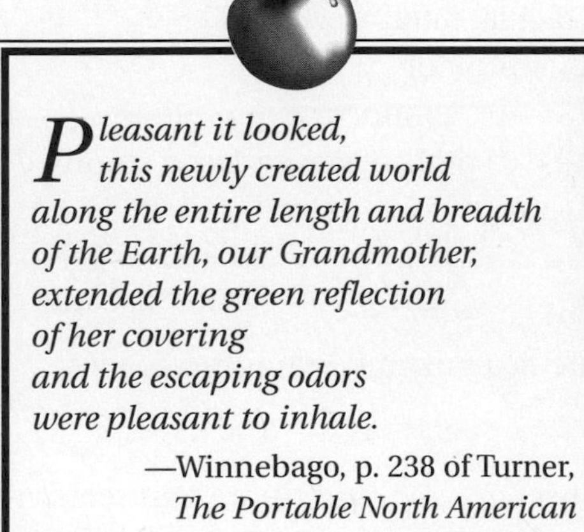

Pleasant it looked,
this newly created world
along the entire length and breadth
of the Earth, our Grandmother,
extended the green reflection
of her covering
and the escaping odors
were pleasant to inhale.

—Winnebago, p. 238 of Turner, *The Portable North American Indian Reader*

Spinach and Broccoli

My friend, A.J., gave me this delicious recipe.

2 tablespoons oil
1/2 teaspoon whole cumin
1/2 teaspoon whole mustard seed
1 large onion, chopped
1 teaspoon turmeric
2 tablespoons fresh ginger, grated
4 cloves garlic, minced
sea salt to taste
4 black cardamom
2 cinnamon sticks
1 teaspoon garam masala
4 curry leaves
1 pound broccoli, finely chopped
1 bell pepper, diced
1/2 bunch cilantro, minced
1 serrano chili, finely minced
2 tablespoons flour
1 large tomato, chopped
5 bunches of spinach, washed and chopped

Add oil to a large stock pot. Sauté whole cumin and mustard seeds.

Add onions and brown lightly. Add turmeric. Sauté for one minute.

Add ginger, garlic, sea salt, and remaining spices.

Add broccoli, bell pepper, cilantro, and chili.

Add flour. Add just enough water to prevent scorching.

Cook for 30 minutes.

Add tomato and spinach. Simmer for 5 minutes.

Discard any spice solids (such as cinnamon stick, curry leaves, etc.) before serving.

Wilted Spinach

People who eat spinach, collards, and kale at least once a day cut their risk of macular degeneration by 43%.

- 3 large cloves garlic, minced
- 1 tablespoon olive oil
- 2 large bunches spinach, stems removed, washed thoroughly
- juice of 1/2 lemon
- sea salt to taste, if desired

Sauté garlic in oil until it just begins to brown.

Add spinach. Cover immediately. Remove from heat. Stir spinach after 30 seconds. Add lemon juice and salt.

Serve immediately.

Variation:
Hardier greens such as kale, collards, and chard work well too, though I would cook the greens for several minutes to soften them.

Winter Vegetables with Horseradish Dill Sauce

- 3 pounds small red potatoes, quartered and reserved in bowl of cold water
- 1 1/2 pounds brussels sprouts, trimmed and halved
- 3/4 pound parsnips, cut diagonally 1-inch thick
- 3/4 pound carrots, cut diagonally 1-inch thick
- 3/4 pound small turnips, cut into sixths

Sauce:

- 3/4 cup oil (use half olive and half flax with 1/2 teaspoon lecithin granules, or try half oil and half butter from Butter recipe)
- 3 tablespoons fresh horseradish, grated (fresh is best, but bottled can be used)
- 3 tablespoons apple cider vinegar
- 3 tablespoons fresh dill, minced
- sea salt to taste

Prepare sauce:

Stir sauce ingredients together in a small bowl. Set aside.

Place vegetable steamer over boiling water. Steam vegetables separately until they are just tender.

Toss veggies with sauce mixture in a large bowl or pan.

Serve immediately, or keep covered and warm in a 200 degree oven.

Tender Thai Vegetables

- 1/2 cucumber
- oil
- 1 small eggplant, sliced into 1/2-inch cubes
- 8 ounces button mushrooms, quartered
- 1 medium zucchini, diced
- 1 tablespoon garlic, minced
- 1 tablespoon ginger, finely minced
- 2 shallots, minced
- 1/4 cup fresh cilantro, chopped
- 1/2 cup green onions, chopped
- 1 medium tomato, diced
- 1 tablespoon arrowroot
- juice of 1 lime

Sauce:

- 1 cup vegetable stock
- 1 tablespoon toasted sesame oil
- 1 tablespoon smooth peanut butter
- 1 tablespoon Bragg Liquid Aminos
- Thai curry paste, red or green (start with 1/8–1/4 teaspoon; adjust to your heat tolerance)

Prepare sauce:

Combine vegetable stock with sesame oil, peanut butter, Bragg's, and curry paste. Set aside.

Cut cucumber in half lengthwise. Scoop out seeds. Cut into 1/2-inch cubes.

Sauté all vegetables, except cucumber and tomato, in a small amount of oil in a hot wok or frying pan. Stir-fry for approximately 2–4 minutes.

Add sauce to vegetables. Simmer until eggplant is very tender, approximately 15 minutes.

Add cucumber and tomato. Stir in arrowroot mixed with water (just enough to dissolve). Simmer until thickened. Remove from heat.

Add lime juice. Serve immediately.

Spanish Rice

- 1 large ripe tomato, pureed (about 1 1/4 cups)
- 2 large onions, chopped fine
- 1 large garlic clove, minced
- 1 large bell pepper, chopped fine
- 1 tablespoon balsamic vinegar
- 1 teaspoon oregano
- 1 teaspoon paprika
- 1/4 teaspoon crushed red pepper flakes
- 1/2 teaspoon sea salt
- 1 1/2 cups long-grain brown rice, rinsed
- 1/2 cup fresh parsley, minced and tightly packed
- 1/2 cup green olives, coarsely chopped

Add tomato puree plus enough water to make 3 cups of liquid to pan. Add onion, garlic, and pepper. Stir until mixture begins to bubble.

Add vinegar, oregano, paprika, crushed red pepper, and salt. Bring to a boil over high heat.

Stir in rice. Reduce heat. Cover. Simmer until almost all liquid has been absorbed, about 45 minutes.

Turn off heat. Let stand, covered, for a few minutes.

Stir in parsley and olives.

Baked Rice Balls

- 1/2 cup of brown rice cooked in 1 1/2 cups of vegetable stock
- 1 onion, diced
- 1 carrot, diced small
- 2 cloves garlic, minced fine
- 1/2 cup parsley, minced fine
- 1/2 cup ground almonds
- sea salt to taste

Preheat oven to 375 degrees.

Combine all ingredients well. If they won't hold a shape, add a little almond or cashew butter. Roll into walnut-sized balls and place on an oiled glass pan.

Bake for 30 minutes or until lightly browned. Cool slightly before removing from pan.

Entrees

Breakfast

1 apple, grated
1 teaspoon lemon juice
1/2 cup vegan yogurt
1 tablespoon sunflower seeds
1/2 cup oats, soaked overnight in 1/3 cup water

Toss apple with lemon juice. Add other ingredients.

Serve immediately.

Cream of Rice Cereal

1/2 cup rice
2 cups water
vegan milk (optional)

Grind rice finely in a spice grinder.

Bring water just to boil. Turn down water to low. Whisk in rice.

Continue whisking for a few minutes. Stir often for 5 more minutes. (Cereal will thicken considerably.)

Serve hot with or without vegan milk.

Quicky Oats

1/2 cup oat groats or steel-cut oats
1 1/4 cup hot water

Place in thermos. Let sit overnight. Ready to eat or process briefly in blender.

Millet Hot Cereal

½ cup millet cooked covered in 1½ cups of water until liquid is absorbed.

Pour in an additional 1 cup of rich nut milk (see recipe in Beverages section), 2 tablespoons brown rice syrup, and a dash of cinnamon, if desired. Cover and cook for another 15 minutes.

Muesli

You will be using 3 different baking sheets for this recipe.

Heat oven to 350 degrees.

On tray 1 place:

5 cups rolled oats
1 cup rye flakes
1 cup sunflower seeds
2 teaspoons cinnamon

On tray 2 place:

1 cup sprouted buckwheat
2 tablespoons millet
¼ cup wheat germ (optional)

On tray 3 place:

¼ cup chopped almonds
¼ cup chopped cashews

Bake all three trays until toasty and smelling good.

Add:

¼ cup date pieces
½ cup raisins

Serve with vegan milk or water.

Variation:
Any of a number of combinations of fruit and nuts. For tropical, try dried mango pieces with toasted coconut and macadamia. My eldest daughter likes dried raspberries, almonds, and walnuts. Experiment to find your favorite.

Cashew French Toast

This is a delicious alternative to egg-based batters. Serve with maple syrup or brown rice syrup (my preference).

- 1 cup cashews
- 1 cup water
- 1/2 teaspoon nutmeg, ground
- 1/2 teaspoon vanilla
- 1/4–1/2 teaspoon Bragg Liquid Aminos
- several drops of stevia liquid (adds enough sweetness so that my daughters do not ask for syrup)
- 8 slices whole-grain bread

Process all ingredients, except bread, in blender until smooth.

Lightly oil a nonstick pan. Place on a medium-high flame.

Pour cashew mixture onto a pie plate.

Dip a slice of bread into mixture, covering both sides (do not soak bread). Place in heated pan. Cook each toast well.

Serve plain or with brown rice syrup.

Variation:

Add 1/4 teaspoon maple flavoring, 1/2 teaspoon cinnamon, and 1/2 banana.

Do not be tempted to check the side being cooked too soon. Wait at least 2–3 minutes until cashew mixture has sufficiently dried. It will be much easier to flip.

My Favorite Scrambler

1 tablespoon olive oil
1 medium onion, chopped
4 garlic cloves, minced
handful spinach, chopped
handful mushrooms, sliced
3–4 artichoke hearts, chopped (optional)
1/2 red bell pepper, chopped
1 pound tofu, drained and crumbled
1/2 teaspoon oregano
1/4 teaspoon turmeric
1 tomato, chopped
1/2 sheet nori sea vegetable, finely shredded (or 1 tablespoon dulse flakes)
Bragg Liquid Aminos, to taste

Sauté onion, garlic, spinach, mushrooms, artichoke, pepper, tofu, oregano, and turmeric in oil.

Add tomato, along with nori and Bragg's.

Waffles

I enjoy these with "Butter" (see recipe in Condiments) and sprinkled with stevia and cinnamon.

1 cup millet
1/2 cup brown rice
1/2 cup oat or rye groats
1 1/2 cups water
1 heaping tablespoon coconut oil
1/2 teaspoon stevia leaf
1 teaspoon vanilla (optional)
1 cup water

Soak grains in water overnight. Drain. Place in blender with remaining ingredients. Process until smooth. Pour into prepared waffle iron.

Pancakes

- 1/2 cup oats, ground if desired
- 3/4 cup buckwheat
- 1/2 cup cornmeal
- 1 teaspoon baking powder
- 1/2 teaspoon stevia leaf
- 1/4 cup coconut oil
- 1 3/4 cups vegan milk

Mix dry ingredients into wet. Let sit for five minutes. Warm a nonstick pan on medium heat. Pour batter into pan to make the size pancakes you prefer. Wait approximately 2 minutes, or until you see bubbles forming on top of pancakes. Flip and brown other side. Serve with syrup of your choice.

Pancakes #2

These are like a dense, chewy, stove-top muffin.

- 1/2 cup ground oats
- 1/2 cup buckwheat
- 1/2 cup spelt
- 2 tablespoons flax, ground
- 1/4 cup pecan meal
- 1 teaspoon baking powder
- 1/2 teaspoon stevia leaf
- 1/4 teaspoon nutmeg
- 1/4 cup coconut oil
- 1 3/4 cups oat or other vegan milk
- 1/4 teaspoon maple flavoring
- 1/2 teaspoon vanilla

Mix dry and wet ingredients separately. Combine together. Let sit 5 minutes. Warm a nonstick pan on medium heat. Pour batter into pan to make the size pancakes you prefer. Wait approximately 2 minutes, or until you see bubbles forming on top of pancakes. Flip and brown other side. Serve with syrup of your choice.

Sandwich Suggestions

vegan mayonnaise or Almonnaise (see recipe in Condiments)
cauliflower, chopped
carrot, shredded
red cabbage, shredded
dill pickle, minced
onions, sautéed in BBQ sauce

mock egg or tuna salad
avocado
tomato
mung bean sprouts
cucumber

1 carrot, shredded
1 tablespoon nutritional yeast
1 tablespoon vegan mayonnaise
1 small pickle, minced

Combine well and layer on bread with sunflower seeds, 1 sheet of nori, tomato, and sprouts.

corn
black beans, mashed
cilantro, minced
rice
roasted bell pepper

Great on chapatis.

roasted bell pepper
tofu (frozen and defrosted) marinated in Italian Dressing
tomato
soy mozzarella

cucumber
leftover curried vegetables
cauliflower
rice

vegan mayonnaise or Almonnaise (see recipe in Condiments)
avocado
carrot, shredded
tomato, sliced
sprouts
romaine lettuce
pumpkin seeds, lightly toasted
whole-grain bread

1 cup sunflower seeds, soaked overnight, drained
1/4 cup parsley
1/4 cup sesame butter or tahini
2–4 tablespoons lemon juice
1 carrot, chopped
2 green onions
1 teaspoon herb of choice
1 tablespoon Vogue Vege Base
2 tablespoons nutritional yeast
sea salt to taste

Process until smooth in processor. Roll in nori sheet or serve on bread.

Reubens

- 1 package tempeh
- 2 tablespoons apple cider vinegar
- 1/4 cup water
- 1 1/2 teaspoons Bragg Liquid Aminos
- 1/2 teaspoon toasted sesame oil
- 1/2 teaspoon garlic powder
- 1/2 teaspoon powdered ginger
- whole-grain prepared mustard
- 4 slices bread
- soy, or other mozzarella- or Swiss-style vegan cheese

Coleslaw:

- 1 carrot, shredded
- 1/4 head cabbage, shredded
- 1/3 cup vegan mayonnaise
- 1 pickle, finely diced
- 2 tablespoons sun-dried tomatoes, reconstituted and finely minced

Preheat oven to broil.

Slice tempeh so that you have 2 thin pieces. Cut each piece in half. Steam for 10 minutes.

Place vinegar, water, Bragg's, oil, garlic powder, and ginger in shallow pan. Add tempeh. Marinate for at least one hour.

Sauté tempeh in a small amount of oil until browned on both sides. Set aside.

Prepare coleslaw.

Spread mustard on 4 slices of bread.

Layer with coleslaw, then tempeh. Top with a slice of vegan cheese.

Place under a broiler briefly, if desired.

Ultimate Sandwich with Creamy Mozzarella

You may add or delete any veggie you wish—kind of like a pizza. This is your choice!

Focaccia:

- 2 teaspoons dry yeast
- 1 1/4 cups warm water
- 1 teaspoon brown rice syrup
- 1 1/2 cups whole wheat or spelt flour
- 1 1/4 cups barley flour
- 3/4 teaspoon sea salt
- 1 teaspoon thyme
- 1 teaspoon rosemary, coarsely ground
- cornmeal
- 1/3 cup olive oil

Vegetables:

- 1 head Roasted Garlic (see recipe in Condiments)
- 1 bell pepper, roasted, skin removed, and slivered
- 1 thinly sliced portobello mushroom
- 1/2 onion, thinly sliced
- 1 small eggplant, thinly sliced
- 1/2 head escarole or other green, rinsed, and torn into pieces
- 1 recipe Creamy Mozzarella (see recipe in Condiments)

Prepare Focaccia:

Dissolve yeast in warm water, along with the rice syrup. Let stand until yeast starts to foam.

Combine flours, salt, and spices in a bowl. Add 2 tablespoons olive oil.

Knead dry and wet ingredients together on a lightly floured surface until dough is smooth and elastic (7–10 minutes). Place dough in an oiled bowl.

Cover loosely with a towel. Let dough rise in a warm, draft-free place until it has doubled in volume (approximately 1 1/2 hours).

Prepare vegetables while dough is rising:

Sauté mushrooms, onion, and eggplant in small amount of olive oil until softened.

Preheat oven to 375 degrees.

Roll dough out to form a 12-inch round. Sprinkle cornmeal into pizza tin or on a baking sheet. Slide sheet under dough. Pinch up edges. Brush surface with 2 more tablespoons of olive oil.

Bake for 15–20 minutes. Cool.

Spread mozzarella on focaccia layer with mushroom mixture, garlic, pepper slivers, then greens. Sprinkle with balsamic vinegar, if desired. Cut into squares.

Spaghetti Squash with Greens

- 1 spaghetti squash
- 1 bunch collards or kale, stems removed, rinsed, and chopped
- 1 large onion, diced
- 2 tablespoons olive oil
- 1/2 cup arame, reconstituted according to package directions
- 1 cup cashews, whole or pieces
- 2 heaping tablespoons Vogue Vege Base
- 1–2 tablespoons apple cider vinegar
- 1/2 teaspoon sea salt
- 1/2 cup water

Preheat oven to 350 degrees.

Scoop out seeds from spaghetti squash. Place cut side down on a baking sheet. Bake for approximately 40 minutes or until softened. Cool. Scrape out squash into a bowl with a fork. Set aside.

Sauté collards and onions in oil until onion is just golden. Add squash, arame, and cashews.

Mix Vogue, vinegar, salt, and water. Pour into veggies. Combine well.

Cover. Simmer 5 minutes. Adjust seasonings, if needed.

Spaghetti Squash and Green Beans

- 1 spaghetti squash, quartered and seeded
- 1 onion, chopped
- 1 tablespoon garlic, minced
- 1 pound green beans, ends cut and beans halved
- 2 tablespoons olive oil
- 1/4 teaspoon thyme
- 1/2 teaspoon sage
- 2 tablespoons Vogue Vege Base
- 1/2 cup water
- 2 tablespoons lemon juice
- 1/4–1/2 teaspoon sea salt
- 2 large tomatoes, chopped
- 1/2 cup pumpkin seeds, toasted*

Preheat oven to 350 degrees.

Place cut side of squash down on baking sheet. Bake for approximately 45 minutes. Cool. Scrape with fork to remove flesh. Set aside.

Sauté onion, garlic, and green beans in oil until crisp tender. Add squash. Add spices, Vogue, and water. Cook 3–5 minutes longer.

Stir in lemon juice and salt.

Toss in tomatoes and pumpkin seeds immediately before serving.

*To dry-toast pumpkin seeds: Heat a skillet. Add pumpkin seeds. Shake occasionally until seeds have popped. Remove from heat.

Asparagus-Tofu Stir Fry

- 1 pound firm tofu, frozen, defrosted and squeezed of all liquid
- 1 bunch asparagus spears
- 1 small onion, diced
- 1 tablespoon garlic, minced
- 1 tablespoon ginger, minced
- 1 small bell pepper, sliced in strips (preferably red or yellow)

coconut oil
1 cup water
1 tablespoon miso
1/8–1/4 teaspoon Thai curry paste
2 tablespoons Bragg Liquid Aminos
1 tablespoon black bean sauce (available in most supermarkets—make sure to select one without preservatives!)
1 tablespoon arrowroot mixed with 1 tablespoon water
1/2 cup toasted almonds, coarsely chopped

Cut tofu into 1/2-inch cubes. Set aside.

Steam asparagus until crisp tender.

Sauté onion, garlic, ginger, and pepper in oil for 3 minutes. Add water, miso, Thai curry paste, Bragg's, and black bean sauce.

Stir in tofu. Simmer for 10 minutes. Add arrowroot/water mixture. Thicken.

Toss in almonds and asparagus.

O Konomi Yaki

You may bake these patties, if desired, on an oiled cookie sheet at 375 degrees for approximately 20–30 minutes, or until lightly browned.

1 small head of Chinese cabbage, thinly sliced
sea salt
1 carrot, shredded
2 tablespoons fresh ginger, grated
2 tablespoons Bragg Liquid Aminos
4 green onions, thinly sliced
1/2 pound fresh shiitake mushrooms, sliced 1/4-inch thick
3/4 teaspoon red pepper flakes
1/2 cup flour (barley, wheat, rice, millet, or oat)
2 tablespoons arrowroot
1 package Mori-Nu firm-style tofu
1 teaspoon toasted sesame oil
2 tablespoons cilantro, chopped
1 tablespoon sesame seed, toasted

Heat a small amount of oil in a large skillet. Add the Chinese cabbage and 1/4 teaspoon salt. Sauté cabbage over medium heat until it begins to wilt, about 3 minutes.

Add carrot, ginger, Bragg's, green onions, mushrooms, and pepper flakes. Cook off excess liquid, if any.

Transfer veggies to a bowl. Cool.

Process flour, arrowroot, tofu, and sesame oil in a blender until smooth. Add mixture to veggies. Add cilantro. Mix well.

Spoon mixture into a lightly oiled skillet (nonstick works best) over medium-high heat, making 3-inch cakes. Brown on both sides.

Sprinkle with sesame seeds.

Serve immediately.

Coconut and Cashew Veggies with Tofu and Orange Sauce

1 pound tofu, frozen and defrosted
combination of veggies, steamed crisp tender (I like carrots, sweet potato, and mushrooms; mushrooms and zucchini do not need to be steamed)
1 teaspoon cayenne
1 teaspoon sea salt
1 teaspoon paprika
3/4 teaspoon black pepper, freshly ground
1 teaspoon garlic powder
1/2 teaspoon onion powder
1/2 teaspoon thyme
1/2 teaspoon oregano
1/2 cup cashews
1 cup water
1 1/2 cups flour (your choice, spelt, rice, millet, oat, etc.)
2 cups unsweetened flaked coconut
coconut oil

Sauce:

- 3/4 cup orange marmalade
- 2 1/2 tablespoons Dijon or coarse-ground mustard
- 2 1/2 tablespoons drained bottled horseradish or fresh peeled and grated, to taste

Prepare Sauce:

Combine all sauce ingredients well. Set aside.

Squeeze tofu. Wrap tofu in kitchen towel for 30 minutes. Cut into 2-inch squares.

Cube or slice veggies 1/4-inch thick. Steam approximately 5 minutes.

Combine spices in a small bowl.

Process the cashews and water in blender until smooth. Pour cashews into another bowl with 1 cup of flour and 2 teaspoons of the spice blend.

Place coconut in another bowl.

Add 1/2 cup of flour to remaining spices.

Heat a small amount of oil in a nonstick pan to medium high.

Dredge tofu and veggies in flour mixture. Shake off excess. Dip in batter. Coat lightly in coconut.

Sauté on each side until golden brown on each side. Transfer to a paper-towel lined bowl. Repeat until finished.

Serve with sauce.

We are so far removed from the Earth, our Mother, that eating is no longer a conscious act.

Nourishment can only be had by awareness, feeding our bodies and souls.

Each thought, each action in the sun-light of awareness becomes sacred.

In this light, no boundary exists between the sacred and the profane.

—Thich Nhat Hanh,
Peace Is Every Step

White Beans with Tomato and Sage

- 1 pound dried white beans, soaked overnight, rinsed
- kombu (sea vegetable), one small frond
- 1/4 cup olive oil
- 4 large cloves garlic, minced
- 15 fresh sage leaves, minced
- 1 bunch collards, stems removed, chopped into 1-inch pieces
- 2 tablespoons Vogue Vege Base
- sea salt to taste
- 2 large tomatoes, diced

Cook beans and kombu in kettle with enough cold water to cover by 2 inches at a bare simmer for 1–1 1/2 hours, or until tender.

Heat oil in large skillet until hot, but not smoking. Add garlic. Remove from heat.

Swirl pan until garlic is just golden. Stir in sage leaves.

Add to beans, along with collards, Vogue, and sea salt. Simmer all for 5 more minutes.

Remove from heat. Stir in tomatoes.

Bean Croquettes

- 2 cups cooked beans
- 1 carrot, diced
- 1/4 onion, diced
- 1 tablespoon chili powder
- 1 teaspoon cumin seeds, ground
- 1/2 cup bread crumbs
- sea salt to taste
- 1/4 cup fresh toasted nuts or seeds

Preheat oven to 350 degrees.

Mash beans.

Sauté carrot, onion, chili powder, and cumin seeds in a small amount of oil until softened.

Mix all ingredients together. Bake for 30–40 minutes, or sauté until browned.

Lentil-Tomato Loaf

- 1 pound lentils
- 1 medium onion, chopped
- 2 stalks celery, chopped
- 2 teaspoons salt
- 4 cloves garlic, minced
- 1 16-ounce can chopped tomatoes (preferably Muir Glen)
- 1/2 teaspoon thyme
- 4 slices bread, crumbled (preferably Ezekiel)
- 2 tablespoons oil

Cook lentils.

Preheat oven to 350 degrees.

Sauté onion, celery, salt, and garlic in small amount of oil.

Add remaining ingredients. Mix well.

Bake in a loaf pan for 45 minutes.

Chipotle and White Bean Pasta

Cilantro would make a delicious addition to this dish, if desired.

- 1 package wheat-free pasta
- 1 ounce sun-dried tomatoes
- 1 chipotle pepper (or scant 1/8 teaspoon chipotle powder)
- 1 onion, chopped
- 4 cloves garlic, chopped
- 2 tablespoons olive oil
- 1 cup corn kernels
- 1 1/2 cups white beans, cooked
- 1–2 tablespoons Vogue Vege Base

Cook pasta according to package directions. Drain. Set aside.

Soak sun-dried tomatoes and chipotle pepper in 1/2 cup hot water until softened. Drain. Reserve liquid.

Sauté onions and garlic in olive oil until tender.

Chop tomatoes. Slice pepper and scoop out seeds to discard (seeds are very hot!). Mince chipotle.

Add tomatoes and chipotle to onions and garlic, including liquid from tomatoes.

Add corn kernels, beans, and Vogue. Heat through. Adjust seasonings, if needed. Toss into noodles.

Serve immediately.

Primavera Pasta

- 1 package soba noodles (or spaghetti squash)
- 1 bunch kale, stems removed and torn into small pieces
- 1/4 cup olive oil
- 4–6 garlic cloves, minced
- 1 onion, diced
- 1/2 bell pepper, diced
- 1 zucchini, diced
- 1/4 teaspoon fennel, coarsely ground or crushed
- 1/2 teaspoon rosemary, coarsely ground or crushed
- 1/2 teaspoon thyme
- 1/4 teaspoon oregano
- 1/4 teaspoon red pepper flakes
- 1 heaping tablespoon Vogue Vege Base
- 3/4 cup water
- 2 large tomatoes, chopped
- 1/3 cup parsley, minced

Cook noodles according to package directions.

Rinse kale. Place in large preheated pot (temperature should be high). Cover immediately. Cook in the rinse water that was still clinging to the leaves. Stir after a few minutes. Add a couple more tablespoons of water if pan is dry. Simmer for a total of 5 minutes. Remove from heat.

Heat olive oil in a large sauté pan.

Add garlic, onion, bell pepper, and zucchini. Sauté until onion is just transparent.

Add spices and Vogue. Cook 2 more minutes.

Add water. Cover. Simmer on low for 5 minutes.

Add tomatoes, parsley, and soba noodles.

Serve immediately.

Primavera Pasta #2

- 1 package soba noodles (or spaghetti squash)
- 2 leeks, rinsed and chopped
- 2 cups broccoli, chopped
- 4 garlic cloves, minced
- 2 tablespoons olive oil
- 1/4 teaspoon marjoram
- 1/2 teaspoon sage
- 1 cup almond or other vegan milk
- 1 tablespoon Vogue Vege Base
- 2 tablespoons arrowroot
- 1 tablespoon Bragg Liquid Aminos
- 1 cup sprouted or cooked garbanzo beans
- 1 yellow bell pepper, slivered
- 1 large tomato, diced

Cook noodles according to package directions.

Sauté leeks, broccoli, and garlic in oil until leeks are softened. Add spices.

Stir in milk, Vogue, arrowroot, and Bragg's. Heat through. Remove from heat.

Stir in garbanzo beans, pepper, and tomato. Pour over soba noodles.

Noodles in Green Sauce

- 1/2 pound soba noodles (or cooked spaghetti squash)
- 1/2 cup shiitake mushroom caps, thinly sliced
- 2 medium carrots, cut in very thin slivers
- 1/2 cup pine nuts, toasted

Sauce:

- 1 1-pound bunch spinach, cleaned, stems removed
- 2 bunches chives, chopped
- 1/2 cup cilantro, chopped
- 1/4 cup basil leaves, chopped
- 3/4 cup vegetable stock
- 2/3 cup cashew cream
- 1/2 teaspoon sea salt
- 1/8–1/4 teaspoon Thai curry paste
- 2 cloves garlic, minced
- 1 tablespoon arrowroot mixed with 1 tablespoon water

Cook noodles according to instructions. (If using squash, quarter and remove seeds. Place cut side down on baking sheet. Bake at 350 degrees for 30–40 minutes. Cool. Scrape out flesh.)

Process first 4 sauce ingredients into puree, using blender or food processor.

Add remaining sauce ingredients, except garlic and arrowroot. Puree again.

Pour into a pan. Sauté garlic in a small amount of oil until lightly browned. Stir in mushrooms. Heat to simmer. Add arrowroot to thicken.

Toss with noodles. Add carrots. Sprinkle with pine nuts.

Serve immediately.

Oriental Noodles with Spicy Ginger and Peanut Sauce

1 package soba or wheat-free noodles
1 broccoli bunch, cut into small flowerets

Sauce:

1/2 cup unsalted peanut butter (preferably organic)
2 1/2 tablespoons fresh ginger, grated
2 small garlic cloves, minced
1/2 cup water
2 tablespoons Bragg Liquid Aminos
1 teaspoon brown rice vinegar
1 teaspoon maple or barley malt syrup
1/4 teaspoon red pepper flakes

Cook noodles per package instructions. Set aside.

Steam broccoli until crisp tender. Set aside.

Process all sauce ingredients in blender until smooth. Add more water, if necessary, to create a medium-thick consistency. Heat briefly. Adjust seasonings, if desired.

Toss into broccoli and noodles.

Asian Spring Rolls

- 1/4 head cabbage, shredded
- 6 shiitake mushrooms, stems discarded, caps sliced thin (save stems for stock)
- 3 garlic cloves, minced
- 3 large shallots, minced
- 1 tablespoon fresh gingerroot, peeled and minced
- 1 large carrot, shredded
- 1/3 cup cilantro, chopped
- 1/3 cup mint leaves, chopped
- 1 cup mung bean sprouts, chopped
- 2 tablespoons Bragg Liquid Aminos
- 1 teaspoon sea salt, or to taste
- 20 spring roll wrappers, or vegan crepes

Dipping Sauce:

- 1/4 cup Bragg Liquid Aminos
- 1/4 cup fresh lime juice
- 2 tablespoons water
- 2 garlic cloves, minced and mashed to a paste with 1/2 teaspoon sea salt
- 2 tablespoons brown rice syrup
- 1 2-inch fresh red or green chili, seeded and minced (wear rubber gloves), or 1/4 teaspoon dried hot pepper flakes, or to taste

Preheat oven to 400 degrees.

Combine all ingredients for spring rolls, except wrappers. Sauté briefly in small amount of oil in a large skillet. Wilt cabbage. Soften remaining veggies.

Wrap spring roll wrappers as you would a burrito, making sure ends are tucked in.

Bake crepes and wrappers for approximately 10–15 minutes.

Mix all ingredients for dipping sauce.

Serve like a wrap sandwich with dipping sauce.

Matar Paneer

This is traditionally made with homemade cheese, but I substitute tofu with excellent results!

- 2 tablespoons fresh gingerroot, peeled and minced
- 2 tablespoons garlic, minced
- 1/4 cup raw cashew nuts
- 1/2 onion soaked in 1/4 cup hot water
- 3 tablespoons sesame oil
- 1/2 teaspoon fenugreek seeds
- 2 1/2 teaspoons turmeric
- 1 teaspoon chili powder
- 2 1/2 tablespoons coriander, ground
- 3 tablespoons sesame oil
- 1 cup cubed tofu
- 1 cup cooked fresh or thawed frozen peas
- 1 1/2 tablespoons garam masala (store-bought or see recipe)
- 1/4 cup fresh coriander, minced
- 1/4 cup gingerroot, peeled and cut into 1 1/2-inch julienne strips
- sea salt to taste

Puree minced gingerroot, garlic, cashew nuts, and onion with water.

Heat oil over low heat. Add fenugreek, turmeric, chili powder, and ground coriander. Cook 30 seconds.

Add gingerroot puree. Cook mixture for 5 minutes. Stir gravy occasionally.

Heat oil in heavy skillet over moderate heat until hot. Sauté tofu for 1 minute. Stir.

Add peas and gravy. Cook 4 minutes. Stir.

Stir in garam masala, half of minced coriander, half of gingerroot, and sea salt.

Transfer to serving dish. Sprinkle with remaining coriander and gingerroot.

Thai Stir Fry

Cashews or toasted pumpkin seeds can be added to this recipe, if desired.

- 1/3 cup arame, soaked in hot water for 15 minutes
- 1/2 pound tofu, cubed (optional)
- 1 onion, chopped
- 1 carrot, chopped
- 1 zucchini, chopped
- 1 cup fresh shiitake mushrooms, sliced
- 1/2 yellow or red bell pepper, cut in slivers
- coconut oil

Sauce:

- 14 ounces coconut milk
- 1/2 cup fresh basil, chopped
- 1/4 cup Bragg Liquid Aminos
- 1 heaping tablespoon Vogue Vege Base
- 1/8–1/2 teaspoon Thai curry paste (to your tolerance)

Prep all veggies. Set aside.

Combine sauce ingredients. Set aside.

Sauté veggies in medium-hot oil until crisp tender, approximately 2–3 minutes.

Stir in sauce. Cover. Simmer approximately 5 more minutes. Serve over grains. Brown basmati would be nice.

Spicy Thai Noodles

Peanuts are a nice addition and keep this dish more authentic, but they are not necessary. Please try to buy organic. There are brands that are tested and are aflatoxin free.

1 package soba noodles
2 cups mung or soybean sprouts
1/2 pound frozen, defrosted, and squeezed tofu, diced
2 tablespoons roasted peanuts, minced
1/3 cup red bell pepper, minced
1/4 cup green onions, minced
1/4 cup fresh cilantro, minced
2 limes

Sauce:

2 cloves garlic, finely minced
1 tablespoon oil
3 tablespoons Bragg Liquid Aminos
3 tablespoons tomato sauce
2 tablespoons lime juice, plus 2 limes
2 tablespoons brown rice syrup
1/4–1/2 teaspoon red Thai curry paste (adjust to your heat tolerance)
1 teaspoon lime peel, finely grated

Prepare sauce:
Combine garlic with oil. Set aside.

Combine remaining ingredients. Set aside.

Cut 2 limes into wedges. Set aside.

Last-minute cooking:
Bring at least 4 quarts water to a vigorous boil. Add noodles. Cook noodles until they lose raw taste, but are still firm, approximately 5 minutes. Drain immediately. Shake out excess water. Transfer to a large bowl.

Sauté garlic mixture in a small skillet over medium-high heat for about 30 seconds. Add remaining sauce ingredients. Bring to low boil. Remove from heat. Add sauce to noodles. Add tofu and bean sprouts. Toss well.

Turn out onto a heated platter. Sprinkle with peanuts, red pepper, green onions, and cilantro.

Serve immediately, accompanied by lime wedges.

Spinach Fritters

- 1 medium onion, diced
- 1 large bunch spinach, rinsed and chopped
- 1 tablespoon olive oil
- 1 package Mori-Nu firm-style tofu
- 1/2 cup flour (rice, spelt, etc.)
- 2 tablespoons arrowroot
- 1 tablespoon Bragg Liquid Aminos
- 1/4–1/2 teaspoon nutmeg

Sauté onion until lightly browned. Place spinach in pan. Cover. Remove from heat. Lift lid after one minute. Drain all liquid.

Process remaining ingredients in a blender until smooth. Mix into spinach mixture.

Drop by spoonfuls (not too large) onto an oiled and heated nonstick pan. Cook until golden brown on both sides.

Serve with lemon wedges and/or fresh Tomato Sauce (see recipe in Condiments).

Coconut Curry Melange

Just the thing to clear your sinuses on a chilly day!

- 1/2 block tofu, frozen and defrosted
- 1 tablespoon Bragg Liquid Aminos
- 1 tablespoon arrowroot
- 1 potato, peeled and diced into 1/2-inch cubes
- 1/2 head cauliflower, chopped into bite-size pieces
- 4 cloves garlic, minced
- 1 tablespoon fresh ginger, finely minced or grated
- 1 red onion, diced
- 1 green bell pepper, diced
- 1/2 cup peas

Sauce:

- 1 cup unsweetened coconut milk
- 1 tablespoon Bragg Liquid Aminos
- 2 tablespoons curry powder
- 2 teaspoons Oriental sesame oil
- 1/8–1/4 teaspoon Thai curry paste, red or green
- 1/4 teaspoon sea salt

Squeeze tofu between 2 plates to remove water. Cube tofu. Set aside.

Mix Bragg's and arrowroot in small bowl. Toss in tofu. Set aside.

Steam potato and cauliflower until just crisp tender. Place all other veggies nearby.

Combine ingredients for sauce in a small bowl.

Heat a small amount of oil on high heat in a wok or large frying pan. Add garlic and ginger first. Stir for 30 seconds. Add remaining veggies, except peas.

Stir-fry until onion pieces separate and green pepper brightens, about 2 minutes.

Add tofu and peas. Pour in sauce. Stir in a little arrowroot and water mixture to thicken, if desired, when sauce comes to a low boil. Adjust seasonings. Serve immediately.

Rice Fritters

2 tablespoons oil
1 onion, diced
4 cups cooked brown rice
4 cups tofu
1/2 cup nut butter (peanut, cashew, or almond)
2–3 tablespoons Bragg Liquid Aminos
1 cup parsley, minced

Sauté onion in oil until golden. Add other ingredients and form into small patties. Bake at 350 degrees, turning to brown on both sides. Serve with Mushroom Gravy if desired.

Italian Beans 'n Greens Over Polenta

1 cup anasazi beans, dried or sprouted
1/3 cup sun-dried tomatoes
1 cup hot water

Polenta:

1 cup yellow corn grits
3 cups water
2 tablespoons olive oil
1/4 teaspoon salt
1 tablespoon olive oil
1 onion, sliced into thin half moons
4 cloves garlic
1 bunch kale, cleaned and chopped
2 tablespoons Vogue Vege Base
salt to taste

Cook beans until tender.

Soak sun-dried tomatoes in hot water for approximately 15 minutes. Remove tomatoes. Reserve water. Mince tomatoes. Set aside.

Prepare polenta. Pour grits slowly into boiling, salted water. Turn temperature to low. Stir constantly. Add olive oil as it thickens. Stir as it thickens, approximately 3–5 minutes. Pour into oiled 10-inch pie pan. Set aside.

Sauté onions in oil until translucent. Add garlic, kale, Vogue, and water from tomatoes. Simmer 5 minutes.

Add beans. Season. Warm through. Pour over polenta. Sprinkle with vegan mozzarella or parmesan, if desired. Slice into wedges.

Baked Polenta with Shiitake Ragout

Elegant entree. Great for nonvegetarian dinner guests.

Ragout:

- 1 large onion, finely chopped
- 4 garlic cloves, minced
- 1 teaspoon dried rosemary, crumbled or coarsely ground
- 3 tablespoons olive oil
- 1 pound white mushrooms, sliced thin
- 1 pound fresh shiitake mushrooms, stems discarded and, if large, the caps quartered
- 1 tablespoon tomato paste
- 3/4 cup dry red wine (preferably organic)
- 1 tablespoon arrowroot
- 1 cup vegetable stock
- 1–2 tablespoons red miso

Polenta:

- 6 cups water
- 1 tablespoon olive oil
- 2 cups yellow cornmeal
- 1/3 cup fresh parsley, minced
- sea salt to taste
- 1/4 pound mozzarella-style vegan or soy cheese, grated

Preheat oven to 400 degrees.

Ragout:

Cook the onion, garlic, and rosemary in a large, deep skillet in oil over moderate heat, until the onion is softened. Stir constantly.

Add mushrooms. Cook mixture over moderately high heat. Stir until liquid from the mushrooms is evaporated.

Stir in tomato paste and wine. Boil mushroom mixture until most of liquid is evaporated.

Stir arrowroot into stock in a small bowl.

Add mixture to the mushrooms. Bring the ragout to a boil, stirring. Simmer the ragout for 2 minutes.

Mix the miso in equal amount of water. Add to ragout. Stir miso in completely.

Polenta:

Boil water with the oil in a large, heavy saucepan.

Add 1 cup of cornmeal, a small amount at a time, stirring.

Reduce heat to low. Add remaining 1 cup cornmeal in a slow stream. Stir constantly. Boil mixture.

Remove the pan from the heat when thickened. Stir in the 2 remaining tablespoons of olive oil, parsley, and sea salt to taste.

Spread 1/3 of the polenta in an oiled 3-quart shallow baking dish. Top with half the ragout. Top ragout with half the mozzarella.

Spread another third of the polenta quickly over the cheese.

Pour remaining ragout over that. Top with remaining cheese. Dot the casserole with remaining polenta.

Bake for approximately 30 minutes.

Polenta Pizza

Toppings are unlimited! Try roasted garlic, or sauté mushrooms with onions. Or marinara, pesto.... Sprinkle with coarsely ground rosemary and oregano and drizzle with olive oil... etc.!

Polenta:

- 1 cup yellow corn grits
- 3 cups water
- 2 tablespoons olive oil
- 1/2 teaspoon sea salt

Topping:

- fresh mushrooms
- tomato slices
- bell peppers
- olive slivers
- roasted garlic

Preheat oven to broil.

Bring water to a boil. Stir in grits, olive oil, and sea salt slowly. Lower heat to a simmer. Stir often, approximately 10 minutes, until creamy.

Pour into oiled baking pan. Top with veggies.

Add cheese, if desired.

Set under broiler briefly, or if using cheese, until bubbly.

Add fresh Tomato Sauce (see recipe in Condiments).

Cashew Nut Casserole

2 tablespoons olive oil
1½ cups cashew pieces
1 large onion, finely chopped
2 garlic cloves, minced
1 large zucchini, diced small
1 medium carrot, diced small
2 large stalks celery, sliced thin
1 teaspoon chili powder
1 teaspoon cumin, ground and toasted
1 heaping tablespoon Vogue Vege Base
1½ cups tomatoes, chopped
4 sun-dried tomatoes, minced
2 teaspoons fresh basil, finely chopped
1½ tablespoons Bragg Liquid Aminos
⅔ cup vegan milk, diluted with ⅔ cup water

Heat 1 tablespoon oil in large stock pot. Toast cashews. Set aside.

Heat remaining oil. Sauté onion until soft.

Add garlic, vegetables, and nuts. Cover. Cook for 10 minutes.

Add chili and cumin powders.

Mix in Vogue, tomatoes, basil, and Bragg's.

Stir in diluted milk.

Season.

Simmer 15–20 minutes.

Creamy Eggplant Casserole

1 cup bulgur
2 medium eggplants, thinly sliced
1 tablespoon olive oil
1 cup onion, diced
2 cups mushrooms, diced
1 large zucchini, diced
4 cloves garlic, minced
1½ tablespoons Vogue Vege Base
1 tablespoon fresh basil, minced
1 tablespoon fresh oregano, minced
3 tablespoons oat flour
½ cup cashews
1 cup water
1 cup mozzarella cheese recipe (optional)
paprika

Preheat oven to 350 degrees.

Soak bulgur in hot water to cover for 10 minutes.

Bake eggplant on an oiled pan until just tender. Set aside.

Sauté onion, mushrooms, zucchini, and garlic in oil until crisp tender. Add Vogue, basil, oregano, and flour. Cook 2 minutes.

Process cashews and water in blender until smooth. Pour into veggie mixture. Stir until gravy thickens. Add more water, if needed, to create a smooth sauce.

Pat down bulgur in an oiled 9 x 13 pan. Add half of the eggplant slices. Pour veggie and gravy mixture over all. Top with remaining eggplant.

Spread generously with cheese, if desired. Dust top with paprika.

Bake for 20 minutes.

Let sit 10 minutes before serving.

Portobello Casserole

- 1/2 cup sun-dried tomatoes
- 2 very large or 4 medium portobello mushrooms, cleaned, stems removed
- 1 onion, sliced into half moons
- 1 zucchini squash, diced
- 3–5 large cloves of garlic, minced
- stems of portobellos, cleaned and diced
- 2 heaping tablespoons Vogue Vege Base
- 1/4 cup olive oil

Preheat oven to 450 degrees.

Reconstitute tomatoes in water. Drain. Reserve water. Chop.

Place mushrooms in large baking dish, top side down.

Cover with vegetables.

Sprinkle with Vogue. Drizzle oil over all.

Add 1/3 cup reserved water to dish. Cover tightly.

Bake for approximately 30 minutes.

Spinach and Rice Casserole with Toasted Almonds

- 1 cup brown rice
- 2 cups water
- olive oil
- 1 onion, chopped
- 4 garlic cloves, minced
- 1/2 package firm-style tofu, rinsed and drained
- 1 tablespoon vegetable stock
- 1–2 teaspoons toasted sesame oil
- 1–2 tablespoons Bragg Liquid Aminos
- 1/3 cup arame, reconstituted according to package directions
- 1 bunch spinach, stems removed, rinsed well, and if large, leaves torn
- 1/3 cup almonds, toasted and coarsely chopped*

Simmer rice in water in a covered pot until all liquid is absorbed.

Sauté onion and garlic in a small amount of oil until softened.

Crumble tofu into pan.

Add stock, sesame oil, and Bragg's. Simmer for a few minutes.

Add rice and arame. Heat through.

Remove pan from burner. Stir in spinach, allowing the heat of the grain to wilt the leaves.

Stir in toasted almonds.

Serve immediately.

*To toast almonds: Place on a cookie sheet a few inches from heat source in your broiler. Shake after a couple of minutes. Remove when lightly browned.

Squash and Bean Casserole

Warming on a cold winter day. These three flavors blend well. Very Native American!

- 1 large kabocha, butternut, or acorn squash
- 3 cups water
- 1 cup corn grits
- 1/4 teaspoon salt
- 2 tablespoons oil
- 1 large onion, diced
- oil
- 4 cups cooked beans (anasazi, pinto, etc.)
- 1 tablespoon Vogue Vege Base
- 1 tablespoon chili powder
- 2 tablespoons Bragg Liquid Aminos
- 1/8–1/4 teaspoon chipotle powder (optional, but nice)

Preheat oven to 350 degrees.

Quarter squash. Remove seeds. Place on baking sheet, cut side down. Bake for approximately 45 minutes. Let cool. Mash. Set aside.

Bring water to boil. Add grits slowly. Turn down temperature to low. Stir continuously until polenta thickens. Add salt and oil. Stir briefly. (Total cooking time should be 7–10 minutes.) Pour immediately into oiled casserole dish. Set aside.

Sauté onion with oil in pan until translucent. Add remaining ingredients, adding a small amount of water, if needed. Adjust seasonings. Cook for 5 minutes. Pour over polenta.

Layer the mashed kabocha squash over beans. Sprinkle with toasted pumpkin seeds, if desired.

Bake at 350 degrees until heated through, approximately 15–20 minutes.

Vegetable Enchilada Casserole

12 corn tortillas

Sauce:

1 tablespoon olive oil
1 medium onion, diced
sea salt to taste
2 teaspoons cumin seed, toasted and ground
2 teaspoons dried oregano, toasted
8 garlic cloves, finely chopped
1 28-ounce can tomatoes, pureed
pinch of chipotle powder

Preheat oven to 350 degrees.

Heat oil in a large pan.

Add onion, 1/2 teaspoon salt, cumin, and oregano.

Sauté over medium heat until onion begins to soften, about 3–4 minutes. Add garlic. Sauté for 1 minute.

Add tomatoes, chipotle, and 1/4 teaspoon salt.

Reduce heat. Cook, uncovered, for 15–20 minutes.

Filling:

- 2 tablespoons oil
- 1 medium onion, diced
- sea salt to taste
- 1/2 teaspoon cumin seed, toasted and ground
- 1 red bell pepper, diced
- 4 medium zucchini, diced
- 2 medium potatoes, cubed and steamed
- 5 garlic cloves, finely chopped
- 3/4 pound mushrooms, thickly sliced
- pinch of chipotle powder

Heat 1 tablespoon oil in large pan.

Add onion, 1/2 teaspoon salt, and half the cumin. Sauté over medium heat for 5–7 minutes.

Add pepper, zucchini, potatoes, 1/2 teaspoon salt, half the garlic, and remaining cumin.

Cook for 10 minutes. Transfer to bowl.

Heat remaining oil. Brown mushrooms over high heat.

Toss mushrooms with other vegetables and chipotle powder.

Place 3–4 corn tortillas in baking dish.

Place filling on top of tortillas. Pour sauce over filling. Repeat 2 or 3 times, ending with sauce.

Bake 10–15 minutes.

Stuffed Pockets

Stuffed pockets are simply pie crust rolled out in 3-inch circles and filled with any combination of bean or lentil leftovers or grain and vegetable leftovers. Fold crust over and seal by pressing with a fork. Bake at 375 degrees for 15–20 minutes. You don't even have to wait for leftovers since kids love these sandwiches. I've filled many pockets with stuffings like sautéed spinach, garlic, onion and shredded veggies, mozzarella cheese, spicy BBQ'd beans and mustard, curried veggies from the Coconut Curry Melange recipe, Coconut Lentils, etc. This is a great time to be creative. Enlist your kids' help to come up with some unusual and delicious combinations.

Asparagus Flan

pie crust recipe of choice (see recipes in Desserts section)
1 tablespoon olive oil
1 large onion, diced small
1 large clove garlic, minced
1 bunch of asparagus, steamed crisp tender
1 block of firm tofu, rinsed and drained
1/4 cup water mixed with 1 tablespoon Vogue Vege Base
2 teaspoons finely grated or minced lemon rind
sea salt to taste

Prepare pie crust.

Preheat oven to 400 degrees.

Sauté onion in oil until golden. Add garlic and sauté for another minute.

Take the pan off the heat. Coarsely chop 1/2 of the asparagus spears and add to pan.

Place tofu in blender along with remaining asparagus and water with vegetable stock. Process until smooth.

Stir into pan with lemon rind, season with salt, and combine all well.

Spread into prepared pie crust and bake for 30 minutes or until firm and lightly browned.

Smoked Tofu and Mushroom Flan

Pie crust recipe of choice (see Desserts section)
1 cup smoked tofu, diced
1/4 cup vegan milk
2 tablespoons olive oil
2 1/2 cups sliced crimini mushrooms
1 onion, diced
4 bay leaves
2 cloves garlic, minced
1 1/2 cups finely chopped mushrooms, crimini and/or shiitake preferred
1 tablespoon Vogue Vege Base
1 1/2 tablespoons fresh rosemary, finely chopped
1–2 tablespoons Bragg Liquid Aminos

Prepare crust.

Preheat oven to 400 degrees.

Process tofu and vegan milk in blender until smooth.

Heat 1 tablespoon oil and sauté the sliced mushrooms until lightly browned. Remove mushrooms to a bowl and set aside.

Add the remaining oil and sauté the onion until golden along with the bay leaves.

Add garlic and chopped mushrooms and cook for another minute.

Remove the bay leaves and mix in Vogue, rosemary, and Bragg's.

Take the pan off the heat.

Add tofu to pan and combine well.

Place sliced mushrooms on bottom of crust. Pour tofu mixture on top and bake for 30 minutes or until firm and lightly browned.

Coconut Lentils

- 1 onion, chopped
- 1 large carrot, chopped
- 2 stalks celery, chopped
- coconut oil
- 1½ cups lentils, rinsed
- 1½ cups coconut milk
- 1 teaspoon curry powder
- 4 cups vegetable stock
- 1 cup minced parsley or spinach leaves
- sea salt to taste

In a large pot, sauté veggies in oil until onion is golden.

Add lentils, coconut milk, curry, and stock and bring to a boil.

Turn heat down and simmer for about 20–30 minutes, or until lentils are soft.

Stir in parsley and sea salt to taste.

Serve over grain of choice.

Vegetable Lasagna

Instead of noodles, we use eggplant!

- 1 large eggplant, thinly sliced and briefly broiled

Tofu Ricotta Sauce:

- 2 onions, chopped
- 4 cloves garlic, chopped
- 1–2 tablespoons olive oil
- 1 pound firm tofu, drained and diced
- 2–3 tablespoons Bragg Liquid Aminos
- ½ cup water
- ½ teaspoon basil, chopped
- ½ teaspoon oregano, chopped
- 1 tablespoon parsley, chopped
- ¼ cup nutritional yeast

Preheat oven to 350 degrees.

Sauté onion and garlic in oil.

Add tofu, Bragg's, water, and herbs. Cover.

Simmer 15 minutes.

Blend half in blender and mash other half for a creamy/chunky texture.

For a meaty texture, add half a package of crumbled tempeh to marinara mixture, or 1/2 cup of bulgur soaked in 1/2 cup hot water until liquid is absorbed.

Marinara Sauce:

- 1/3 cup sun-dried tomatoes
- 3–4 large garlic cloves, minced
- 1 large onion, diced
- 1–2 tablespoons olive oil
- 1 28-ounce can chopped tomatoes (preferably Muir Glen)
- 1/2 teaspoon basil, chopped
- 1/2 teaspoon oregano, chopped
- 1 bay leaf
- 1/8 cup balsamic vinegar
- pinch of red pepper flakes
- sea salt to taste

Soften sun-dried tomatoes in 1/2 cup boiling water. Remove from heat. Let sit until cooled. Drain. Reserve liquid. Chop. Set aside.

Sauté garlic and onion in olive oil until softened. Add remaining ingredients, using reserved water from sun-dried tomatoes as needed to loosen mixture. Simmer 20 minutes.

Filling:

- 1 bunch spinach
- 1 carrot, shredded
- 6–8 ounces mushrooms, sliced

Remove stems from spinach. Rinse well. Wilt briefly in covered pan. Chop.

Mix spinach, carrots, and mushrooms into ricotta sauce.

Layer a pan with marinara sauce first, then eggplant, ricotta, and sauce. Repeat once or twice more. Finish with marinara on top.

Cover. Bake 20–25 minutes until bubbly.

Chestnut, Apple, and Cornbread Stuffed Squash

2 butternut squash

Stuffing:

1 pound fresh chestnuts, or 3/4 pound canned chestnuts
1 large onion, chopped
2 celery stalks, chopped
2 tablespoons sage leaves, minced (or 1 tablespoon dried)
2 tablespoons thyme leaves, minced (or 2 teaspoons dried)
1 tablespoon rosemary, minced (or 1 teaspoon dried)
1/2 cup parsley, minced
2 Granny Smith apples, cut into 1/4-inch pieces
1/4 cup "Butter" (see recipe in Condiments)
1 cup vegetable stock

Cornbread for stuffing:

3/4 cup flour (spelt, barley, or wheat pastry)
1 1/4 cups yellow cornmeal
1 tablespoon nonaluminum baking powder
1/2 teaspoon sea salt
1 cup vegan milk

Preheat oven to 375 degrees.

Cut squash in half. Clean. Bake, cut side down, until tender, approximately 30–45 minutes.

Shell and peel chestnuts. Roast in a hot oven (400–450 degrees) until tender, approximately 20–30 minutes. Chop coarse.

Prepare cornbread:
Mix dry and liquid ingredients separately. Stir together. Pour batter into greased 8-inch square baking pan. Bake in preheated 425 degree oven for 20–25 minutes, or until top is pale golden and a tester comes out clean. Remove from pan. Break into coarse chunks to cool and dry out completely.

Cook onion and celery with salt and pepper to taste over moderately low heat. Stir until vegetables are softened. Transfer the mixture to the bowl of cornbread.

Add chestnuts and herbs. Adjust seasonings, if necessary. Toss mixture gently until combined well. Let cool. Stir in apples. Stuff cooked squash. Return to oven. Pour vegetable stock over all.

Bake for another 30–45 minutes.

Mediterranean Stuffed Collard Greens

I love these little rolls served warm or cold. Try them with hummus and pita or my version of tzatziki for a complete meal.

- 1 large bunch of collard greens, stems removed
- 1/2 cup coarse cracked wheat or bulgur
- 1/3 cup green lentils
- 1 1/2 tablespoons fresh parsley, finely minced
- 1 1/2 tablespoons fresh dill, finely minced
- 1 1/2 tablespoons fresh mint, minced
- 1/4 cup raisins, chopped (optional)
- 1 cup onion, finely chopped
- 8 tablespoons olive oil
- 6 tablespoons fresh lemon juice
- about 1 cup vegetable stock
- lemon wedges as an accompaniment

Blanch collard greens, a few leaves at a time, in a large pot of hot (not boiling) water for 15–30 seconds. Remove. Cool.

Make the Filling:
Soak bulgur in a small bowl of hot water to cover for 15 minutes. Drain. Press hard to extract water.

Simmer lentils in a small pan of boiling water for 20 minutes. Drain. Add to bulgur. Add parsley, dill, mint, and raisins.

Cook onion in 3 tablespoons of oil in a skillet over moderate heat. Stir until golden. Add to grain mixture.

Stir in 3 tablespoons lemon juice and the remaining 2 tablespoons oil. Add salt and pepper to taste.

Stuff the Leaves:
Spoon a heaping teaspoon of filling on each leaf (if leaves are large, cut in half).

Roll the filling up tightly in the leaf, folding the sides. Squeeze the roll to compact the filling (rolls should be about the size of your forefinger).

Line the bottom of a 3-quart heavy saucepan with leftover collard greens. Arrange the rolls in layers close together, seams down. Season each layer with a small amount of salt, if desired.

Drizzle remaining oil and lemon juice over rolls. Cover with an inverted heatproof plate slightly smaller than the diameter of the pan. Press down lightly.

Add just enough stock to come up to the rim of the plate. Bring to a boil.

Reduce heat to low. Cook rolls, covered with the plate and the lid, for 45 minutes, or until most of the liquid is absorbed.

Remove from heat. Let cool, covered.

Serve at room temperature or chilled. Arrange on a plate with lemon wedges.

Veggie Rolls

Whole-grain bread may tear when you try to roll it. Briefly steaming bread will make it more pliable.

- 1 onion, chopped
- 1 cup greens, shredded
- 1/2 cup carrot, shredded
- 1/4 cup bell pepper, slivered
- 1/2 cup mushrooms, minced
- oil
- 1 tomato, chopped
- 2 tablespoons flour
- 1/2 teaspoon sea salt
- 8 slices bread
- olive oil
- dulse gomacio (see recipe in Condiments)

Sauté onion, greens, carrots, bell peppers, and mushrooms in a small amount of oil until softened. Add tomato. Stir in flour and salt. Cool.

Preheat oven to 375 degrees.

Steam bread briefly. Flatten bread. Spread veggies in center of each. Roll. Brush each with oil. Sprinkle with dulse gomacio.

Place on baking sheet, seam down. Bake for approximately 20 minutes, or until browned.

Chili and Corn-Filled Zucchini

Try guacamole and tomato salsa as an accompaniment on a bed of mixed greens.

6 medium zucchini

Filling:

1 tablespoon olive oil
1 onion, chopped
1 teaspoon cumin seeds, ground
sea salt (start with 1/4 teaspoon)
ground chipotle pepper or cayenne (start with 1/8 teaspoon)
3 cups corn kernels
5 garlic cloves, minced
1 teaspoon marjoram, ground
scooped zucchini flesh
2 tablespoons cilantro, chopped
1 cup cooked adzuki, anasazi, or other beans
toasted pumpkin seeds

Cut the zucchini in half lengthwise. Leave ends on.

Scoop out centers, leaving about a 1/4-inch shell. Save the scooped flesh to add to the filling. Save shells.

Preheat oven to 375 degrees.

Prepare filling. Sauté all ingredients in oil, except cilantro and beans, for 5 minutes.

Toss in cilantro and beans. Adjust seasonings, if needed.

Mound the filling into reserved zucchini shells. Sprinkle with pumpkin seeds.

Place in an oiled baking dish. Cover.

Bake for 30 minutes. Let rest 10 minutes before serving.

Millet-Stuffed Zucchini

6 medium zucchini

Filling:

1/2 cup pine nuts
1/3 cup millet
1 cup water
4–6 cloves garlic, minced
1 heaping tablespoon Vogue Vege Base
1 onion, chopped
scooped zucchini flesh
1/3 cup sun-dried tomatoes, reconstituted in water and minced
1 tablespoon fresh basil, minced
1 tablespoon fresh oregano, minced
sea salt to taste
olive oil

Preheat oven to 375 degrees.

Cut the zucchini in half lengthwise, leaving the ends on. Scoop out the centers of the zucchini. Leave about a 1/4-inch shell. Save the scooped flesh to add to the filling. Save shells.

Toast pine nuts. Set aside.

Cook millet in water in a small covered saucepan until all liquid is absorbed.

Sauté all ingredients, except pine nuts, in approximately 2 tablespoons of olive oil until onions are softened.

Mix in millet and pine nuts. Mound into zucchini boats.

Place in a lightly oiled baking dish. Cover.

Bake for 30 minutes.

Stuffed Cabbage Stroganoff

6–8 large cabbage leaves (or large collard greens, stems removed)

Filling:

3 cups cooked barley (not pearled, which is highly refined)
3/4 cup onion, chopped
1 1/2 cups mushrooms, chopped
3/4 cup almonds, toasted and coarsely chopped
1/4 cup parsley, minced
1 tablespoon Bragg Liquid Aminos
1 cup vegan yogurt

Sauce:

1/3 cup onion, chopped
1 1/2 tablespoons oil
1 1/2 cups mushrooms, thinly sliced
1/8–1/4 teaspoon red pepper flakes
2 tablespoons arrowroot
2 tablespoons Bragg Liquid Aminos
2 tablespoons nutritional yeast
1 cup vegan milk

Preheat oven to 350 degrees.

Combine all filling ingredients.

Spoon into cabbage leaves. Place in large shallow baking pan.

Sauté onion in oil for 2 minutes. Add mushrooms and red pepper flakes. Cook for 2 minutes. Add remaining ingredients slowly. Stir over moderate heat until thickened.

Pour sauce over cabbage.

Bake, covered, for 20 minutes.

Savory Stuffed Portobellos

Great with roasted potatoes, with peppers, and Italian Chopped Salad.

- 3 portobello mushrooms
- small handful parsley
- 4–5 garlic cloves, minced fine
- 1/2 onion, minced fine
- 2 tablespoons olive oil
- 2 slices bread, toasted, finely ground
- 1 tablespoon nutritional yeast
- 2 tablespoons Bragg Liquid Aminos
- 1/4 teaspoon marjoram, ground
- lemon
- Creamy Mozzarella Cheese Recipe (optional) (see recipe in Condiments)

Remove stems from mushrooms. Hollow partially to stuff. Set aside.

Preheat oven to 350 degrees.

Sauté parsley, garlic, and onion in olive oil until soft. Mix with remaining ingredients.

Stuff mushrooms and sprinkle with juice from 1 lemon.

Bake for 30–40 minutes.

Spread mozzarella over top. Sprinkle with additional parsley.

Squash and Leek Turnovers

Filling:

- 1 1/2 pounds butternut squash
- 5 garlic cloves, finely chopped
- 2 tablespoons olive oil
- 2 large leeks, white parts only
- 1/2 teaspoon salt
- 1/2 teaspoon dried thyme
- 2 tablespoons miso

1 tablespoon fresh thyme, chopped (or 1/4 teaspoon dried)
3/4 cup vegan cheese (mozzarella, Monterey jack, etc.) (optional)

Pastry:

3 1/2 cups flour
1/4 cup oil (or 3 tablespoons coconut oil)
1 1/2 teaspoons sea salt
1 tablespoon sweetener
1 cup water

Preheat oven to 400 degrees.

Peel, seed, and cut butternut squash into 1/2-inch cubes. Set aside.

Prepare filling:
Combine 2 cloves of chopped garlic with 1 tablespoon oil. Place cubed squash in baking dish. Toss with garlic oil and 1/2 teaspoon salt.

Cover. Bake 25–30 minutes, until squash is tender, but still holds its shape. Do not overcook.

Heat remaining oil in large skillet. Add leeks, salt, and thyme. Sauté over medium heat for approximately 2 minutes, until softened. Add remaining garlic. Cover pan, allowing leeks to steam until tender, about 5 minutes.

Add miso, mixed with a small amount of water.

Toss the squash, leeks, and thyme gently together. Add cheese, if desired. Season filling well so its flavor comes through the pastry.

Prepare pastry:
Mix flour and oil until crumbly.

Dissolve salt and sweetener in water.

Combine flour mixture and sweetened water. Mix to form a dough. Roll out dough on floured board. Cut into 8-inch rounds. Place approximately 1/3 cup filling on each piece. Wet edges. Press with fork to seal.

Bake for 15–20 minutes, or until light brown.

Sweet Squash Stuffed with Wild Rice

- 1/4 cup olive oil
- 2 cloves garlic, minced
- 1 small red onion, finely chopped
- 4 ribs celery, minced
- 1 small zucchini, diced
- 1/4 pound mushrooms, chopped
- 1/2 of a 10-ounce bag frozen peas
- 1/2 teaspoon rosemary
- 1/2 teaspoon sage
- 1 1/2 tablespoons Vogue Vege Base
- 5 cups cooked wild and brown rice
- sea salt to taste
- 1/4 cup pecans, chopped
- 1 large squash (butternut) or 2 smaller (acorn), cut in half and seeded

Preheat oven to 450 degrees.

Heat olive oil in a large skillet over medium-low heat. Add all veggies and spices. Cook several minutes, until softened. Stir in rice, salt, and pecans.

Divide the stuffing into each squash half. Arrange in a baking pan. Pour water into pan to 3/4-inch. Cover pan tightly.

Bake for 1–1 1/2 hours, or until squash is tender when pierced.

Enchilada Pie

Sauce:

- 1 cup onions, chopped
- 3 cups tomatoes, chopped
- 2 garlic cloves, minced
- pinch of cayenne
- 1 tablespoon chili powder
- 1 tablespoon brown rice syrup
- sea salt to taste
- 1/2 teaspoon ground cumin

- 8 soft corn tortillas
- 1 1/2 cups pinto beans, cooked and mashed
- 1/4 pound black olives, sliced
- 1/4–1/2 pound cheddar-style cheese, grated
- corn kernels (optional)
- green onions, chopped (optional)

Simmer onions, tomatoes, garlic, cayenne, chili powder, rice syrup, salt, and cumin, uncovered, for 30 minutes.

Preheat oven to 350 degrees.

Pour a small amount of sauce on bottom of baking dish.

Begin layering ingredients, starting with tortillas, then beans, olives, cheese (at this point you could add corn kernels or green onions). Continue layering.

Finish with sauce and cheese.

Bake until bubbly.

Quick and Easy Soft Tacos

For those nights when you're pressed for time!

- 2 cups quinoa, cooked
- 1 cup beans, cooked
- 1 cup salsa
- 1/2 cup corn
- corn tortillas, steamed briefly

Condiment suggestions:

- cheddar-style cheese, grated
- salsa
- vegan sour cream
- avocado slices
- chopped tomatoes
- mixed salad greens
- sprouts
- dulse gomacio
- pumpkin seeds

Combine all ingredients well. Warm on stove.

Steam tortillas briefly to soften.

Build soft tacos with filling and condiments to taste.

Veggie and Black Bean Tacos

2 cups broccoli, coarsely chopped
1 cup onions, sliced into half moons
1 red bell pepper, cut in strips
1 large portobello mushroom, sliced
1/2 teaspoon ground cumin
2 teaspoons chili powder
1 tablespoon olive oil
1/4 cup water
1 heaping tablespoon Vogue Vege Base
2 tablespoons lime juice
2 cups of cooked and drained beans (your choice, anasazi, pinto, black)
2 medium tomatoes, chopped
12 tortillas

Condiments:

vegan cheese (optional)
lettuce, shredded
salsa
tofu sour cream (recipe in Condiments section)
cilantro

Sauté first 6 ingredients in olive oil for five minutes.

Add water and Vogue. Simmer 2 minutes. Remove from heat.

Stir in lime juice, beans, and tomatoes.

Build tacos by using veggie mix. Add condiments to taste.

Spicy Sausage and Soba Noodles in Paprika Sauce

This is a very spicy dish. For those of you with a low heat tolerance, you may cut down on the paprika and cayenne.

2 tablespoons garlic, minced
1 tablespoon shallot, minced
3/4 package of vegan sausage, chopped (store-bought or try Tempeh Sausage recipe)
1/8 cup olive oil
2 tablespoons sweet paprika
1/4 teaspoon cayenne powder
2 tablespoons fresh basil, minced (or 2 teaspoons dried)
2 tablespoons fresh oregano, minced (or 2 teaspoons dried)
1 cup vegetable stock
1/2 cup plain vegan yogurt*
1/2 cup Tofu Sour Cream (see recipe in Condiments)
1 package soba noodles, cooked as per instructions
1/3 cup scallions, finely chopped
1 medium tomato, chopped
sea salt to taste

Cook garlic, shallot, and sausage in a large skillet in olive oil until garlic is golden and sausage begins to brown.

Add paprika, cayenne, basil, and oregano.

Stir in stock and simmer mixture until liquid is reduced by half.

Stir in yogurt and sour cream. Simmer mixture until liquid is slightly reduced.

Toss the soba noodles, scallions, and tomato into sauce mixture. Add salt, if desired.

* I use White Wave soy yogurt.

Chickpea, Eggplant, and Tomato Stew

This is a time-intensive recipe . . . but worth it!

- 1/2 pound dried chickpeas (or sprouted, which will cut the preparation time dramatically)
- 1 pound eggplant
- 1 teaspoon salt, plus additional for sprinkling the eggplant
- 2 onions, chopped
- 2 1/2 teaspoons hot green chili, chopped (wear rubber gloves)
- 1 green bell pepper, seeded and chopped
- 1/4 cup olive oil
- 14–16 ounce can whole tomatoes, including juice (preferably Muir Glen)
- 1/2 cup fresh parsley, chopped
- 1 1/2 teaspoons garlic, crushed
- 1 teaspoon dried oregano
- 1 bay leaf

Soak chickpeas in a large bowl in water to cover by 2 inches overnight. Drain. Transfer to a saucepan. Add fresh water to cover. Boil. Lower heat. Cover. Simmer for 45 minutes, or 15 minutes if using sprouted chickpeas. Drain in a sieve. Reserve the cooking liquid.

While chickpeas cook, peel eggplant. Cut into 1-inch cubes. Place in colander. Sprinkle lightly with additional salt. Allow to stand for 1 hour. Rinse eggplant. Squeeze dry.

Preheat oven to 300 degrees.

Sauté onions, chili, and bell pepper in a large skillet in oil over moderately high heat for 3 minutes. Stir constantly.

Stir in eggplant. Sauté mixture for 2 minutes. Stir constantly, being careful not to let eggplant brown.

Stir in tomatoes, including juice, parsley, garlic, oregano, and remaining 1 teaspoon sea salt. Simmer mixture for 10 minutes. Stir often.

Stir together chickpeas, 1 3/4 cups of reserved cooking liquid, bay leaf, and eggplant mixture in a 4-quart casserole. Cover.

Bake for 2 1/2 hours, or 30 minutes if using sprouted chickpeas.

Sausage and Potato Skillet

- 4 vegan sausage links, diced (or 1 recipe Tempeh Sausage rolled into small balls)
- olive oil
- 1/2 onion, diced
- 2 cloves garlic, minced
- 1/2 bell pepper, diced
- 1/2 block firm tofu, crumbled
- 1–2 tablespoons Vogue Vege Base
- 1 tablespoon Bragg Liquid Aminos
- 2–3 potatoes, cooked and diced*
- 1 tomato, chopped

Brown sausage links in oil.

Add onion, garlic, and bell pepper.

Cook until veggies are slightly softened.

Add tofu, Vogue, and Bragg's.

Stir until combined and just heated through.

Toss in potatoes and tomatoes.

*If you have leftover baked potatoes, this would be the time to use them—or steam cubed potatoes.

Cashew Burgers

2 medium carrots, finely diced
2 cloves garlic, minced
1 onion, diced
oil
2 cups cooked rice or moist cooked millet
1 cup cashews
2/3 cup sunflower seeds
1/3 cup sesame seeds
1/2 cup parsley, minced
1 teaspoon sage, minced
2 tablespoons nutritional yeast
2 tablespoons Vogue Vege Base
1 teaspoon sea salt

Preheat oven to broil.

Sauté carrots, garlic, and onion until softened in a small amount of oil.

Grind all nuts and seeds.

Mix all ingredients together well. Form into patties.

Broil until browned on both sides, approximately 10 minutes total.

Earth Burgers

Use Cashew Burgers recipe. Substitute pumpkin and sunflower seeds for cashews and sesame.

Add 2 tablespoons tomato paste and 1 teaspoon chili powder instead of sage.

Cook as above.

Nut Burgers In-the-Raw

- 1 cup sprouted wheat
- 1/4 cup water
- 1 cup walnuts, ground
- 1/2 cup sunflower seeds, chopped
- 1/3 cup almond or cashew butter
- 1 small stalk celery, chopped
- 2 tablespoons parsley, chopped
- 2 tablespoons onion, chopped
- 1/4 cup water mixed with:
  - 1 tablespoon miso
  - 1 teaspoon Bragg Liquid Aminos
- pinch of marjoram
- pinch of dill

Combine all ingredients in a large bowl. Mix thoroughly. Form into burgers. Add more water if too dry. Serve burgers with salsa!

Tempeh Sausage Patties

- 1 package tempeh
- 1/2 cup vegetable stock
- 1 tablespoon olive oil
- 1/2 onion, finely chopped
- 1/4 teaspoon fennel seeds, crushed
- pinch red pepper flakes
- 1 teaspoon sage
- 1/2 teaspoon oregano
- 2 tablespoons nutritional yeast
- 1/4 cup rolled oats
- 1–2 tablespoons Bragg Liquid Aminos

Simmer tempeh in vegetable stock. Cool. Grate. Reserve stock. Set aside.

Sauté onion until golden. Mix ingredients together, using enough reserved stock as necessary to hold patties together. Brown in a skillet with a small amount of oil.

Millet Seed Patties

- 1 medium onion, diced
- 1 cup millet, cooked in 3 cups water
- 1/2 cup rice, cooked in 1 cup water
- 1 cup pumpkin seeds, ground
- 1/4 cup almond or cashew butter
- 3 tablespoons olive oil
- 1 teaspoon sea salt
- 2 tablespoons Vogue Vege Base
- 1 teaspoon sage

Sauté onion in small amount of oil. Cool.

Mix remaining ingredients well. Form into patties. Brown in lightly oiled pan.

Serve plain, with gravy or salsa.

Pecan Patties

These keep well in the refrigerator for several days.

- 1/2 cup oatmeal
- 1/4 cup water
- 1 medium onion, diced
- 1 tablespoon oil
- 3/4 cup pecans, ground
- 1–2 tablespoons Bragg Liquid Aminos
- 1/4 teaspoon thyme
- 1 heaping tablespoon Vogue Vege Base

Mix oatmeal in water. Let sit for a few minutes.

Sauté onion in oil. Cool.

Mix all ingredients well. Form into patties. Let sit for 30 minutes.

Brown lightly in skillet. Serve warm or cold.

Millet Nut and Seed Balls – Rhiannon's "Booger Balls"

- 1/2 cup millet
- 1 1/2 cups water
- 1 large stalk kale, stem removed, very finely minced
- 1/4 teaspoon onion powder
- 2 tablespoons Bragg Liquid Aminos
- 2 heaping tablespoons Vogue Vege Base
- 1 heaping tablespoon cashew butter
- 1/4 cup raw pumpkin seeds, finely ground

Simmer millet with water until almost absorbed.

Add kale. Cover. Let sit for 5 minutes.

Combine onion powder, Bragg's, Vogue, and cashew butter well. Mix into millet and kale mixture, along with pumpkin seeds. Adjust seasonings, if needed.

Form into walnut-sized balls (smaller balls for smaller fingers).

Baked Tofu with Cabbage and Wild Rice

A large green salad, raw corn and red bell salad, mashed potatoes, and a cranberry relish or chutney would make this a terrific holiday meal!

- 1/4 cup wild rice
- 1 1/4 cups water
- 1/2 package tempeh
- 1 1-pound package tofu, sliced in 4 pieces
- 1 cup red cabbage, chopped
- 1 cup red onion, chopped
- 1/2 cup apple cider
- 1/2 teaspoon sage
- 1/4 teaspoon thyme
- 1/4 teaspoon marjoram
- 2 tablespoons Bragg Liquid Aminos
- 1 tablespoon Vogue Vege Base
- whole-grain prepared mustard
- nutritional yeast

Cook rice in water over low heat for approximately 40 minutes. Drain.

Steam tempeh for 10 minutes. Cool. Grate. Set aside.

Wrap tofu in clean kitchen towel for 30 minutes.

Preheat oven to 375 degrees.

Combine cabbage, onion, and cider. Cover. Simmer until cabbage is just tender. Add tempeh, sage, thyme, marjoram, Bragg's, and Vogue. Set aside.

Spread each slice of tofu generously with mustard on both sides. Dip in nutritional yeast. Place on a baking sheet. Bake for 30 minutes.

Place a scoop of dressing on a plate topped with a tofu cutlet.

Serve with a simple brown gravy (try mine without the mushrooms and finely chop the onions).

Rosemary Tofu Sauté

- 1 pound extra-firm or firm tofu
- 1/4 cup nutritional yeast
- 1 slice of bread, ground in spice grinder*
- 1 tablespoon Vogue Vege Base
- 1/2 teaspoon garlic powder
- 1/2 teaspoon paprika
- 3/4–1 teaspoon rosemary, coarsely ground
- olive oil
- 1 lemon, juiced
- kale or spinach, cleaned, stems removed, and chopped

Wrap tofu in kitchen towel for 30 minutes.

Mix yeast, bread, Vogue, garlic powder, paprika, and rosemary. Set aside.

Cube tofu into 1/2-inch pieces. Place tofu in a bowl. Stir in 1 tablespoon olive oil.

Add dry ingredients. Toss to cover. Let sit for a few minutes.

Heat a heavy pan over medium high. Add 2 or more tablespoons of olive oil. Heat until hot, but not smoking.

Add tofu cubes and any excess breading. Cook until browned on all sides.

Add lemon juice. Stir. Pour onto a serving platter.

Bring heat to high. Add kale or spinach (do not shake off rinse water). Cover immediately. If you are using spinach, turn the heat off and let sit for 45 seconds. If using kale, add 1–2 tablespoons water and bring heat down to low. Simmer for 5 minutes until just tender.

Serve immediately.

*If you do not have a spice grinder, let the bread dry out completely (overnight), then crush with a rolling pin. It is not necessary to use dry bread in grinder.

Salisbury Steaks

- 2 packages tempeh
- 1 cup vegetable stock
- 1/2 block firm tofu, crumbled
- 1/2 cup moist cooked millet or rice
- 1/4 cup parsley, finely minced
- 1/4 cup celery, finely minced
- 1/4 cup mushrooms, finely minced
- 1/2 cup onion, finely minced
- 1 clove garlic, minced
- 1 teaspoon dry mustard
- 1 teaspoon paprika
- 2 tablespoons Bragg Liquid Aminos
- 2 tablespoons Vogue Vege Base

Simmer tempeh in vegetable stock for 10 minutes. Cool. Grate.

Mix all ingredients well (this works best with your hands). Form 3–4 inch patties.

Sauté in small amount of olive oil until golden brown on both sides.

Serve with Mushroom-Onion Gravy (see recipe in Condiments).

BBQ-Style Tempeh

- 1 package tempeh
- 1 tablespoon olive oil
- 1 large onion, diced
- 1 celery stalk, diced
- 2 large carrots or 1 red bell pepper, diced
- 1 cup BBQ sauce (try "Annie's" brand)
- 1/2 cup vegetable stock

Steam tempeh for 10 minutes. Cut into cubes. Set aside.

Sauté veggies in oil for 2 minutes. Add sauce and stock. Stir.

Add tempeh. Bring to boil. Reduce heat. Cover. Simmer 15 minutes.

Serve over grains.

Deli-Style Tempeh

- 1 package tempeh
- 1 large onion, diced
- 2 medium carrots, diced
- 1 tablespoon oil
- 1 bunch of collards, stems removed, chopped
- 2 cups sauerkraut, rinsed
- 1–2 tablespoons whole-grain prepared mustard, or to taste
- 1/2 cup water
- 1 tablespoon Vogue Vege Base

Steam tempeh for 10 minutes. Cool.

Sauté tempeh, onion, and carrots in oil until onions are translucent.

Stir in remaining ingredients. Reduce heat to low. Cover. Simmer 5 minutes.

Hot and Pungent Tempeh with Broccoli

1 package tempeh, cubed
1 tablespoon Bragg Liquid Aminos
2 tablespoons plus 2 teaspoons arrowroot
1–2 tablespoons oil
3 cloves garlic, minced
1 bunch broccoli, cut into small flowerets, blanched

Sauce:

1/4 cup vegetable stock
2 tablespoons Bragg Liquid Aminos
1 1/2 tablespoons brown rice vinegar
1 tablespoon Oriental sesame oil
1 tablespoon brown rice syrup
1/4 teaspoon sea salt
1/4–1/2 teaspoon red Thai curry paste
2 tablespoons cilantro, minced

Place tempeh in a bowl. Add Bragg's and 2 teaspoons arrowroot. Set aside.

Combine ingredients for sauce in a small bowl. Set aside.

Place wok or pan over medium high heat. Add 1 tablespoon oil.

Add tempeh. Stir-fry until browned. Add more oil if pan dries out. Remove tempeh from pan.

Add garlic and broccoli. Stir-fry just until heated through.

Return tempeh to wok. Pour in sauce. Bring sauce to a low boil. Simmer for several minutes.

Stir in a little arrowroot (mixed with equal water) until lightly thickened.

Serve immediately.

Lettuce-Wrapped Tempeh Meatballs

1 package tempeh
1 cup vegetable stock
2 green onions, minced
2 tablespoons cilantro, minced
2 tablespoons Bragg Liquid Aminos
2 tablespoons sesame butter or tahini
1 teaspoon orange peel, minced
3/4 teaspoon nutmeg, ground
1/4 teaspoon chili sauce or Thai curry sauce
4 cloves garlic, minced
1 tablespoon ginger, minced
oil
lime juice to taste
lettuce leaves

Simmer tempeh in vegetable stock. Drain. Cool. Grate.

Mix all ingredients, except oil and lime juice, well. Form into small balls. Sauté in a small amount of oil until browned.

Squeeze lime juice over meatballs.

Serve wrapped in lettuce leaves. Eat like soft tacos.

Rio Grande Tempeh Meatloaf

Serve with salsa if desired or try my Corn and Sun-Dried Tomato Relish . . . yummy!

12 ounces tempeh
1/2 cup onion, chopped
1/2 cup green bell pepper, chopped
1/2 cup fresh cilantro, chopped
2 jalapeno peppers, minced and seeded
1 tablespoon Vogue Vege Base
2 tablespoons olive oil
1/4–1/2 teaspoon sea salt

2 teaspoons cumin, ground
2 teaspoons chili powder
3 large garlic cloves, minced
1 1/2 cups cooked black beans
1/2 cup silken tofu
2 tablespoons Bragg Liquid Aminos
approximately 2 cups tortilla chips, crushed
1/2 cup vegetable stock

Preheat oven to 375 degrees.

Steam tempeh for 10 minutes. Cool. Grate.

Combine all ingredients well. Pack mixture into an oiled loaf pan.

Bake for 50 minutes.

Let meatloaf stand 10 minutes before serving.

Tempeh Hash

1 package tempeh
2 large potatoes, diced small
1 large onion, diced
1 teaspoon cumin seeds
1 tablespoon olive oil
1 cup small veggies, diced (such as corn, carrot, peas, etc.)
1/2 yellow or red bell pepper, slivered
1 tablespoon chili powder
1–2 tablespoons Bragg Liquid Aminos
pinch red pepper or chipotle pepper (optional)

Simmer tempeh in 1 cup of vegetable stock. Cool. Grate.

Broil potatoes until brown on all sides.

Sauté onion and cumin seeds in oil for 2 minutes. Add tempeh. Brown lightly.

Add remaining ingredients. Heat through.

Tri-Grain Hash

1 cup quinoa
3/4 cup millet
1/4 cup amaranth
5 cups water
2 tablespoons olive oil
1 large potato, diced
1 large onion, diced
1 large carrot, diced
1 roasted red bell pepper, chopped
1–2 heaping tablespoons Vogue Vege Base
1/2 cup water
1 zucchini, diced
1/2 cup corn
1–2 tablespoons chili powder
1/2–3/4 cup cheddar-style vegan cheese (optional)
1 teaspoon sea salt

Simmer quinoa, millet, and amaranth in water, covered, until liquid is absorbed (approximately 20 minutes).

Sauté potato, onion, and carrot in olive oil.

Add remaining ingredients. Stir in cooked grain.

Adjust seasonings, if needed.

Tempeh in Shiitake Cream Sauce

1 medium carrot, shredded
1 green onion, shredded
1 package tempeh
2 tablespoons olive oil
1/2 cup shiitake mushroom caps, sliced thin
1 tablespoon ginger, finely minced
1/2 cup cashew cream (1/4 cup each water and cashews blended until smooth)
1 tablespoon Bragg Liquid Aminos

1 tablespoon Oriental sesame oil
1/2 teaspoon orange peel, finely grated
1/8–1/4 teaspoon Thai curry paste

Blanch carrot and green onion by pouring boiling water over them through a sieve. Set aside.

Slice tempeh in half. Slice again. Split them into 4 thin scallops. Steam for 10 minutes.

Heat olive oil in pan. Add tempeh. Brown on both sides. Remove from pan. Add mushrooms and ginger to hot sauté pan.

Combine Bragg's, oil, orange peel, and curry paste in small bowl to make sauce.

Add sauce. Bring to boil. Simmer 5 minutes.

Spoon sauce over tempeh slices. Garnish with carrots and green onions.

Serve immediately.

Tempeh in Red Wine Sauce

Great served over mashed potatoes or millet.

1 package tempeh
1 tablespoon oil
1 onion, diced small
2 carrots, diced small
1 celery or celeriac root, outer skin discarded, cut into 1/4-inch cubes
1/4 teaspoon thyme
1 heaping tablespoon Vogue Vege Base
1/4 cup organic red wine
2 heaping tablespoons tomato paste
1 bay leaf
1/4 cup Bragg Liquid Aminos
1 cup vegetable stock
1 tablespoon arrowroot mixed with 2 tablespoons water
sea salt to taste

Steam tempeh for 10 minutes. Cool. Cut into 1/2-inch cubes. Set aside.

Sauté veggies in oil for 5 minutes.

Add thyme, Vogue, and red wine. Cook 2 minutes.

Add tomato paste, bay leaf, Bragg's, and stock. Simmer 15 minutes.

Add arrowroot mixture. Stir in tempeh. Simmer 10 additional minutes.

Add salt to taste.

Tempeh with Lemon Ginger Glaze

1 package tempeh
1/2 cup lemon juice
1/4 cup brown rice syrup
1/4 cup vegetable stock
2 tablespoons Bragg Liquid Aminos
1/2 teaspoon sea salt
2 teaspoons lemon peel, grated
2 teaspoons fresh ginger, grated
1–2 tablespoons oil
3 garlic cloves, finely minced
2 tablespoons arrowroot
2 tablespoons water

Steam tempeh for 10 minutes. Cool. Slice into slender fingers or dice into 1/4-inch pieces.

Place lemon juice, rice syrup, vegetable stock, Bragg's, salt, lemon peel, and ginger in a small saucepan. Set aside sauce.

Sauté garlic and tempeh in oil until tempeh is golden brown.

Simmer sauce for 5 minutes. Dissolve 2 tablespoons of arrowroot into equal amount of water. Stir into sauce until a thick glaze is achieved. Stir sauce into tempeh.

Serve immediately.

Tempeh Skillet Dinner

1 package tempeh
1/2 pound green beans, cut into 1-inch pieces
olive oil
1 onion, diced
2 medium potatoes, diced
2 tablespoons Vogue Vege Base
2 tablespoons Bragg Liquid Aminos
1/2 teaspoon dry mustard
2 large tomatoes, diced (or 1 14-ounce can Muir Glen diced tomatoes)
water

Steam tempeh 10 minutes. Cool. Cube.

Steam green beans until crisp tender.

Sauté onion, potatoes, and tempeh in oil until lightly browned.

Add Vogue, Bragg's, and dry mustard.

Stir in tomatoes and approximately 1/3 to 1/2 cup water.

Cover. Simmer until potatoes are tender. Mix in green beans.

Serve immediately.

Tempeh Millet Loaf

Delicious served with Mushroom-Onion Gravy.

1 package tempeh
1 cup hot vegetable stock
2 cups cooked millet
1 large onion, chopped
2 teaspoons olive oil
1/2 cup parsley, minced
2 teaspoons Bragg Liquid Aminos
2 teaspoons fresh sage, minced
1 teaspoon fresh oregano, minced
2–3 teaspoons whole-grain prepared mustard

Simmer tempeh in vegetable stock for 10 minutes. Cool. Reserve liquid. Grate tempeh.

Preheat oven to 350 degrees.

Pour hot stock over millet.

Sauté onion in oil.

Mix tempeh, millet, and onions with parsley.

Mix in remaining ingredients. Pat into a well-oiled loaf pan. Cover.

Bake for 20–30 minutes.

Serve as is or with Mushroom-Onion Gravy (see recipe in Condiments).

Desserts

Cherry Whip

Stevia can enhance the effect of other sweeteners. Adding it to recipes as a dietary supplement can help reduce the amount of sweetener you would need.

- 1 cup cashews
- 2 cups water
- 1/2 cup brown rice syrup
- 2 cups cherries
- 1/3 cup coconut oil
- 1/2 teaspoon stevia liquid
- 1 teaspoon slippery elm powder
- 2 tablespoons soy milk powder
- 1 teaspoon vanilla
- 1/2 teaspoon lemon extract
- 1/4 teaspoon salt

Process all but 1 cup cherries and coconut oil in blender until smooth. Slowly add coconut oil. Pour into container and place in freezer.

Stir in 1 cup of cherries after dessert has thickened some. Serve before it becomes too hard.

You can easily substitute a different fruit, such as peaches, to this recipe. Just delete lemon extract.

Agar Fruit Gel

This is a vegan version of Jell-O.

- 4 tablespoons agar flakes
- 4 cups apple, peach, or apricot juice
- 2 cups fresh fruit, chopped, pureed, or both
- 1 teaspoon vanilla
- juice of 1/2 lemon

Place agar and juice in a saucepan. Let sit for a few minutes to soften.

Bring to a boil. Simmer for 5 minutes.

Remove from heat. Stir in fruit and flavoring. Pour into a bowl or mold. Allow to set.

Sesame Custard

- 2 cups apple juice
- 2½ tablespoons brown rice syrup
- ¼ teaspoon agar powder
- 2½ tablespoons arrowroot
- 2 tablespoons water
- ¼ cup sesame butter or tahini

Combine apple juice and syrup. Bring to a boil. Add agar powder. Simmer for 2 minutes.

Make a paste of arrowroot and water. Stir into hot juice. Cook over low heat until thick.

Stir in sesame butter. Cook until smooth.

Pour into large bowl or into 4 individual dishes.

Cool to room temperature. Chill.

Carob Pudding

- 1 package Mori-Nu tofu
- 2 tablespoons carob powder
- 1 tablespoon grain coffee (preferably Pero)
- 2 tablespoons cashew butter
- ¼ teaspoon stevia or 2–4 tablespoons brown rice syrup
- 1 teaspoon vanilla

Process all ingredients in blender until smooth.

Chill and serve.

Creamy Fruit Pudding

- 3/4 cup cashews
- 1/2 cup water
- 2 large bananas
- 2 cups fresh or frozen fruit, chopped
- stevia to taste
- 1 teaspoon vanilla

Process cashews, water, and bananas in blender until smooth.

Add stevia and vanilla and process briefly.

Stir fruit into mixture.

Chill or serve immediately.

*If you want a sweeter taste, add more stevia or 1 tablespoon of brown rice syrup.

Tapioca Pudding

Though not a traditional recipe, this conjures up memories of cold childhood winters spent in a toasty, warm kitchen, my hands warmed by a bowl of freshly made pudding.

- 1 cup cashews
- 4 cups water
- 1/2 cup tapioca pearls
- 1/3 cup maple syrup or barley malt syrup
- 1 teaspoon vanilla
- 1/2 cup unsweetened coconut, shredded
- 1/2 cup dates, chopped (optional)

Blend 1 cup cashews with 1 cup water until smooth. Pour into saucepan with remaining water.

Add tapioca pearls. Soak 15 minutes.

Add maple syrup. Bring to boil. Reduce heat. Simmer 10 minutes.

Remove from heat. Add vanilla, coconut, and dates, if desired.

Cool before serving.

Carob Fudge

2/3 cup brown rice syrup
1/3 cup carob powder
1 cup ground almonds
1/2 cup ground pecans
1 cup unsweetened flaked coconut
1/2 cup walnuts
1 1/2 teaspoons vanilla

Mix all together well. It will be stiff, so start with a spoon, but you may have to use your fingers to incorporate everything well.

Pat into a glass pan to about 1/2-inch thickness.

Refrigerate prior to slicing and serving.

Lemon Mousse

1 package Mori-Nu tofu
1 1/2 tablespoons smooth cashew butter
2 tablespoons brown rice syrup
1/4 teaspoon stevia powder
1/4 teaspoon sea salt
2 tablespoons lemon juice
1/2 tablespoon lemon zest, finely grated
1 teaspoon vanilla extract
pinch of turmeric dissolved in the lemon juice

Blend all ingredients in a food processor or blender.

Refrigerate before serving.

Strawberry Mousse

- 1/2 cup apple juice
- 1 tablespoon agar flakes
- 1 package Mori-Nu silken tofu
- 1/4 teaspoon stevia powder
- 3 cups strawberries
- 1 teaspoon vanilla
- 1 teaspoon lemon rind, finely grated

Simmer juice in a saucepan over low heat. Add agar. Stir until dissolved, approximately 5 minutes.

Combine all ingredients in a blender or processor.

Pour into dessert dishes.

Chill about one hour.

Sesame Crunchies

- 1/2 cup peanut butter
- 1/2 cup sesame butter or tahini
- 1/2 cup brown rice syrup
- 1 teaspoon vanilla
- 1/2 cup oil
- 3/4 cup oats, ground
- 3/4 cup millet flour
- 1/2 cup coconut, shredded
- 1/2 cup sunflower seeds
- 1/2 cup carob chips

Preheat oven to 350 degrees.

Combine all ingredients.

Drop by spoonfuls on oiled cookie sheets. Press slightly.

Bake for 10–15 minutes.

Cool before removing from pans.

Banana Spice Bars

Wet ingredients:

3 tablespoons flax seed, finely ground
1/2 cup water
2/3 cup brown rice syrup
1/4 cup oil
1/2 cup plain soy yogurt
1 teaspoon vanilla extract

Dry ingredients:

1 1/2 cups flour (barley, spelt, rye, or oat)
1 cup rice flour
1 tablespoon arrowroot
1 tablespoon baking soda
1/2 teaspoon sea salt
1 teaspoon stevia leaf
2 teaspoons cinnamon, ground
1/2 teaspoon nutmeg, ground
1 teaspoon allspice, ground

Nut mixture:

1/2 cup pecans, chopped
2 tablespoons sesame seeds
2/3 cup sunflower seeds
1 1/2 cups bananas, mashed

Preheat oven to 350 degrees.

Mix flax seeds with water. Set aside.

Blend flax mixture with wet ingredients.

Stir dry ingredients together. Add to wet ingredients.

Stir in nut mixture.

Pour into oiled 9 x 13-inch pan.

Bake for 30–35 minutes or until done. Cut into squares while still warm.

Almond Balls

- 1/2 cup raw almond butter
- 1 tablespoon brown rice syrup
- 1 tablespoon oat flour
- 1/4 teaspoon vanilla
- raisins
- carob powder

Mix first four ingredients.

Make balls. Press raisins inside each.

Roll in carob powder.

Carob Chews

- 1/2 cup peanut or cashew butter
- 1/2 cup almond butter
- 2/3 cup brown rice syrup
- 1/2 teaspoon vanilla
- 3 tablespoons carob flour
- 1 1/4 cups oats

Combine butters, sweetener, and vanilla. Mix well.

Combine dry ingredients. Add to wet. Roll into balls.

Store in refrigerator.

Options:
Add 3/4 cup raisins, or
1–2 teaspoons grated orange or tangerine peel.
Roll in flaked coconut or crushed nuts.
Place a surprise dry fruit filling in middle (apricots, for example).
Use your imagination!

Fruit and Nut Balls

Great source of calcium, phosphorus, and protein. Kids eat them up!

1 cup cashews
1 cup almonds
1 cup raisins
½ cup figs (or 1 cup dates)
½ cup dates
coconut, shredded (or carob powder)

Grind nuts in food processor.

Add dry fruit slowly.

Process until you are able to roll into balls.

Add a small amount of water if too dry.

Roll in shredded coconut or carob powder.

Almond Clusters

1 cup almonds, ground
½ cup brown rice syrup
½ teaspoon ground cinnamon
½ teaspoon vanilla
3 tablespoons almond or cashew butter
3 cups boxed flake cereal (preferably Erewhon Corn or Amaranth Flakes)

Mix all ingredients except flakes.

Stir in flakes. Mix well. Shape into small balls. Chill.

Sunflower-Apricot Patties

1 cup sunflower seeds, ground
1 cup dried apricot, finely chopped
pinch of sea salt
3/4 teaspoon vanilla
carob powder

Combine sunflower seeds, apricot, salt, and vanilla.

Roll and pat into half-dollar size.

Coat in carob powder.

Sprouted Wheat Surprises

These freeze well.

1 1/4 cups sprouted wheat (tail should be 1/8-inch to 1/4-inch long)
2 cups dates, pitted
1 cup nuts, chopped
1/2 cup sesame seeds
2 tablespoons nut butter
2 tablespoons orange or lemon rind, grated
1/4 teaspoon sea salt
shredded coconut (optional)

Put wheat and dates through a food grinder or processor. Work in remaining ingredients with hands.

Form into balls. Place an additional nut half in center of ball, if desired.

Roll each ball in shredded coconut, if desired.

Double Dip Fruit Bits

When kids want something sweet and I'm busy, these are fast and satisfying!

strawberries (or other fresh or dried fruit, except melons)
finely ground nuts (preferably almonds)
plain vegan yogurt

Dip fruit in yogurt. Dip in nuts. Eat!

Carob Frosting

Great on Carob Cupcakes or Peanut Butter Cake.

1 cup cashew or almond butter
6 tablespoons brown rice syrup
2 teaspoons vanilla
6 tablespoons carob powder
3–6 tablespoons vegan milk

Blend all ingredients well.

Add enough milk to achieve a spreading consistency.

Cashew Cream

Wonderful with pumpkin or apple pie!

1 cup raw, unsalted cashews
approximately 1/4 cup water
2–3 tablespoons maple syrup (or a pinch of stevia, with or without 1/4 teaspoon maple extract flavoring)
1 teaspoon vanilla

Chop nuts coarsely in a blender.

Add remaining ingredients gradually to the blender with the motor running. Taste. Add additional syrup, if desired.

Blend to desired consistency. Add more water, if needed.

Carob Ganache, a Pourable Icing

- 1/2 cup brown rice syrup
- 1/4 cup vegan milk
- 1 cup nondairy carob chips
- 2 tablespoons "Butter" (see recipe in Condiments)
- 1/2 teaspoon vanilla extract

Heat syrup and milk to a simmer. Add chips and butter. Cook until chips melt. Remove from heat. Stir in vanilla.

Use to dip fruits or pour over cakes.

Vanilla Tofu Cream

This is a wonderful cream to serve over strawberries and shortcake, or as a parfait with carob pudding.

- 1 pound silken tofu
- 1/3 cup coconut oil
- 1/2 cup maple syrup
- 1 tablespoon lemon juice
- 1/4 teaspoon salt
- 3/4 teaspoon agar powder (or 4 teaspoons agar flakes)
- 1 cup water
- 1/4 cup arrowroot powder
- 1 cup vegan milk
- 1/4 cup vanilla extract

Combine tofu, oil, maple syrup, lemon juice, and salt in a blender.

Combine agar powder and cold water in a heavy-bottomed saucepan.

Stir over medium flame until mixture reaches a boil.

Combine arrowroot with milk and vanilla in a separate bowl. Add to boiling liquid.

Cook until mixture begins to bubble. Stir continuously. Remove from heat.

Add hot mixture to blender. Blend until smooth.

Pour into container. Place in refrigerator about one hour to cool before serving.

Ginger Cookies

Fresh ginger is what makes this cookie!

- 1/2 cup oil
- 1/2 cup barley malt syrup
- Egg Replacer for 1 egg
- 1/2 cup brown rice syrup
- 1 teaspoon cinnamon, ground
- 3 tablespoons ginger, freshly grated
- 2 teaspoons baking soda
- 1/4 cup oat bran
- 2 cups oat flour

Preheat oven to 350 degrees.

Combine wet ingredients in a medium bowl. Mix well.

Mix dry ingredients in another bowl.

Combine wet and dry ingredients thoroughly . . . do not overmix!

Drop by spoonfuls onto a greased cookie sheet.

Bake for approximately 15 minutes.

Coconut Macaroons

1 cup coconut, grated
1 cup oatmeal flour
1/4 cup brown rice syrup
1/8 teaspoon sea salt
1 teaspoon vanilla
1 teaspoon lemon zest
2 tablespoons flax meal
water (enough to hold everything together)

Mix all ingredients. Roll into small balls. Set aside for a few hours.

Store in refrigerator.

Oatmeal Date Cookies In-the-Raw

These may be stored in the refrigerator for several days.

2 cups oatmeal, ground
1 tablespoon flax seed, ground
1 teaspoon lecithin
1/4 teaspoon sea salt
1/2 teaspoon cinnamon, ground
1/2 teaspoon allspice, ground
2 teaspoons vanilla
1/2 cup dates, blended in 1/2 cup apple juice
1/4 cup pecans or walnuts, ground

Mix all ingredients well. (The dough will be stiff.) Roll into small balls.

Let sit for an hour.

Quick and Easy Oatmeal Cookies

- 3 bananas
- 1/2 cup nuts, chopped
- 1 cup dates, chopped
- 1 cup figs, chopped
- 1/2 teaspoon salt
- 1 tablespoon vanilla
- 2 cups oats

Preheat oven to 400 degrees.

Mash bananas, leaving some chunks. Add nuts, dates, and figs. Beat well.

Add salt, vanilla, and oats.

Drop from spoon onto ungreased cookie sheet. (You can spread cookie sheet with a small amount of lecithin or oil, if needed.)

Bake approximately 25 minutes.

Sesame Crunch Cookies

If not eaten immediately, refrigerate in an airtight container.

- 1 cup rolled oats
- 3/4 cup toasted sesame seeds
- 1 1/2 cups barley flour
- 1 teaspoon baking soda
- pinch sea salt
- 3 tablespoons lemon rind, finely minced
- 1/3 cup coconut oil
- 1/2 cup maple syrup
- 2 tablespoons lemon juice

Preheat oven to 375 degrees.

Grind oats and sesame seeds coarsely. Add flour, baking soda, and salt.

Mix liquid ingredients. Stir into dry ingredients, creating a soft dough.

Roll dough into smooth balls about the size of a small walnut.

Place about 2 inches apart on lightly oiled cookie sheets.

Press balls gently to flatten them slightly.

Bake until lightly browned on the bottom, approximately 20 minutes.

Cool completely.

Sesame Millet Cookies

- 1/4 cup millet
- 1/2 cup water
- 1 cup barley malt syrup
- 1 1/2 cups sesame butter or tahini
- 1 teaspoon vanilla
- 1/4 cup cornmeal
- 1/4 cup rye flour
- 1/2 cup toasted sesame seeds

Preheat oven to 350 degrees.

Simmer millet in water in a covered pan until water is absorbed.

Add remaining liquid ingredients.

Mix dry ingredients in separate bowl.

Add wet ingredients to dry ingredients. The dough will be very sticky.

Spoon dough onto oiled cookie sheets. Flatten with wet fingers.

Bake for approximately 15 minutes or until browned.

Cool. They will firm as they cool.

Banana Raisin Ice Cream

- 2/3 cup raisins
- 1/2 cup water
- 2 cups cashews, ground
- 2 pounds very ripe bananas
- 1 teaspoon vanilla

Soak raisins in water overnight.

Process all ingredients in blender.

Pour into container. Freeze.

Banana Chipsicle

- 1 banana
- nut butter
- vegan carob chips or raisins
- ground nuts or coconut

Cut banana in half. Insert popsicle stick.

Spread banana with nut butter. “Stud” banana with chips or raisins. Roll in ground nuts or coconut.

Crepes

Any of these would be great with a dollop of Vanilla Tofu Cream (see recipe in Desserts).

- 1 cup barley flour
- 1 cup spelt, kamut, or pastry flour
- 1/4 cup nutritional yeast
- 1/2 teaspoon baking powder
- dash of sea salt
- 3 1/2 cups water
- 2 tablespoons oil
- 1 cup silken tofu
- oil to coat pan

Puree all ingredients in a blender until smooth.

Heat a 9-inch nonstick crepe pan (or regular pan) over medium-high heat until a drop of water sizzles. Coat pan with oil.

Pour in 1/4 cup of batter. Tilt and swirl pan so that batter forms an even layer over the whole surface. Cook until edges loosen from side of pan and top starts to bubble.

Flip crepe over. Cook on other side until flecked with gold.

Stack finished crepes in a dish to cool. (Makes approximately 24 crepes.)

Fill crepes with your choice of fillings.

Crepe Fillings

Variation 1:

- 2 apples, chopped
- 1/4 cup raisins
- 1/4 cup apple juice
- 1/2 teaspoon cinnamon
- 1 teaspoon lemon juice
- 1 tablespoon arrowroot mixed with 2 tablespoons fruit juice

Simmer all ingredients, except arrowroot mixture, in saucepan until apples are tender.

Mix in arrowroot. Simmer until thickened.

Fill and roll crepes.

Variation 2:

- 3/4 pound tofu
- 1/3 cup carob powder
- 1/4 cup brown rice syrup
- 2 tablespoons oil
- 1 1/2 teaspoons vanilla
- 1 teaspoon lemon juice
- pinch of salt

Blend all ingredients until smooth and creamy.

Chill until set. Roll crepes.

Serve with dollop of tofu whipped cream or cashew cream. Sprinkle with nuts.

Variation 3:

1 cup raspberries
2 bananas, sliced
2 teaspoons lemon juice
2 tablespoons flaked unsweetened coconut

Mix all ingredients well in bowl.

Chill. Fill and roll crepes.

Pie Crust

Enough for one 10-inch pie.

1½ cups sunflower seeds
1½ cups almonds
pinch of salt
1½ teaspoons baking powder
2 tablespoons oil*
3 tablespoons water

Preheat oven to 375 degrees.

Grind seeds and nuts. Combine with salt and baking powder.

Stir in oil and water with a fork, adjusting to create a moist dough.

Pat into a lightly oiled pie plate.

Bake for 15 minutes, or until golden brown.

Cool. Fill.

**Variation:*
You can delete oil and add cashews and walnuts.

Pie Crust #2

- 3/4 cup barley flour, chilled
- 3/4 cup spelt flour, chilled
- 3 tablespoons coconut oil
- pinch of sea salt
- 1/2 cup ice water

Add oil to flour. Work in until it forms a crumbly meal. Stir salt into water. Add to flour. (Do not worry if dough seems too wet; it will dry up.)

Roll out each half of dough on a floured surface. Transfer to pie plate. Trim and crimp edges.

Place in a 400 degree oven for 10–15 minutes if you are prebaking the shell.

Fruit Mousse Pie

Crust:

- 1/3 cup sunflower seeds
- 1/3 cup cashews
- 1/3 cup almonds
- 1/3 cup coconut
- 1/2–1 cup raisins (enough to hold mixture together)
- 1 cup soft dates

Grind seeds, nuts, and coconut to a fine meal in a food processor.

Add the fruit. Process, adding additional raisins as necessary.

Press crust into a lightly oiled 9-inch pie plate. Fill crust.

Filling:

- 1 bag frozen berries
- 1–3 tablespoons brown rice syrup or 1/4 teaspoon stevia liquid
- 1 package Mori-Nu tofu
- 1/2 cup cashews

Blend all ingredients in blender until smooth. Pour into pie crust.

Refrigerate immediately until ready to serve.

Lemon Pie

- 1 tablespoon agar flakes or 3/4 teaspoon agar powder
- 1/4 cup boiling water
- 1 1/2 cups water
- 1/2 cup lemon juice
- 1 cup apple juice
- 2/3 cup cashew nuts
- 2/3 cup brown rice syrup
- 1/3 cup coconut
- 6 tablespoons arrowroot powder
- 2 tablespoons lemon rind
- 1/4 teaspoon sea salt

Prepare pie crust (see Pie Crust recipe choices).

Mix agar with boiling water. Let sit one minute.

Pour agar mixture into blender. Add remaining ingredients to blender.

Process until very smooth.

Place over heat. Stir constantly until thickened.

Pour into a 10-inch pie shell.

Place in refrigerator to chill.

Pumpkin Pie

Cashew Cream makes a wonderful accompaniment to this pie.

Crust:

- 3/4 cup barley flour
- 3/4 cup oats
- 1/2 cup toasted almonds, finely chopped
- 1/2 teaspoon cinnamon
- pinch of sea salt
- scant 1/8 teaspoon stevia powder
- 1/4 cup oil

Blend dry ingredients.

Stir in oil. Add 1–2 tablespoons of water, if needed.

Press into an oiled 9-inch pie plate. Spread to cover all surfaces.

Pie:

- 2 cups cooked pumpkin, kabocha, or butternut squash
- 1 pound firm or extra-firm tofu
- 1/2 cup brown rice syrup
- 1 rounded teaspoon of cinnamon, ground
- 1/2 teaspoon nutmeg, ground
- 1/2 teaspoon ginger, ground
- 1/4 teaspoon allspice, ground
- 1/4 teaspoon cloves, ground
- 1/2 teaspoon sea salt
- 1/4 teaspoon stevia powder

Preheat oven to 375 degrees.

Combine all ingredients in blender. Process. Add water only if the mixture seems very thick.

Pour into pie crust. Bake on the middle shelf for 30 minutes.

Cool and firm up on a rack for at least 2 hours before serving.

Carob Cupcakes

1 2/3 cups barley or wheat pastry flour
1/2 cup roasted carob powder
2 tablespoons grain coffee (preferably Pero)
3/4 teaspoon sea salt
2 teaspoons baking powder
2/3 cup brown rice syrup
1/8–1/4 teaspoon stevia liquid
1/3 cup coconut oil
1 cup vegan milk
2 teaspoons vanilla
1/3 cup vegan carob chips

Preheat oven to 350 degrees.

Mix dry ingredients in one bowl and wet ingredients in another. Add together. Stir just until combined.

Pour into oiled or papered muffin tins. (I like to use paper cups but oiling the muffin tins is fine as well.)

Bake for approximately 18–20 minutes, or until a toothpick inserted in the center comes out clean.

Cool. Serve as is or with Carob Frosting (see recipe in Desserts).

Variations:
Try lightly toasted almond slivers instead of carob chips. Decrease vanilla to 1 1/2 teaspoons and add 1/2 teaspoon almond flavoring.

Mix cherries into dry ingredients and omit vegan carob chips.

Black Forest Cake

- 1 1/2 cups water
- 1 1/4 cups maple syrup
- 1 1/2 teaspoons vanilla
- 3/4 cup applesauce
- 3 cups flour (spelt, wheat pastry, or combine with barley)
- 1 cup carob powder
- 1 1/2 tablespoons baking powder
- 1 1/2 teaspoons baking soda
- cherries or strawberries, sliced
- Carob Ganache (see recipe in Desserts)
- 1/2 Vanilla Tofu Cream (see recipe in Desserts)

Preheat oven to 350 degrees.

Mix liquid ingredients.

Mix dry ingredients.

Stir dry ingredients into wet.

Pour into 2 oiled and floured 9-inch cake pans.

Bake for about 35 minutes, or until done. Cool for 10 minutes. Remove from pans. Invert on cooling rack. Cool completely. Split each layer in half lengthwise with a serrated knife to form 4 round layers.

Make Ganache and Vanilla Cream (see recipes).

Place one layer of cake on a serving plate. Spread with 1/3 of Ganache.

Place another layer of cake on top of Ganache. Layer strawberries or cherries. Place another layer of cake on top of strawberries. Spread with Vanilla Cream. Place the last layer on top and pour the remaining Ganache over the cake, spreading it with a knife.

Cool in refrigerator until ready to serve. Place a few strawberries or cherries decoratively over cake, if desired.

> *What is enough?*
> *It's the key to bringing our lives into alignment with what the Earth can sustain. It can also be the key to a personal fulfillment—to a life that is simpler, less cluttered, yet rich with purpose and meaning.*
>
> —from *In Context,* a Quarterly of Human Sustainable Culture (Summer 1990)

Carrot Cake

This is my favorite cake. I use only fruit as a sweetener, and it is still sinfully rich.

- 2 cups finely ground carrots (or carrot pulp from juiced carrots)
- 1 cup raisins, soaked in water about 1 hour (save soak water)
- 1 cup dates
- 1 cup nuts (walnuts, pecans, almonds, brazil nuts, etc.)
- 2 cups oat flour
- 1 1/2 teaspoons cinnamon, ground
- 1 1/2 teaspoons nutmeg, ground
- 1 lemon zest
- 1 orange zest
- 1/4 cup dried pineapple, diced small
- 2 teaspoons vanilla
- 1/4 teaspoon sea salt

Frosting:

2 cups cashews
1/2 cup raisin soak water, adding more if necessary
2 tablespoons lemon juice
several drops of stevia liquid
2 teaspoons vanilla
1 lemon zest

Press excess liquid from carrots, if necessary. Process raisins, dates, and nuts in food processor until finely ground. Combine well with remaining ingredients.

Prepare frosting. Process all ingredients in blender until smooth. Add more raisin soak water, if necessary, to achieve desired consistency.

Line a 10-inch pie pan with plastic wrap. Press half of cake mixture into pan. Turn pan over onto serving plate. Remove pan and plastic wrap.

Spread half of frosting over top. Repeat molding with remaining mixture. Gently release on top of first layer. Spread remaining frosting on top and sides of cake.

Garnish with cinnamon and chopped nuts, if desired.

Peanut Butter Cake

Try this with the Carob Frosting recipe.

3 tablespoons flax seed
1/2 cup water
1/2 cup organic peanut butter
1/3 cup oil
3/4 cup brown rice syrup
1 1/2 teaspoons vanilla
1 cup vegan milk
2 cups barley or wheat pastry or spelt flour
1 teaspoon baking powder
3/4 teaspoon sea salt

1/2 teaspoon cinnamon, ground
1/2 cup vegan carob chips
1/2–3/4 cup organic peanuts, coarsely chopped (optional)

Preheat oven to 350 degrees.

Mix wet ingredients.

Mix dry ingredients in separate bowl.

Add wet ingredients to dry. Combine well.

Pour into an oiled and floured 9-inch pan.

Bake for approximately 45 minutes, or until center springs back when touched.

Strawberry Shortcake

Vanilla Tofu Cream (see recipe in Desserts)

Cake:

2 cups barley flour
2 cups spelt flour
1/2 teaspoon stevia leaf
4 teaspoons baking powder
2 teaspoons baking soda
2/3 cup oil
1 1/2 cups barley malt syrup
1 1/2 cups water
2 teaspoons apple cider vinegar
1 teaspoon salt
2 teaspoons vanilla extract

Strawberry Sauce:

1 pint strawberries, hulled and stemmed
1/2 teaspoon lemon juice
1/4 teaspoon vanilla
1/4 teaspoon stevia liquid
pinch of sea salt
1 pint of strawberries, sliced

Preheat oven to 350 degrees.

Sift flours, stevia, baking powder, and baking soda together in one bowl.

Whisk together remaining ingredients in another bowl.

Mix wet and dry ingredients together. Pour into oiled pans.

Bake for approximately 25 minutes, until toothpick inserted in center comes out clean and cake is golden brown. Cool.

Prepare sauce:
Blend all ingredients except last pint of strawberries.

Stir in sliced strawberries.

Serve shortcake with Vanilla Tofu Cream (see recipe in Desserts) and Strawberry Sauce.

Beverages

In 1997 the average American consumed 576 12-ounce servings of sodas annually. That amount has only increased over the last several years. Phosphorus (the bubbly in soda), caffeine, and sugar leach alkaline mineral reserves, such as calcium, from the body, and aspartame and other toxins create chemical warfare within.

Oat Milk

This is a nice "milk" to add to cereals, or just cold from the fridge.

- 2/3 cup rolled oats
- 2 cups water

Soak overnight. Place in blender with:

- 1 teaspoon vanilla
- 1/3 cup cashews
- 1/2 cup dates
- 1/8 teaspoon sea salt

Process until smooth. Pour into glass container with enough water to make two quarts.

Nut Milk

This is a variation of a recipe provided by a member of our local chapter of the Vegetarian Society. This works best with a Vita Mix Blender. If you don't have one, try grinding the nuts first in a spice grinder.

- 1/2 cup each almonds and cashews
- 2 tablespoons each sesame, sunflower, and flax seeds
- 1 tablespoon pumpkin seeds
- 1 tablespoon each granular lecithin, brown rice flour, and barley malt powder
- 1/4 teaspoon each sea salt and slippery elm powder
- 1 1/2 teaspoons vanilla (optional)
- 1/3 cup brown rice syrup or stevia liquid to taste

Put all dry ingredients in blender. Process until ground fine.

Stir rice syrup into 1 1/2 cups warm water, then add this slowly to blender ingredients. Increase to high speed for 30 seconds.

Turn down blender to low and add remaining water, then increase to high speed for 30 seconds.

Store in refrigerator in glass containers.

This is a thick nut milk that can be thinned with more water, if desired.

If you use this recipe in any of the following recipes, you can delete the nuts or seeds suggested in that recipe.

Most other nut milks are made with single nuts or seeds as opposed to putting several together as in this recipe. This may prove to be too rich or "raw tasting" for some, so experiment with just single nut and seed milks.

Usually 1/4 cup of nuts or seeds to each 4 cups of water is a good place to start. Ingredients like flax, lecithin, rice flour, and slippery elm are added for texture, so you can add or delete them in the recipe as you create your own individual nut milk.

You may also strain the milk if desired.

Apple Milk

- 1 cup fresh apple juice
- 1 cup almond milk
- 1 medium banana
- 1/4 teaspoon cinnamon

Blend all ingredients in blender.

Coconut Milk

2 small coconuts (make sure there are no cracks)

Test the 3 "eyes" of the coconut with an ice pick to find the weakest one. Pierce it to make a hole.

Drain liquid and reserve 1/2 cup. (Add cold water to make 1/2 cup, if necessary.)

Bake coconut in preheated 400 degree oven for 15 minutes. Break with a hammer. Remove flesh from the shell, taking it out carefully with the point of a strong knife. Cut coconut meat into small pieces.

Coarsely grind half the coconut meat with half the reserved coconut liquid in a food processor. Let mixture drain in a cheesecloth-lined sieve set over a bowl. Squeeze mixture in cheesecloth to extract the thick coconut milk. Transfer the ground coconut from the cheesecloth to a bowl. Reserve it for making a batch of light coconut milk.

Repeat the procedure with the remaining coconut milk and liquid.

To make light coconut milk:
Finely grind half the reserved ground coconut with 3/4 cup boiling water. Let mixture drain in the cheesecloth-lined sieve. Squeeze it in the cheesecloth to extract the thin coconut milk. Discard the finely ground coconut.

Lemonade for One

juice of 1 lemon
12 ounces water
1/8 teaspoon stevia liquid, or to taste

Stir all ingredients together.

Carob Nut Drink

2 tablespoons cashews
2 tablespoons almonds
1 cup soy milk
1 tablespoon carob powder
1/4 teaspoon vanilla
1 tablespoon grain coffee (preferably Pero)
1/8 teaspoon stevia liquid

Blend all ingredients in blender until smooth.

Carob Shake

1 cup almond milk
2 teaspoons unsweetened carob powder
1 tablespoon stevia liquid
1 1/2 frozen medium bananas

Blend all ingredients in blender.

Hot Carob Drink

2 cups vegan milk
1 heaping tablespoon carob powder
1–2 tablespoons brown rice syrup
1/4 teaspoon vanilla
sea salt to taste

Heat all ingredients in saucepan. Whisk until frothy and free of lumps.

Blueberry, Fig, and Date Shake

2 cups almond milk
1 tablespoon sweetener (optional)
1/2 teaspoon cinnamon, ground
1/2 cup pitted dates
1/4 cup figs
1 cup blueberries

Blend all ingredients in blender.

The Meeny Greeny Banana Shake

1 frozen banana
1/2–3/4 cup vegan milk
small handful of almonds
1 teaspoon spirulina or chlorella
1 teaspoon flax oil

Process ingredients in blender until smooth.

Dreamy Date Shake

1/2 banana, frozen if possible
3–4 dates, pits removed
1/4 cup almonds
1/4 teaspoon nutmeg, ground
1/4 teaspoon maple flavoring
vegan milk

Place all ingredients, except milk, in blender.

Pour milk to the 1 1/2 cup line.

Process until smooth.

Cashew-Apricot Drink

1/3 cup dried apricots
3 cups hot water
1/2 cup cashews
1/2 teaspoon vanilla

Soak apricots in hot water for 5 minutes.

Blend all ingredients in blender until smooth.

Just Peachy! Shake

2 medium ripe peaches
1 frozen banana
small handful almonds
small handful cashews
almond milk
1/4 teaspoon vanilla (not needed if almond milk is flavored)

Blend all ingredients in blender until smooth.

Fruit Smoothie

1 banana, fresh or frozen
1 cup frozen berries (raspberries are sweetest)
2 tablespoons sunflower seeds
1 cup juice of choice (I usually dilute with water 50%)
1/2 teaspoon spirulina (optional)
acidophilus powder (optional)

Blend all ingredients in blender until smooth.

Cranberry Yogurt Shake

3/4 cup plain yogurt (preferably vegan)
1/4 cup distilled water
1/3 cup cranberries, fresh or frozen
2 tablespoons sunflower seeds
1/8 teaspoon stevia liquid
acidophilus powder (optional)

Blend all ingredients in blender until smooth.

Carrot Drink

1 medium carrot
1/2 apple, quartered and cored
1/2 lemon, peel and seeds removed
1 tablespoon flax oil (optional)
1 cup or more water

Blend all ingredients in blender until smooth.

Carrot Drink #2

1 medium carrot
1/4 beet
1/2 apple, cored and quartered
1/4 lemon, peel and seeds removed
1/4 cup parsley
1 tablespoon Kyogreen (or other microalgae)
1 cup or more water

Blend all ingredients in blender until smooth.

Glossary of Special Ingredients

Amaranth—An extraordinarily nutritious seed, high in protein, normally used as a side dish, though not by itself. It has quite a strong taste and so is usually combined with other grains in small amounts. My family likes it in rice, in which I may add an additional 2–3 tablespoons of amaranth while cooking. Try popping it in a heavy, dry pan; it will look like miniature popcorn.

Apple cider vinegar—Made from freshly pressed apple juice, touted as a tonic for many ailments. Purchase only organic, unfiltered, and not pasteurized vinegar to ensure purity and quality. Used in most of my recipes calling for vinegar.

Arrowroot—Used as a thickener, it looks much like cornstarch, though it is derived from a tropical starchy tuber and is superior nutritionally to cornstarch. Use equivalent amounts.

Barley malt syrup—Thick, amber-colored sweetener made from sprouted barley. Not as sweet as sugar and comprised of primarily maltose, a complex sugar, less destructive to the body's mineral balance.

Bragg Liquid Aminos—A nonfermented seasoning similar to soy sauce and made with just soybeans. Highly concentrated with a high sodium content. Use sparingly.

Carob—Ground and roasted pods from a tropical tree. Good source of calcium, iron, magnesium, and vitamins A & B. Use in place of cocoa powder.

Coconut oil—One of my favorite oils. Check out the Fats section and the foreword page in the Breads section for more information and availability.

Egg Replacer—An egg substitute product available at natural food markets and some supermarkets. Look in the Substitutions section in the front of this book for more egg replacement ideas.

Flax seeds—Rich in the essential omega-3 fatty acids and vitamin E. Store in freezer and grind as you need them. Sprinkle on your hot cereal or bake into breads or muffins for a rich, nutty flavor. Three tablespoons ground seed mixed with 1/2 cup water is equivalent to 2 eggs when replacing in quick bread recipes.

Kudzu—Used as a thickener, it can replace cornstarch or arrowroot in equal amounts. It is valued in Chinese medicine for a variety of ailments including digestive disorders, colds, and headaches. Usually comes in chalky white chunks. Press with the back of a spoon to break it up before using.

Lecithin—I prefer granules over the liquid variety. Extracted from soybeans, it is used extensively as a flavor enhancer and acts as a preservative. Lecithin helps to emulsify cholesterol in the body as well as aid in the utilization of fats.

Microalgae—Chlorella, spirulina, and wild blue-green algae are the three most widely available. These chlorophyll-rich foods enrich the blood and are higher in protein, beta carotene, and nucleic acids than any other food. These foods renew human cells and help to reverse aging.

Millet—A gluten-free, alkaline cereal grain with a high amino-acid profile and high iron content. May be cooked into a dry pilaf or a smoother mashed potato texture by adding more water. Dry toasting it prior to cooking gives it a richer, nuttier flavor. Its mild taste lends itself well to a myriad of different seasonings, gravies, or sauces.

Miso—A fermented paste made from soybeans and a grain such as rice or barley. Ranges in color from blond to brown, with the taste being stronger in the darker shades. Wonderful flavor when stirred into a soup or sauce just before serving, yet works great in dressings and some desserts as well. A concentrated protein source. Very salty and should be used in moderation.

Nut butters—Thick paste made by grinding nuts, the most popular being peanut. Use organic when possible and watch the ingredients. Supermarket brands usually use hydrogenated oil as an emulsifier and other ingredients which simply do not have to be there. A wide variety is available including almond, cashew, and more exotic ones like filbert. If you have a strong blender, making your own with fresh or freshly roasted nuts is best.

Nutritional yeast—Do not confuse with brewer's or baking yeast. A rich source of B vitamins and protein, this is an inactive yeast and will not ferment. Adds wonderful flavor to gravies and sauces.

Quinoa—An easy to digest grain that contains the highest amount of protein of any other grain. Also rich in iron, calcium (more than milk), phosphorus, B vitamins, and vitamin E. Easy to prepare. Rinse first. Cooks in 15 minutes.

Rice syrup—Like barley malt syrup, this is comprised predominantly of maltose, a slowly digested carbohydrate. It is not as sweet as honey or sugar in baked goods, though I still like the subtle flavor and couple it with stevia powder if I want a sweeter flavor. We like rice syrup on pancakes and it makes great-tasting popcorn balls!

Sea salt—Containing all trace elements, including iodine, this is superior to commercial salt, which is highly refined and contains many additives. Sea salt is evaporated and impurities are removed. A much superior taste to the harsh, chemically treated brands.

Seaweed—Many varieties to explore, some of which are dulse (my favorite), kombu (used primarily in soups and stews, makes beans more user friendly!), wakame, arame, nori (popular in sushi rolls), hijiki, and agar-agar (kanten). Agar is used as a gelling agent. Sea vegetables are an extremely valuable food source with a full spectrum of minerals, rich in iodine, calcium, and iron.

Sesame butter—Use in place of tahini or peanut butter. This is a paste made from whole, roasted sesame seeds. Because of its high Vitamin E content, it will have a longer shelf life than other nut butters.

Soy yogurt—Available in health food stores in plain or flavored varieties. Can also be made easily at home by mixing 1 teaspoon dairy yogurt or yogurt starter into a quart of soy milk and letting it sit uncovered in a warm spot for 14–18 hours. Alternatively try boiling 1 cup of water with 1/4 cup soy powder and 2 teaspoons of rice or barley syrup and leave to sit 48 hours. Then add 1 quart soymilk and let sit an additional 14 hours.

Stevia—An herb that is 30–300 times sweeter than sugar. Available in leaf form or as a clear liquid or white powder. See section on Sweeteners for more info.

Tempeh—A traditional Indonesian food made by splitting, cooking, and fermenting soybeans. Fresh is best and easy to make, though it takes 30 hours to incubate. Inoculated by a culture that forms fuzzy white/gray/black mycelium enzymes, which bind the beans together, creating a hardy, meaty, texture. When homemade it is rich in vitamin B_{12} and contains high amounts of protein, which is easy to assimilate. My family loves the flavor and the versatility of this wonderful and nutritious food. Check out *The Tempeh Cookbook* by Dorothy R. Bates for making your own. I double my recipes and freeze them to always have some on hand. Do not eat raw.

Toasted sesame oil—Highly aromatic and intensely flavored oil made from toasted sesame seeds. Not used as a cooking oil. You only need a few drops to flavor grains, beans, or stir fries.

Vogue Vege Base—A great product made from dehydrated vegetables. Adds depth of flavor to many recipes. Use for stock. If unavailable, use any strong-flavored vegetable stock.

References and Resources

My search for answers to my health questions has led me on an extraordinary journey of discovery. I am constantly looking for new sources of information. In this section, I have included a partial list of books, periodicals, and organizations that I have found very helpful. I urge anyone who wants to make changes in their lives to obtain as much knowledge as possible. It is the only way to break from a victimized stance to one of self-worth and confidence. Being aware gives us back the power to make the important decisions in our own life, and the realization of the consequences of our actions. This, in turn, will create a more responsible family and community-minded individual.

Cookbooks:

The American Vegetarian Cookbook from the Fit for Life Kitchen, by Marilyn Diamond.

Recipes from an Ecological Kitchen, by Lorna J. Sass.

The Tempeh Cookbook, by Dorothy R. Bates.

Ten Talents, by Frank and Rosalie Hurd.

The Uncheese Cookbook, by Joanne Stepaniak.

Books and Periodicals:

The Body Ecology Diet: Recovering Your Health and Rebuilding Your Immunity, by Donna Gates.

Diet for a New America, May All be Fed, and *The Food Revolution,* by John Robbins.

Diet for a Small Planet, by Frances Moore Lappé.

The Environmental Magazine, 28 Knight Street, Norwalk, CT 06851, 203-854-5559, www.emagazine.com.

Environmental Research Foundation, Rachel's Environment and Health Weekly, PO Box 5036, Annapolis, MD 21403-7036, 410-263-1584, erf@rachel.org.

Fast Food Nation, by Eric Schlosser.

Fats That Heal, Fats That Kill: The Complete Guide to Fats, Oils, Cholesterol and Human Health, by Udo Erasmus.

Food and Healing, by Annemarie Colbin.

Food and Water, 398 Vermont Route 215, Walden, VT 05873.

Foods That Heal: A Guide to Understanding and Using the Healing Powers of Natural Foods, by Bernard Jensen.

Healing with Whole Foods, by Paul Pitchford.

Hormonal Chaos, The Scientific and Social Origins of the Environmental Endocrine Hypothesis, by Sheldon Krimsky.

How to Grow Fresh Air: 50 Houseplants to Purify Your Home or Office, by B. C. Wolverton.

Living Downstream, by Sandra Steingraver.

Mad Cowboy, by Howard F. Lyman.

Natural Cleaning for Your Home: 95 Pure and Simple Recipes, by Casey Kellars.

Natural Health Magazine, PO Box 7442, Red Oak, IA 51591-0440, 800-526-8440.

The New Our Bodies, Ourselves, by the Boston Women's Health Book Collective.

The Nutrition Bible: A Comprehensive, No-Nonsense Guide to Foods, Nutrients, Additives, Preservatives, Pollutants and Everything Else We Eat and Drink, by Jean Anderson and Barbara Deskins.

Organic Gardening, 33 East Minor Street, Emmaus, PA 18098, 610-967-5171, www.organicgardening.com.

Prescription for Nutritional Healing, by James F. Balch, M.D., and Phyllis A. Balch, C.N.C.

Silent Spring, by Rachel Carson.

Spontaneous Healing: How to Discover and Enhance Your Body's Natural Ability to Maintain and Heal Itself, by Andrew Weil.

Vegetarian Times, 4 Highridge Park, Stamford, CT 06909, 800-829-3340, www.vegetariantimes.com.

Organizations:

American Natural Hygiene Society, PO Box 30630, Tampa, FL 33630, 813-855-6607.

American Vegan Society, 501 Old Harding Highway, Malaga, NJ 08328.

Center for Science in the Public Interest/Americans for Safe Food, 1501-16th Street, NW, Washington, DC 20036, 202-332-9110.

Greenpeace, 1611 Connecticut Avenue, NW, Washington, DC 20009, 202-462-1177.

Natural Law Party, PO Box 1900, Fairfield, IA 52556, 515-472-2040, www.natural-law.org.

North American Vegetarian Society, PO Box 72, Dolgeville, NY 13329.

Price-Pottenger Nutrition Foundation, PO Box 2614, La Mesa, CA 91943-2614, 800-366-3748, price-pottenger.org.

Sierra Club, PO Box 7603, San Francisco, CA 94120-9826, 415-776-2211.

Index

D

U

V

North Atlantic Books Series: Food as Medicine, Food as Consciousness

North Atlantic Books has developed a series of unique books on food as medicine and the relationship between diet and consciousness. These books transcend traditional categories of nutrition, alternative medicine, and spiritual practice to discuss health, diet, and consumption in terms of our actual human situation. The three titles presently comprising the series are *Healing with Whole Foods: Oriental Traditions and Modern Nutrition* by Paul Pitchford (published originally in 1993; revised and updated in 1997; revised and updated again in 2002); *Conscious Eating* by Gabriel Cousens, M.D. (published originally by Essene Vision Books in 1992; enlarged, revised, and republished by North Atlantic Books in 2000); and *How We Heal: Understanding the Mind-Body-Spirit Connection* by Douglas W. Morrison (published originally by Health Hope Publishing House as *Body Electronics Fundamentals* in 1993; enlarged, revised, and republished by North Atlantic Books in 2001; revised and expanded in 2006).

These books propose that every food is a medicine (and has long-term secondary effects on both our organs and our psyche) and that each medicine is likewise a food (and directly affects metabolic balance and energetic capacity).

In all three "food as medicine, food as consciousness" books, consumption is viewed not just as a mechanical event of nutrition and bodily maintenance nor as sensual recreation but also as a total psychospiritual process. Dietary sources and preparation, cooking procedures and utensils, levels of taste and consumption awareness, and diverse facets of digestion and fasting are explored. The authors are concerned with the assimilation and transmutation of what enters the body-mind (including enzymes, minerals, oils, type of water, type of air, etc.) rather than what is either enjoyable and pleasing to consume or rumored to be healthy. Each of these books explores the deeper cellular satisfaction and resonance that come from eating, drinking, and combining foods as part of a serious daily practice. Each ask: what makes food alive?; how does eating teach you who you are?; how can whole foods and conscious eating help you find your destiny?

Each of the books also deals with the impact human beings have on the Earth and its sentient beings (the role of compassion and responsibility in diet), plus the reciprocal effects of the planet's environment on health and food. They presume that eating must be attuned to communities and ecosystems.

Note: These books (and others listed here) were written independently of one another. The individual authors' advice, while overlapping in some areas, disagrees in others, sometimes even offering contradictory solutions to the same issues (for instance, the advantages and drawbacks of cooking and consuming food raw). None of the authors specifically recommends the other two books or has any connection to them.

North Atlantic Books as a publisher is presenting these separate visions for readers to consider in creating their own diets and addressing their own self-healing. Individuals will find ideas in one or another book better suited to their own constitutions and temperaments, so every reader should use sound personal judgment and intuition in choosing a path of food.

- information on making a gentle transition from an animal-products-based diet to one centered on whole grains and fresh vegetables; there are over three hundred healthful vegan recipes presented, as well as detailed information on the healing properties of plant and animal foods.
- sections on weight loss, heart and vascular renewal, female health, digestive problems, candida yeast infections, root canals, food combining, fasting, children, pregnancy, and aging; includes insights from Ayurvedic medicine of India.
- detailed "regeneration diets" and herbal treatments for cancer, arthritis, mental illness, drug and alcohol abuse, AIDS, and other degenerative conditions; also features a "parasite purge program" tailored to specific body types.

Paul Pitchford is a healer, teacher, and nutrition researcher. He has taught at various learning centers, including universities and schools of East Asian medicine, and lectured at numerous healing events. Pitchford currently lives in Northern California, where he directs the Heartwood Institute Wellness Clinic and Oriental Healing Arts Program, located in Garberville, CA.

www.northatlanticbooks.com

How We Heal: Understanding the Mind-Body-Spirit Connection

By Douglas W. Morrison
ISBN: 1-55643-579-7
$29.95 trade paper, 497 pp.
illustrations

". . . for healing to be possible, we must desire this healing and yet have no attachment to it: we must remain willing to not heal. We must be willing to put our full effort into the process and yet have no attachment to the outcome of that effort."—from the book

This book addresses healing in the broadest conceivable context. Though *How We Heal* is a comprehensive resource on the physical basis of health, it goes far beyond the physical to examine the emotional and spiritual elements that cause illness and can block even the most powerful healing methods from success. Morrison's genius lies in explaining the full nature of the healing crisis and the role of resistance in preventing us from getting well. This book serves as an excellent introduction to the frontiers of healing, where the most advanced realms of molecular science meet the most esoteric aspects of spirit.

How We Heal explores some of the more cutting-edge methods of diagnosis and healing, including iridology, sclerology, and Body Electronics.

An extensive section on nutrition includes cooking methods, the research of Dr. Weston A. Price, diet versus supplements, digestion, elimination, the role of friendly microbes within our digestive system, and the use of probiotics. Topics such as sleep, air and breathing, quantity and quality of water, exercise methods, bodywork techniques, and the dangers of amalgam dental fillings, root canals, fluoride, electromagnetic fields, vaccinations, drugs, and tobacco are considered in a clear, informative way. Yet, as thoroughly as Morrison presents all these physical factors, the author never loses sight of the much larger picture, and it is his ability to integrate the physical, emotional, mental, and spiritual aspects of health that is truly at the heart of this book.

Douglas W. Morrison studied Body Electronics with its founder, Dr. John Whitman Ray, and has been teaching seminars since 1988. He is a graduate of Harvard University and holds doctorate degrees in naturopathy, nutritional counseling, and alternative medicine.

www.northatlanticbooks.com

Conscious Eating

By Gabriel Cousens, M.D.
ISBN: 1-55643-285-2
$35.00 trade paper, 874 pp.
illustrations, charts, recipes

Long viewed as the bible of vegetarianism, *Conscious Eating* is a comprehensive effort to bring clarity and light to the most essential questions regarding our food choices and the process of living healthfully, happily, and in increased harmony with all beings on the planet.

Conscious Eating not only serves as an encyclopedia of vegetarian, vegan, live-food, and organic nutrition, but is really four books in one: Principles of Individualizing the Diet; The Choice of Vegetarianism; Transition to Vegetarianism and Live-Foods; and The Art of Live-Food Preparation. The mystery and mastery *of Conscious Eating* is that it integrates all four books into one. Read one book at a time, the entire text, or use it as a reference.

Conscious Eating, in a revolutionary approach, addresses the uniqueness of each human and empowers readers to deal with this scientific reality as opposed to the "one diet serves all" approach of fad books. Readers will learn how to individualize their diets for their particular psycho-physiological types-including four main perspectives: fast/slow oxidizer; parasympathetic/sympathetic autonomic; ayurvedic; and blood type-to optimize their health on all levels.

Explore chapter after chapter of new information including:

- How to heal the "biologically-altered brain"-the result of genetic weakness compounded by generations of poor diet and present poor diet combined with environmental and emotional toxicities.
- A mind-body-spirit approach to the vegetarian way of life.
- The importance of vegetarianism in healing self and ecology of the planet.
- The most complete scientific explanation of vegetarianism and vitamin B_{12}.
- How a vegan diet protects you from the dangers of radiation.
- Live-food and nutrition: from biophysics to metaphysics.
- An extensive chapter on enzymes-the secret of health and longevity.
- New theory of nutrition: why the material/mechanistic theory of nutrition (nutrition focusing on calories) is inadequate, misleading, and an inaccurate way of understanding nutrition.
- Nutrition for pregnancy-extensive vegetarian/vegan information on pregnancy and post-pregnancy.
- The art of live-food preparation: two hundred recipes included.
- In-depth discussion on the transition to vegetarianism, veganism, and live-foods.

Gabriel Cousens, M.D., M.D. (H) and Diplomat of Ayurveda, is one of the foremost medical proponents of a vegetarian/vegan, live-food, one-hundred-percent organic diet as a key component to maximum health and spiritual awareness. He is the founder/director of the Tree of Life Rejuvenation Center located in Patagonia, Arizona.

www.northatlanticbooks.com

Other Titles—Food and Diet

Brain-Building Nutrition: The Healing Power of Fats and Oils

By Michael A. Schmidt

ISBN: 1-58394-048-0
$16.95 trade paper, 312 pp.

Fats are a natural past of the human diet and are needed by the body, mind, and nervous system for optimum health. Written in an easy-to-understand style, this book identifies fats that are necessary, looks at the effects of too much saturated fat, and recommends how to transition from bad fats to good ones.

Coconut Cookery

By Valerie MacBean

ISBN: 1-58394-018-9
$15.95 trade paper, 216 pp.

Coconut Cookery extols the virtues of the humble coconut with 130 original recipes that are crafted to please the palates of epicures, vegans, and food adventurers alike. Coconut oil is perhaps the best cooking oil. It is very stable at high temperatures because it contains negligible amounts of unsaturated fatty acids.

The Folk Art of Japanese Country Cooking: A Traditional Diet for Today's World

By Gaku Homma

ISBN: 1-55643-098-1
$18.95 trade paper, 288 pp.
illustrations, b&w photos

Homma explains nabemono (one-pot cooking), traditional Japanese foods, and how to incorporate these foods in entire meals. Cooking methods include techniques for chopping vegetables, making udon and soba noodles, making tofu, and using tofu products.

The Magic of Chia:
Revival of an Ancient Wonder Food

By James Scheer
ISBN: 1-58394-040-5
$12.95 trade paper, 290 pp.
recipe section

Chia is a plant that has grown wild in Latin America and the southwestern United States for centuries. Used by Native Americans for endurance and a staple in their diet, chia delivers high nutritional value and sustained energy. Over the last twenty years, scientists have been involved in learning how to domesticate and grow chia seed.

"James Scheer has unlocked the secrets of chia...through easy-to-use recipes he tells us how to discover the magic in this ancient, natural, and healthy food."—Earl Mindell, author of *The Vitamin Bible* and *Prescription Alternatives*

The Raw Food Gourmet:
Going Raw for Total Well-Being

By Gabrielle Chavez; Foreword by Victoria Boutenko
ISBN: 1-55643-613-0
$14.95 trade paper, 200 pp.
recipe section

Far from taking away familiar comforts, a raw foods diet brings new vitality and an increased sense of physical and spiritual well-being. Chavez takes us along on her own voyage of discovery as she describes how to use the wide range of fruits, nuts, grains, vegetables, and seasonings that make up the repertory of a raw food lifestyle.

Vegetarian Turkish Cooking

By Carol Robertson
ISBN: 1-58394-038-3
$15.95 trade paper
268 pp., b&w photos

Robertson relates her travel adventures in the first half of the book. The second half is dedicated to vegetarian foods and recipes-with over one hundred Turkish dishes, including Spinach with Yogurt Sauce, Eggplant Purée, assorted Sis Kebabs, Minted Pea Pilav, Vegetable Dolmas, and Baklava.

Other Titles—General Healing

The Book of Herbal Wisdom: Using Plants as Medicines

By Matthew Wood
ISBN: 1-55643-232-1
$20.00 trade paper
590 pp., illustrations

Wood discusses thirty-six healing herbs and their medicinal qualities and then cross-references herbs to the compatible, similarly plant-based systems of homeopathy and Bach flower essences. This book is broadly applicable to physical maladies as well as psychological and spiritual growth.

Planet Medicine: Origins

By Richard Grossinger
ISBN: 1-55643-369-7
$30.00 trade paper
645 pp., illustrations

The main subject of *Planet Medicine: Origins* is the emergence of medicinal practices among primitive bands and tribes and the development of those practices into full-blown therapeutic systems and medical theory. *Planet Medicine* establishes seven main categories of healing: technological, manipulative, herbal, energetic, shamanic, psychoanalytic, and constitutional.

Planet Medicine: Modalities

By Richard Grossinger
ISBN: 1-55643-214-3
$25.00 trade paper
625 pp., illustrations

Planet Medicine: Modalities is an excellent source for someone trying to choose a particular therapy. Topics include: spirit healing, psychic surgery, Reiki, rebirthing, martial arts as medicine, sexuality, osteopathy, chiropractic, applied kinesiology, visceral manipulation, craniosacral therapy, Alexander technique, Bates method, Eutony, Feldenkrais method, Rolfing, Polarity, Chi Gung, Breema, Zero

Balancing, Continuum, Body-Mind Centering, sound, scent, color, food, herbs, drugs, planetary hygiene, and political issues in healing and the future of medicine.

Relearning to See: Improve Your Eyesight-Naturally!

Revised edition
By Thomas R. Quackenbush
$27.50 trade paper, ISBN: 1-55643-341-7
$35.00 cloth, ISBN: 1-55643-205-4
575 pp., illustrations
color plates

In this accessible presentation of the famous Bates method, Quackenbush (who teaches the Bates method in California and Oregon) describes how eyesight can improve naturally-at any age and regardless of heredity. With this simplified, practical, self-help approach to improving eyesight you can relearn to see-naturally and clearly, without glasses or surgery. This is a virtual encyclopedia of natural eyesight improvement.

Wind in the Blood: Mayan Healing and Chinese Medicine

Hernán García, Antonio Sierra, and Gilberto Balám
Translated by Jeff Conant
ISBN: 1-55643-304-2
$20.00 trade paper
320 pp., b&w photos

Wind in the Blood is a detailed look at Mayan medicine on Mexico's Yucatan peninsula and its similarities to Chinese traditional medicine. It was originally published in Spanish as a manual for health workers in Mayan areas to bridge the gulf between Western medical techniques and Mayan medical knowledge.

Your Inner Physician and You:
Craniosacral Therapy and Somatoemotional Release

John E. Upledger, DO, OMM

ISBN: 1-55643-246-1

$14.95 trade paper

235 pp., illustrations

Dr. Upledger recounts his personal experiences exploring and developing CranioSacral Therapy. CranioSacral Therapy follows the pressure of the cerebrospinal fluid and the movements of the cranial and sacral bones, subtly manipulating them to achieve balance. This method has been successful treating autism, post-traumatic stress syndrome, and many injuries, illnesses, and traumas.